D1110112

Competing Voices
The American Novel,
1865–1914

Twayne's Critical History of the Novel

Herbert Sussman, Series Editor
Northeastern University

Competing Voices

The American Novel, 1865–1914

Susan V. Donaldson
College of William and Mary

Twayne Publishers
An Imprint of Simon & Schuster Macmillan
New York

Prentice Hall International
London   Mexico City   New Delhi   Singapore   Sydney   Toronto

Twayne's Critical History of the Novel Series

Competing Voices: The American Novel, 1865–1914
Susan V. Donaldson

Twayne Publishers
An Imprint of Simon & Schuster Macmillan
1633 Broadway
New York, NY 10019

Library of Congress Cataloging-in-Publication Data
Donaldson, Susan Van D'Elden, 1951 –
    Competing voices : the American novel, 1865–1914 /
Susan V. Donaldson
        p.   cm. — (Twayne's critical history of the novel)
    Includes bibliographical references (p.   ) and index
    ISBN 0-8057-7854-3 (alk. paper)
    1. American fiction—19th century—History and
criticism. 2. American fiction—20th century—History and
criticism.
    I. Title. II. Series.
    PS377.D66   1998
    813'.409—dc21   98-39993
                                                         CIP

This paper meets the requirements of ANSI/NISO
Z3948-1992 (Permanence of Paper).

10 9 8 7 6 5 4 3 2 1

Printed in the United States of America

For my mother,
Genette V. Donaldson,
and
in memory of my father,
Grady W. Donaldson
(1919–1994)
"Integer vitae scelerisque purus"

Contents

Preface

The novel is of all pictures the most comprehensive and the
most elastic. It will stretch anywhere—it will take in absolutely
anything. All it needs is a subject and a painter. But for its subject, magnificently, it has the whole human consciousness.

—Henry James, "The Future of the Novel" (1899)

In 1850 an American periodical called *The Literary World* observed,
with a certain degree of wonder, "The novel is now almost recognized with the newspaper and the pamphlet as a legitimate mode of
influencing public opinion."[1] A year later, as though to underscore
the accuracy of that observation, *Uncle Tom's Cabin* began appearing
in serial form in the *National Era* and then was issued as a separate
volume in 1852. So immense was its popularity—selling 350,000
copies in its first year alone and earning its author, Harriet Beecher
Stowe, $10,000 in just three months—that public discussions of slav-
ery both North and South would never be the same.[2] Stowe's use of
the novel as a vehicle for voicing antislavery sentiments was readily
accepted by nineteenth-century audiences, who took it as a matter
of course that novels could serve, in the words of Barbara Bardes
and Suzanne Gossett, as "agents of cultural transmission" and as
"participants in cultural conflict."[3] Novels had, after all, long served
as a form of education for women barred from institutions of higher
learning and as political weapons waging wars on issues ranging
from temperance to prostitution.[4] In the hands of white women, like
Stowe's cohort of fellow domestic novelists, including Lydia Maria
Child, Catherine Maria Sedgwick, Caroline Stansbury Kirkland,
Susan Warner, Maria Jane McIntosh, and E.D.E.N. Southworth, and
African Americans like William Wells Brown, an escaped slave
turned writer, the novel at mid-century could also serve as a vehicle
for asserting and exploring new identities and demanding recognition for those identities from readers and the American public at
large.

By the second half of the nineteenth century, as the country was undergoing the turbulent transformation of a loosely tied union of largely rural regions into a corporate, urban, industrialized society, the novel had become a highly contested arena for negotiating new and often competing identities, for articulating previously unheard voices, and for limning the outlines of new and multiple stories. Indeed, the changes sweeping American society in the years after Appomattox to the beginning of World War I in Europe—large-scale demographic shifts from the countryside into the cities, waves of immigrants from Asia and from once-unfamiliar regions in eastern and southeastern Europe, and the rise of new industries and bureaucracies for organizing business—largely made the emergence of new identities and new stories possible; these were stories like those of the New Woman, anxious to enter the halls of education and business, of recently arrived immigrants seeking to understand a new culture often at odds with their own traditions, and of African Americans determined to carve out places for themselves in the aftermath of slavery. For these groups the increasingly fluid nature of American society made it possible to define and assert new identities for themselves, and as the nineteenth century drew to an end, the novel more and more came to be seen as a particularly effective means of exploring and articulating those identities. Not surprisingly, for those segments of the American population that were beginning to view the rapid changes of the era with growing alarm, the novel could also serve as a powerful tool for imposing order and structure, for establishing the boundaries of social categories like region, race, class, and gender, and even for scrutinizing and interrogating some of those new identities and stories accompanying the period's wide-scale changes.

To a striking degree, novels helped to construct postbellum America's public sphere and offered revealing glimpses of that realm as well. Making sense of just what that sphere involved requires a brief examination of the famous definition offered by German theorist Jürgen Habermas, who saw this realm as distinct from the "public" on one hand and a mere crowd on the other. "By the public sphere," he wrote in 1964, "we mean first of all a realm of our social life in which something approaching public opinion can be formed. Access is guaranteed to all citizens. A portion of the public sphere comes into being in every conversation in which private individuals assemble to form a public body." In this kind of gathering, he adds, participants "behave neither like business or professional people transacting private affairs, nor like the members of a constitutional order subject to the legal constraints of a state bureaucracy." Rather, he notes, those who help make up the public sphere "behave as a public body when they confer in an unrestricted fashion—that is, with the guarantee of freedom of assembly and association and the freedom to express and publish their opinions—about matters of general interest." In a particularly large public realm, then, the means of providing communication and information—like newspapers and magazines, for example—become especially important because of the way they define the issues under discussion and, in many respects, the far boundaries of the public arena.[5]

A good many commentators have taken issue with Habermas's veneration of the public sphere as well as its implicitly homogeneous and masculine definition, but the term and the concept are nonetheless useful for understanding something about the public arena of nineteenth-century American culture and the role the novel played in constructing, complicating, and revealing that arena. Mary Ryan builds upon Habermas's discussion of the public sphere in *Women in Public: Between Banners and Ballots, 1825–1880*. From a feminist perspective, Ryan says, the term *public* covers four crucial aims in making sense of the notion of an American public arena: "as a reference for cultural values, as a crudely serviceable classification of social behavior, as a space denoting especially blatant gender asymmetry and inequality, and as a center of concentrated power." Defining the antebellum American public realm in terms of mass-based parties, public meetings, city halls, and the popular press, Ryan also suggests that its perimeters extended to the country's first theaters in this period, as well as to restaurants, merchants' exchanges, and mechanics' institutes. What emerged by 1840, she notes, was "a relatively one-dimensional gender picture"—a peculiarly white and male public world where females, if they were included at all, generally served as symbols of femininity in patriotic parades and celebrations—as Liberty and Columbia—and as passive audiences on the sidelines.[6]

By the 1850s, though, that public arena of political exchange, festivities, and leisure had become fissured and contentious as local municipal politics increasingly reflected the growing presence of working-class men and Irish immigrants. Increasingly, actors in the public sphere allied themselves with certain social groups defined

by class or ethnicity, whether they were Know-Nothing party affili-
ates protesting the new presence of immigrants in American life or
foreign-born political activists defiantly asserting their right to be
heard in local party organizations. The result was the emergence of
a pluralized, multisegmented, and even fragmented public arena.
"Once seen as an Olympian citadel of virtuous and idealistic male
citizens," Ryan observes, "the American urban public had become a
wide-open arena of political contention."[7]

This was a period, in short, that political theorist Charles Taylor
would describe as being defined by an emerging politics of identity
and recognition; if anything, this particular description can be
applied even more aptly to the country's turbulent postbellum era
as white and black women and men of color, as well as immigrants
and inhabitants of marginal regions, increasingly insisted upon
making themselves heard—and listened to—in arenas of public
exchange, in newspapers, political forums, and novels. Taylor
argues that with the gradual collapse in the late eighteenth and
early nineteenth century of traditional social hierarchies that
bestowed upon individuals ready-made, inherited, and unambigu-
ous notions of identity, there emerged what we would recognize as
"the modern preoccupation with identity and recognition." The
demise of old hierarchies, Taylor asserts, made it possible to insist
upon the dignity of all participants in a culture and imposed upon
individuals the responsibility of discovering and articulating one's
own inward-defined, original identity. But this identity, Taylor has-
tens to add, could not be arrived at in isolation. Discovering one's
self required engaging in dialogue or debate with others, and
therein lies the importance of recognition in modern identity and
politics. In an earlier time, Taylor notes, recognition of one's identity
was something one could take for granted in assuming a sense of
self already defined by one's family and community, but a modern
notion of identity, presupposing an inner, original sense of self,
requires dialogue and debate with others and in particular requires
their *recognition* of that original and inner sense of self. Hence Taylor
concludes: "What has come about with the modern age is not the
need for recognition but the conditions in which the attempt to be
recognized can fail. That is why the need is now acknowledged for
the first time. In premodern times, people didn't speak of 'identity'
and 'recognition'—not because people didn't have (what we call)
identities, or because these didn't depend on recognition, but rather

because these were then too unproblematic to be thematized as such." Indeed, the politics of recognition attributes crucial importance to the way recognition—or its absence, or even misrecognition—can determine one's individual identity; "and so," Taylor notes, "a person or group of people can suffer real damage, real distortion, if the people or society around them mirror back to them a confining or demeaning or contemptible picture of themselves."[8]

It is one of the central contentions of this study that the postbellum American novel played a crucial role in the politics of recognition that emerged in an increasingly heterogeneous and contentious public sphere. For novels gave access to the public sphere and the exchanges it promoted to groups traditionally barred from participation in its debates and ceremonies—to white women, particularly middle-class women, who increasingly had come to be defined within the confines of the home by the late 1840s, and to black men and women struggling to cast off the identities bestowed upon them by the institution of slavery.[9] In novels, those traditionally confined to the margins of American culture—or those, like immigrants, newly introduced to that culture—could begin to stake out social spaces for themselves, to assert their identities and the stories of how they acquired those identities on their own terms, and to demand recognition for those identities and stories from other inhabitants of the public sphere.[10]

To carve out that space, to discover one's own identity, to tell one's own new story—these were aims that became particularly important in the aftermath of the Civil War's enormous upheavals and the changes wrought upon governmental structures, everyday life, and even individual selfhood. Historian Anne Rose, for one, has argued against the tendency to see the war as a watershed of social and cultural change; she insists instead that a certain continuity of romantic values and culture defined the white middle-class Victorian family.[11] But if one moves beyond the perimeters of the white middle-class family, as do the historians contributing to the essays in *Divided Houses: Gender and the Civil War*, the massive disruptions of racial and gender categories become readily apparent. It was a war, after all, in which black men eagerly sought out the opportunity to serve in the Union army in order to achieve the manhood denied to them by both southern and northern white society but most particularly by slavery, and it was also a war in which white elite southern men explicitly recognized that for black men to

achieve manhood was to offer a direct threat to white elite definitions of manhood premised upon the subordination—and assumed
unmanliness—of black slaves. It was a war too in which white
northern men saw themselves arrayed against a competing notion
of masculinity represented by white southern planters who seemed
diametrical opposites of the figure of self-mastery, discipline, frugal-
ity, and restraint increasingly coming to define white middle-class
masculinity in the North. It was also a war in which white women,
northern and southern, were able to expand their activities and their
influence farther into the public arena than they ever had before and
in which black slave women began to envision a separate domestic
refuge for black families over which they could, for the first time,
genuinely preside as wives and mothers. To change any of these categories, the essays in *Divided Houses* make clear, was to affect them
all eventually. Hence one could argue that the end of the war
brought with it a new and unsettling fluidity to social categories of
race, gender, and class.[12]

For some that new fluidity could be perceived as providing
opportunities to break out of the confines of old identities and old
narratives, but for others the fluidity of the immediate postbellum
period, as well as the increasing heterogeneity of the public sphere,
appeared deeply disturbing and desperately in need of order. It is
within the context of this growing heterogeneity, of the increasingly
noisy arena of competing voices the American public sphere was
fast becoming, that the postbellum era's new preoccupation with literary professionalism, with imposing sharply defined and reassuring standards upon novels—the ways they were written and the
ways they should be read—should be examined. For the calls to
establish standards by which to judge novels and to repudiate old
habits of the past—particularly idealism, romanticism, and sentimentalism—revealed anxiety about a public arena that seemed
increasingly chaotic, fissured, and unmanageable. What was
needed, declared commentators in some quarters, was a Great
American Novel that could offer the country a model of a unified
single story, and what the "profession" of writing required were
standards distinguishing good novels from bad ones and genuine
literary professionals from rank amateurs writing quickly and
promiscuously for money. For a country just emerging from an
internecine conflict, consensus and unity took on a new and
poignant appeal. Accordingly, it is probably not at all surprising

upon reflection that the growing pluralism of voices and stories beginning to define the postbellum novel was often greeted with counterassertions of the need for stability, tradition, and carefully defined boundaries that designated what novels and their readers were. It is probably also not surprising that in this period many novels and their writers placed a new premium upon certainty and resolution, upon the empirical evidence provided by what appeared to be the least ambiguous of all the human senses—vision and the sights it uncovered. To see was to know, many postbellum novels counseled, and, accordingly, the act of visual perception took on a new—and sometimes desperately asserted—importance.

The emergence of literary modernism at the end of this era, as the country moved into the twentieth century, suggests that those efforts to see, to know, and to impose order were not, ultimately, successful. The era that began with novelist John W. De Forest's much-heralded call for a Great American Novel, telling Americans a single story and weaving a sense of communal unity that they had lost during four years of bloody conflict, ended, ironically enough, with the novel itself undergoing fragmentation into multiple stories and even multiple forms. By the end of the nineteenth century, writers like Charles Chesnutt, Abraham Cahan, and Sarah Orne Jewett were producing novellas and short story sequences that questioned the very validity of novelistic unity and the sense of consensus it implied, and writers like Stephen Crane and Gertrude Stein were to take that interrogation of the novel even further in texts that self-consciously flaunted their resistance to narrative order and unity and foregrounded instead discontinuity and fragmentation. In doing so, experimental and iconoclastic writers like Crane and Stein took as both the form and content of their works the fluidity and heterogeneity of the public arena itself, an arena that resonated with voices and stories competing for the right to be heard and, finally, to be recognized.

Acknowledgments

As the product of several years of scholarship and teaching, this book is in many respects very much a collaborative effort. The narrative I have tried to trace here of the late nineteenth- and early twentieth-century American novel would have been very different indeed without the support, criticism, and suggestions I have received over the years from colleagues and students. My biggest debt of gratitude is owed to the series editor, Herbert Sussman, who carefully nurtured this project from the beginning, offered trenchant suggestions for improvements, and demonstrated extraordinary patience throughout a prolonged process of research and writing. I am also greatly indebted to several colleagues who took precious time out from their own work to read and comment on early versions of chapters, especially Martha Houle and Elsa Nettels, who read every word, took me to task for unclear language, and cheered me on. Noel Polk and Judith Sensibar as well offered valuable advice and criticism at crucial stages, and Susan Glisson conscientiously checked citations and references. Finally, I owe a debt of thanks to Anne Davidson, my editor at Twayne, who has been supportive, patient, and understanding from start to finish, and to Michael J. Burke for his meticulous copy-editing.

In addition, I received much-needed support for this project from the College of William and Mary, which provided me with a research leave and a summer grant to pursue research at the beginning stages. Time and space to write were also made available to me at the Virginia Center for the Humanities in Charlottesville, where I was able to complete an early draft of a chapter while working on two other projects. I am grateful to both institutions for their assistance. Thanks go as well to Eleonore and Ferdinand van Notten for their hospitality while I was finishing the manuscript during a teaching stint at Leiden University in The Netherlands.

Above all, I would like to express my gratitude to my students at the College of William and Mary, especially those in my late-nineteenth-century American literature classes. The fruits of our discussions and debates appear in every chapter.

Chronology

1865   Alice Cary, *Married Not Mated; or, How They Lived at Woodside and Throckmorton Hall*. Elizabeth Stuart Phelps, *Up Hill; or, Life in the Factory*. Elizabeth Stoddard, *Two Men*. Walt Whitman, *Drum-Taps* and *Sequel to Drum-Taps* (1865–66). End of the Civil War. Thirteenth Amendment abolishing slavery passed. President Abraham Lincoln assassinated. Black Codes passed in southern states.

1866   Augusta J. Evans, *St. Elmo*. Herman Melville, *Battle-Pieces and Aspects of the War*. John Greenleaf Whittier, *Snow-Bound*. Maria Cummins dies. Congress passes legislation ending the Black Codes.

1867   Lydia Maria Child, *A Romance of the Republic*. John W. De Forest, *Miss Ravenel's Conversion from Secession to Loyalty*. Elizabeth Stoddard, *Temple House*. Mark Twain, *The Celebrated Jumping Frog of Calaveras County and Other Sketches*. Catherine Maria Sedgwick dies. Military Reconstruction Act passed.

1868   Louisa May Alcott, *Little Women* (completed 1869). Horatio Alger, *Ragged Dick*. Alice Cary, *A Lover's Diary*. Rebecca Harding Davis, *Dallas Galbraith* and *Waiting for the Verdict*. Elizabeth Stuart Phelps, *The Gates Ajar*. Susan Warner, *Daisy*. Fourteenth Amendment giving African Americans citizenship ratified.

1869   Augusta J. Evans (Wilson), *Vashti: or "Until Death Do Us Part."* Frances Ellen Watkins Harper, *Minnie's Sacrifice*. E.D.E.N. Southworth, *The Fatal Marriage*. Harriet Beecher Stowe, *Oldtown Folks*. Mark Twain, *The Innocents Abroad*. Sarah Elizabeth Hopkins Bradford, *Scenes in the Life of Harriet Tubman*. Prohibition Party is established. Union Pacific and Central Pacific railroads meet at Promontory Point, Utah. American Woman's Suffrage Association founded.

1870   Louisa May Alcott, *An Old-Fashioned Girl*. Rebecca Harding
        Davis, *Put Out of the Way*. Sara Willis Parton (as Fanny
        Fern), *Ginger-Snaps*. Elizabeth Stuart Phelps, *Hedged In*.
        William Gilmore Simms dies. Incorporation of Standard Oil
        Company of Ohio.

1871   Louisa May Alcott, *Little Men*. Edward Eggleston, *The
        Hoosier School-Master*. Elizabeth Stuart Phelps, *The Silent
        Partner*. Harriet Beecher Stowe, *Pink and White Tyranny* and
        My Wife and I. Walt Whitman, *Democratic Vistas*. Charles
        Darwin, *The Descent of Man and Selection in Relation to Sex*.
        Knights of Labor founded.

1872   John W. De Forest, *Kate Beaumont*. Edward Eggleston, *The
        End of the World*. Frances Ellen Watkins Harper, *Sketches of
        Southern Life*. William Dean Howells, *Their Wedding Journey*.
        Sara Willis Parton (as Fanny Fern), *Caper-Sauce*. Mark
        Twain, *Roughing It*. Susan Warner, *A Story of Small Begin-
        nings*. Victoria Woodhull runs for president of the United
        States on the Equal Rights Party ticket.

1873   Louisa May Alcott, *Work: A Story of Experience*. John W. De
        Forest, *The Wetherel Affair*. Edward Eggleston, *The Mystery of
        Metropolisville*. Mark Twain and Charles Dudley Warner, *The
        Gilded Age*. Adeline Whitney, *The Other Girls*. Herbert
        Spencer, *The Study of Sociology*. Financial panic.

1874   Rebecca Harding Davis, *John Andross*. Edward Eggleston,
        The Circuit Rider: A Tale of the Heroic Age. William Dean
        Howells, *A Foregone Conclusion*. Women's Christian Temper-
        ance Union is established.

1875   Louisa May Alcott, *Eight Cousins*. John W. De Forest, *Honest
        John Vane* and *Playing the Mischief*. Augusta J. Evans (Wil-
        son), *Infelice*. Henry James, *Roderick Hudson*. Congress
        passes Civil Rights Act.

1876   Eliza Andrews, *A Family Secret*. Frances Ellen Watkins
        Harper, *Sowing and Reaping* (completed 1877). Helen Hunt
        Jackson, *Mercy Philbrick's Choice*. Mark Twain, *The Adven-
        tures of Tom Sawyer*. Alexander Graham Bell receives patent
        for telephone. Combined forces of Oglala Sioux, Cheyenne,
        and Hunkpapa Sioux under the leadership of Crazy Horse,
        Two Moons, and Gall defeat Col. George Armstrong Custer

and his Seventh Cavalry expeditionary force at the Battle of the Little Bighorn.

1877   Henry James, *The American*. Sarah Orne Jewett, *Deephaven*. Elizabeth Stuart Phelps, *The Story of Avis*. E.D.E.N. Southworth, *The Bride's Ordeal*. Susan Warner, *Diana, Bread and Oranges* and *Pine Needles*. Nationwide railroad strike. Reconstruction ends. Chief Joseph and the Nez Perce surrender to U.S. military forces.

1878   Louisa May Alcott, *Rose in Bloom*. Rebecca Harding Davis, *A Law unto Herself*. Edward Eggleston, *Roxy*. Henry James, *Daisy Miller* and *The Europeans*. Harriet Beecher Stowe, *Poganuc People*.

1879   John W. De Forest, *Irene the Missionary*. William Dean Howells, *The Lady of the Aroostook*. Albion Tourgée, *A Fool's Errand*. Susan Warner, *My Desire*. Henry George, *Progress and Poverty*. Electric light bulb is invented.

1880   Henry Adams, *Democracy*. Joel Chandler Harris, *Uncle Remus: His Songs and His Sayings*. William Dean Howells, *The Undiscovered Country*. Mark Twain, *A Tramp Abroad*. Lew Wallace, *Ben-Hur*. Susan Warner, *The End of a Coil*.

1881   John W. De Forest, *The Bloody Chasm*. William Dean Howells, *Dr. Breen's Practice*. Henry James, *The Portrait of a Lady* and *Washington Square*. Helen Hunt Jackson, *A Century of Dishonor*. Booker T. Washington starts teacher training school at Tuskegee, Alabama. President James A. Garfield assassinated. Washerwomen's strike in Atlanta.

1882   William Dean Howells, *A Modern Instance*. Elizabeth Stuart Phelps, *Doctor Zay*. Elizabeth Stoddard, *The Unloved Life*. Susan Warner, *Nobody*. Ralph Waldo Emerson dies. Henry Wadsworth Longfellow dies. Chinese Exclusion Act sets restrictions on the immigration of Chinese laborers for a decade.

1883   Edward Eggleston, *The Hoosier School-Boy*. Mary Hallock Foote, *The Led-Horse Claim*. Edgar W. Howe, *The Story of a Country Town*. William Dean Howells, *A Woman's Reason*. Laura Jean Libbey, *A Fatal Wooing*. Mark Twain, *Life on the Mississippi*. Albion Tourgée, *Hot Plowshares*. Constance Fenimore Woolson, *For the Major*. Frances E. Willard, *Women and*

Temperance. Civil Rights Act of 1875 declared unconstitutional by the U.S. Supreme Court.

1884   Henry Adams, *Esther.* Helen Hunt Jackson, *Ramona: A Story.* Sarah Orne Jewett, *A Country Doctor.* Katherine McDowell (as Sherwood Bonner), *Sewanee River Tales.* Mary Noailles Murfree (as Charles Egbert Craddock), *In the Tennessee Mountains.* E.D.E.N. Southworth, *Why Did He Wed Her?* Susan Warner, *A Red Wallflower.* William Wells Brown dies.

1885   George Washington Cable, *The Grandissimes.* Henry Harland (as Sidney Luska), *As It Was Written: A Jewish Musician's Story.* William Dean Howells, *The Rise of Silas Lapham.* Sarah Orne Jewett, *A Marsh Island.* Mary Noailles Murfree (as Charles Egbert Craddock), *A Prophet of the Great Smoky Mountains.* Clarissa Minnie Thompson, *Treading the Winepress* (completed in 1886). Mark Twain, *Adventures of Huckleberry Finn.* Susan Warner, *Daisy Plains.* Martin Delany dies. Susan Warner dies. Helen Hunt Jackson dies.

1886   Louisa May Alcott, *Jo's Boys and How They Turned Out.* Rebecca Harding Davis, *Natasqua.* Henry Harland (as Sidney Luska), *Mrs. Peixada.* William Dean Howells, *Indian Summer* and *The Minister's Charge.* Henry James, *The Bostonians* and *The Princess Casamassima.* Sarah Orne Jewett, *A White Heron and Other Stories.* Luigi Donato Ventura, *Peppino.* Emily Dickinson dies. Haymarket Riot in Chicago. American Federation of Labor organized. Kansas passes legislation allowing women to vote in municipal elections.

1887   Augusta J. Evans (Wilson), *At the Mercy of Tiberius.* Harold Frederic, *Seth's Brother's Wife.* Mary E. Wilkins Freeman, *A Humble Romance and Other Stories.* Henry Harland (as Sidney Luska), *A Land of Love* and *The Yoke of the Thorah.* William Dean Howells, *April Hopes.* Harriet Waters Preston, *A Year in Eden.* John Dewey, *Psychology* (rev. 1889, 1891). Interstate Commerce Commission created.

1888   Edward Bellamy, *Looking Backward 2000–1887.* Edward Eggleston, *The Graysons: A Story of Abraham Lincoln.* Frances Ellen Watkins Harper, *Trials and Triumphs.* William Dean Howells, *Annie Kilburn.* Henry James, *The Aspern Papers.* Grace King, *Monsieur Motte.* Amélie Rives, *The Quick or the Dead?* Louisa May Alcott dies.

1889   Rose Terry Cooke, *Steadfast*. Henry Harland (as Sidney
        Luska), *Grandison Mather, or An Account of the Fortunes of Mr.
        and Mrs. Thomas Gardiner*. Lafcadio Hearn, *Chita*. William
        Dean Howells, *A Hazard of New Fortunes*. Mark Twain, *A
        Connecticut Yankee in King Arthur's Court* (as *A Yankee at the
        Court of King Arthur*). Constance Fenimore Woolson, *Jupiter
        Lights*. Jane Addams founds Hull House in Chicago.

1890   Octavia Victoria Rogers Albert, *The House of Bondage, or,
        Charlotte Brooks and Other Slaves*. Kate Chopin, *At Fault*.
        Emily Dickinson, *Poems*. Lafcadio Hearn, *Youma*. William
        Dean Howells, *The Shadow of a Dream*. Sarah Orne Jewett,
        Strangers and Wayfarers. George Washington Cable, *The
        Negro Question*. William James, *The Principles of Psychology*.
        Jacob Riis, *How the Other Half Lives*. Mississippi passes laws
        restricting voting by African Americans. Sherman Anti-
        Trust Act passed. Formation of General Foundation of
        Women's Clubs.

1891   Sophia Alice Callahan, *Wynema*. Edward Eggleston, *The
        Faith Doctor*. Mary E. Wilkins Freeman, *A New England Nun
        and Other Stories*. Alice French (as Octave Thanet), *We All*.
        Hamlin Garland, *Main-Travelled Roads*. William Dean How-
        ells, *An Imperative Duty*. Emma Dunham Kelley, *Megda*. José
        Martí, "Our America." James Russell Lowell dies. Herman
        Melville dies.

1892   Mary Hallock Foote, *The Chosen Valley*. Charlotte Perkins
        Gilman, "The Yellow Wall-Paper." Frances Ellen Watkins
        Harper, *Iola Leroy, or Shadows Uplifted*. William Dean How-
        ells, *Mercy*. Annie Nathan Meyer, *Helen Brent, M.D.* Anna
        Julia Cooper, *A Voice from the South*. Ida B. Wells, *Southern
        Horrors: Lynch Law in All Its Phases*. Walt Whitman dies. John
        Greenleaf Whittier dies. Homestead strike. Populist Party is
        founded.

1893   Stephen Crane, *Maggie: A Girl of the Streets* (rev. 1896).
        Edward Eggleston, *Duffels*. Mary E. Wilkins Freeman, *Giles
        Corey, Yeoman* and *Jane Field*. Henry Blake Fuller, *The Cliff-
        Dwellers*. William Dean Howells, *The World of Chance*. Henry
        James, *The Real Thing and Other Tales*. Grace King, *Balcony
        Stories*. Victoria Earle Matthews, *Aunt Lindy*. Ruth McEnery
        Stuart, *A Golden Wedding and Other Tales*. Worst economic

depression of the nineteenth century begins. World's Columbia Exposition held in Chicago. Pullman strike.

1894   Gertrude Atherton, *Before the Gringo Came* (rev. in 1902 as *The Splendid Idle Forties*). Kate Chopin, *Bayou Folk*. Mary E. Wilkins Freeman, *Pembroke*. William Dean Howells, *A Traveler from Altruria*. Harriet Prescott Spofford, *A Scarlet Poppy and Other Stories*. Ruth McEnery Stuart, *The Story of Babette* and *Arlotta's Intended*. Mark Twain, *Pudd'nhead Wilson* (enlarged edition as *The Tragedy of Pudd'nhead Wilson, and The Comedy of Those Extraordinary Twins*). Havelock Ellis, *Man and Woman: A Study of Secondary and Tertiary Sexual Characters*. Henry Demarest Lloyd, *Wealth against Commonwealth*. Oliver Wendell Holmes dies. Josephine St. Pierre Ruffin founds *The Woman's Era*, first black women's newspaper, in Boston. Pullman strike broken by federal troops.

1895   Stephen Crane, *The Red Badge of Courage* and *The Black Riders and Other Lines*. Alice Dunbar-Nelson, *Violets and Other Tales*. Mary "Molly" Moore Davis, *Under the Man-Fig*. Mary E. Wilkins Freeman, *The Long Arm*. Elizabeth Stuart Phelps (Ward), *A Singular Life*. Ida B. Wells, *Red Record*. Frederick Douglass dies. Booker T. Washington delivers the "Atlanta Compromise" speech at the Cotton States and International Exhibition in Atlanta.

1896   Abraham Cahan, *Yekl: A Tale of the New York Ghetto*. Stephen Crane, *George's Mother*. Rebecca Harding Davis, *Doctor Warrick's Daughters* and *Frances Waldeaux*. Paul Laurence Dunbar, *Lyrics of Lowly Life* and *The Uncalled*. Mary E. Wilkins Freeman, *Madelon*. Harold Frederic, *The Damnation of Theron Ware*. Joel Chandler Harris, *Sister Jane*. Sarah Orne Jewett, *The Country of the Pointed Firs*. Charles M. Sheldon, *In His Steps*. Ruth McEnery Stuart, *Sonny*. Joseph Le Conte, *Evolution: Its Nature, Its Evidences, and Its Relation to Religious Thought*. Harriet Beecher Stowe dies. Harriet Jacobs dies. U.S. Supreme Court upholds segregation in *Plessy v. Ferguson*.

1897   Kate Chopin, *A Night in Acadie*. Mary E. Wilkins Freeman, *Jerome, a Poor Man*. Ellen Glasgow (anon.), *The Descendant*. Henry James, *The Spoils of Poynton* and *What Maisie Knew*. Harriet Prescott Spofford, *An Inheritance*. Havelock Ellis,

Studies in the Psychology of Sex (1897–1910). First subway opens in Boston.

1898   Gertrude Atherton, *The Californians* (rev. 1935). Abraham Cahan, *The Imported Bridegroom and Other Tales of the New York Ghetto*. Stephen Crane, *The Open Boat and Other Tales of Adventure*. John W. De Forest, *A Lover's Revolt*. Ellen Glasgow, *Phases of an Inferior Planet*. Henry James, *The Turn of the Screw*. Emma Dunham Kelley (Hawkins), *Four Girls at Cottage City*. Charles Major, *When Knighthood Was in Flower*. Charlotte Perkins Gilman, *Women and Economics*. Spanish-American War. U.S. acquires Philippines, Puerto Rico, and Guam and annexes Hawaii.

1899   Charles Chesnutt, *The Conjure Woman*. Kate Chopin, *The Awakening*. Sutton E. Griggs, *Imperium in Imperio*. Henry James, *The Awkward Age*. Frank Norris, *McTeague*. John Dewey, *The School and Society*. Sigmund Freud, *On the Interpretation of Dreams*. Thorstein Veblen, *The Theory of the Leisure Class*. E.D.E.N. Southworth dies.

1900   James Lane Allen, *The Reign of Law*. Charles Chesnutt, *The House Behind the Cedars*. Theodore Dreiser, *Sister Carrie*. Paul Laurence Dunbar, *The Love of Landry*. Alice Dunbar-Nelson, *The Goodness of St. Rocque and Other Stories*. Winnifred Eaton (as Onoto Watanna), *Miss Nume of Japan*. Mary E. Wilkins Freeman, *The Heart's Highway*. Ellen Glasgow, *The Voice of the People*. Pauline Hopkins, *Contending Forces*. Mary Johnston, *To Have and to Hold*. Harriet Prescott Spofford, *The Maid He Married*. Mark Twain, *The Man That Corrupted Hadleyburg and Other Stories and Essays*. Edith Wharton, *The Touchstone*. Stephen Crane dies.

1901   Gertrude Simmons Bonnin (Zitkala-Sa), *Old Indian Legends*. Charles Chesnutt, *The Marrow of Tradition*. Paul Laurence Dunbar, *The Fanatics*. Winnifred Eaton (as Onoto Watanna), *A Japanese Nightingale*. Mary E. Wilkins Freeman, *The Portion of Labor*. Pauline Hopkins, *Hagar's Daughters* (completed 1902). Henry James, *The Sacred Fount*. Sarah Orne Jewett, *The Tory Lover*. Frank Norris, *The Octopus*. Jacob Riis, *The Making of an American*. J. P. Morgan organizes U.S. Steel as the first billion-dollar corporation. President William McKinley assassinated.

1902   Thomas Dixon, *The Leopard's Spots*. Paul Laurence Dunbar,
        The Sport of the Gods. Winnifred Eaton (as Onoto Watanna),
        The Wooing of Wisteria. Augusta J. Evans (Wilson), *A Speckled
        Bird*. Ellen Glasgow, *The Battle-Ground*. Sutton E. Griggs,
        Unfettered. Joel Chandler Harris, *Gabriel Tolliver: A Story of
        Reconstruction*. Pauline Hopkins, *Of One Blood* (completed in
        1903). Henry James, *The Wings of the Dove*. Ruth McEnery
        Stuart, *Napoleon Jackson: The Gentleman of the Plush Rocker*.
        Edith Wharton, *The Valley of Decision*. Owen Wister, *The Vir-
        ginian*. Charles Alexander Eastman, *Indian Boyhood*. William
        James, *The Varieties of Religious Experience*. Frank Norris dies.
        U.S. coal strike.

1903   Winnifred Eaton (as Onoto Watanna), *The Heart of Hyacinth*.
        Henry James, *The Ambassadors*. Jack London, *The Call of the
        Wild*. Frank Norris, *The Pit*. Mary Austin, *The Land of Little
        Rain*. W. E. B. Du Bois, *The Souls of Black Folk*. First commer-
        cially successful film, *The Great Train Robbery*, released.
        Orville and Wilbur Wright make their first successful flight
        at Kitty Hawk, North Carolina. Ford Motor Company is
        established.

1904   Winnifred Eaton (as Onoto Watanna), *Daughters of Nijo* and
        The Love of Azalea. Ellen Glasgow, *The Deliverance*. Henry
        James, *The Golden Bowl*. Mary Johnston, *Sir Mortimer*. Eliza-
        beth Stuart Phelps (Ward), *Trixy*. Edith Wharton, *The
        Descent of Man and Other Stories*. Henry Adams (anon.),
        Mont-Saint Michel and Chartres. Lincoln Steffens, *The Shame
        of the Cities*. Ida Tarbell, *The History of the Standard Oil Com-
        pany*. Kate Chopin dies.

1905   Charles W. Chesnutt, *The Colonel's Dream*. Thomas Dixon,
        The Clansman. Mary E. Wilkins Freeman, *The Debtor*. Sutton
        E. Griggs, *The Hindered Hand; or, The Reign of the Repression-
        ist*. David Graham Phillips, *The Deluge*. Marie Van Vorst,
        Amanda of the Mill. Edith Wharton, *The House of Mirth*. Nia-
        gara movement, forerunner of the NAACP, is established.

1906   Winnifred Eaton (as Onoto Watanna), *A Japanese Blossom*.
        Ellen Glasgow, *The Wheel of Life*. Jack London, *White Fang*.
        Ernest Poole, *The Voice of the Street*. Upton Sinclair, *The Jun-
        gle*. Harriet Prescott Spofford, *Old Washington*. Meat Inspec-
        tion and Pure Food and Drug acts passed.

1907   Thomas Dixon, *The Traitor*. Edith Wharton, *The Fruit of the Tree* and *Madame de Treymes*. Henry Adams, *The Education of Henry Adams*. Henry James, *The American Scene*. William James, *Pragmatism*. Financial panic.

1908   Mary E. Wilkins Freeman, *The Shoulders of Atlas*. Ellen Glasgow, *The Ancient Law*. Jack London, *The Iron Heel*. Helen Reimensynder Martin, *The Revolt of Anne Royle*. Edith Wharton, *The Hermit and the Wild Woman and Other Stories*. Joel Chandler Harris dies. General Motors is established.

1909   Mary Austin, *Lost Borders*. Ellen Glasgow, *The Romance of a Plain Man*. Jack London, *Martin Eden*. Thomas Nelson Page, *John Marvel, Assistant*. Ezra Pound, *Personae*. Gertrude Stein, *Three Lives* (composed 1905–6). William James, *A Pluralistic Universe*. Sarah Orne Jewett dies. Sigmund Freud lectures on psychoanalysis at Clark University. Model T car produced by Henry Ford. Largest women's strike in American history by shirtwaist workers. National Association for the Advancement of Colored People (NAACP) is founded.

1910   Winnifred Eaton (as Onoto Watanna), *Tama*. Mary E. Wilkins Freeman, *The Green Door*. Charlotte Perkins Gilman, *What Diantha Did*. Corra Harris, *A Circuit Rider's Wife*. Edith Wharton, *Tales of Men and Ghosts*. Jane Addams, *Twenty Years at Hull-House*. Rebecca Harding Davis dies. Mark Twain dies. First U.S. newsreel made.

1911   Theodore Dreiser, *Jennie Gerhardt*. W. E. B. Du Bois, *The Quest of the Silver Fleece*. Charlotte Perkins Gilman, *Moving the Mountain*. Ellen Glasgow, *The Miller of Old Church*. Mary Johnston, *The Long Roll*. Edith Wharton, *Ethan Frome*. Charles Alexander Eastman, *The Soul of the Indian*. Charlotte Perkins Gilman, *The Man-Made World; or Our Androcentric Culture*. Frederick Winslow Taylor, *Principles of Scientific Management*. National Council of Women Voters founded. Triangle Shirtwaist Co. fire in New York City results in the deaths of 146 employees and brings national attention to exploitative working conditions.

1912   Mary Austin, *A Woman of Genius*. Willa Cather, *Alexander's Bridge*. Theodore Dreiser, *The Financier*. Edith Maud Eaton (as Sui Sin Far), *Mrs. Spring Fragrance*. Winnifred Eaton (as

Onoto Watanna), *The Honorable Miss Moonlight*. Zane Grey, *Riders of the Purple Sage*. James Weldon Johnson (anon.), *The Autobiography of an Ex-Coloured Man*. Edith Wharton, *The Reef*. Mary Antin, *The Promised Land*. Harriet Monroe founds *Poetry: A Magazine of Verse* in Chicago. Strike against American Woolen Company in Lawrence, Massachusetts, led by IWW.

1913   Willa Cather, *O Pioneers!* Robert Frost, *A Boy's Will*. Ellen Glasgow, *Virginia*. Mary Johnston, *Hagar*. Jack London, *The Valley of the Moon*. Mary White Ovington, *Hazel*. Eleanor H. Porter, *Pollyanna*. Edith Wharton, *The Custom of the Country*. First Imagist manifesto issued. Transcontinental calls begin with the establishment of connections between New York City and San Francisco. New York Armory exhibition of Post-Impressionist paintings. Congressional Union for Woman Suffrage established by Lucy Burns, Crystal Eastman, and Alice Paul. Paterson Silk Strike in New Jersey.

1914   Theodore Dreiser, *The Titan*. Robert Frost, *North of Boston*. Mary Johnston, *The Witch*. Frank Norris, *Vandover and the Brute* (written 1894–95). Gertrude Stein, *Tender Buttons*. *Des Imagistes*, edited by Ezra Pound, appears in England and the United States as the first Imagist anthology. Margaret Anderson founds *Little Review*. Wallace Stevens publishes first major postcollege poems in *Poetry*'s special war issue, edited by Harriet Monroe. World War I begins in Europe.

1

Sentimentalism versus Professionalism: Augusta J. Evans and Henry James

"We are utterly weary of stories about precocious little girls," a very young Henry James wrote in an 1865 review, and probably no words more aptly summed up the battle for domain over the American novel in the second half of the nineteenth century—or, for that matter, the striking prominence and success of sentimental novels, often about those precocious little girls, by women writers throughout the nineteenth century.[1] James's words, oddly enough, anticipated both the wild popularity of yet another "precocious little girl"—the noble and erudite heroine Edna Earl of Augusta J. Evans's best-selling 1866 novel *St. Elmo*—and the critical condemnations of that novel and the whole agenda of literary sentimentalism, condemnations voiced by a good many postbellum writers and critics who yearned to establish some sort of order over the flood of words and novels sweeping over the American public in the middle decades of the nineteenth century. The most striking feature about American novels in the 1850s and 1860s, when male writers like Henry James were coming of age, was the fact that so many of those novels were unapologetically sentimental narratives—featuring stereotyped characters, sensationalized plots, seemingly pat endings, highly emotional appeals, and openly didactic agendas designed to influence their readers and reform the public sphere according to the values of hearth, home, and piety.

They were also novels written, not insignificantly, by women, and singularly successful women at that, like Susan Warner, Harriet Beecher Stowe, E.D.E.N. Southworth, and Augusta J. Evans. *St. Elmo*, which traces the emotional trials and literary triumphs of that "precocious little girl" Edna Earl, was so popular throughout the entire century that a special single edition of the volume required

1

the printing of 100,000 copies.[2] Indeed, so prominent were best-selling women writers like Evans in American letters that by mid-century terms like "culture" in general and "literature" in particular had very nearly come to be defined as inherently feminine. As David Leverenz has pungently observed, "To be a man of culture had become an effeminating oxymoron in America well before the Civil War."[3] And no one was more acutely aware of that effeminat-ing quality than ambitious young male writers like Henry James and William Dean Howells, who resolutely repudiated the senti-mental novel as a valid literary endeavor and set about to redefine the call of writing as something very like an exclusively male pro-fession, and the world of letters itself—and by implication the pub-lic sphere—as staunchly masculine.

Explicitly in their criticism and implicitly in their novels, James and Howells in particular came to define literary professionalism as the very antithesis of the sentimentalism so characteristic of best-sellers like *St. Elmo*. Sentimental writers like Alabamian Augusta J. Evans, in turn, found themselves thoroughly exasperated by what Edna Earl herself caustically refers to as "these self-elected officials of the public whipping-post"—by which she means, of course, male critics who savaged best-selling novels by women writers as ama-teurish at best and excessively emotional and calculatingly commer-cial at worst.[4] Hence what emerged in the postbellum literary marketplace was something very like a pitched gender battle—between, on the one hand, sentimental women novelists like Evans, who stoutly insisted upon their right of access to the public arena of political and literary exchanges and upon the literary worth of their lucrative novels, and ambitious young male writers like James, who were just as determined to eject the sentimental, the commercial, and the popular from the realm of art.

Indeed, no two novels could appear at first glance to be more unlike than Evans's *St. Elmo* and James's novella *The Aspern Papers*, published much later, in 1888, but they share a common concern with authorship and the proper way it should be defined. More to the point, perhaps, each novel envisions the agenda of the other as its dark opposite. *St. Elmo* presents its explicitly sentimental agenda of remaking the public sphere according to the values of hearth, home, and piety partly in opposition to the values associated with literary professionalism—to a certain exclusiveness and elitism, and to critics sneering at the pretensions of women authors and jealously guarding the doors of the literary realm. In contrast, *The Aspern Papers* poses the necessity of rescuing genuine literature—or rather, the undiscovered papers of a long-dead poetic genius—from the custodianship of women lacking the knowledge or the taste to appreciate their true worth. The two novels bear no ostensible relation to one another, but so compelling are the concerns they share—the effects of authorship and the articulation of literary standards—that *St. Elmo* and *The Aspern Papers,* separated by more than 20 years, nonetheless engage in a debate of sorts between a female-oriented agenda of sentimentalism and a male-oriented agenda of literary professionalism.

Evans's novel follows the trials of the young orphaned Edna Earl, the granddaughter of a humble Tennessee blacksmith, who early on in her life is "seized" by the "daring scheme of authorship" and pursues it to great success, producing one highly pious and learned novel after another and exerting a pronounced influence to the good not just upon her adoring public but upon the man she loves but has dismissed for his reprobate rakishness (125). She achieves these impressive results, Evans's narrator repeatedly and pointedly observes, despite the caviling of literary critics who denounce Edna's work for every possible reason. Having attained her greatest goals and left a considerable legacy among her readers and the public at large, Edna ultimately renounces the profession of writer to devote herself to her reformed rake.

James's novel, in contrast, sides with the world of critics—or at least appears to—for his first-person narrator and protagonist is a literary critic willing to pursue any subterfuge, pay any amount of money, for the private papers of a much-heralded and now-dead American poet. As the self-appointed guardian of the poet's art and memory, the narrator of *The Aspern Papers* asserts repeatedly that it is his duty to wrest the papers from the improper and vaguely scandalous custodianship of the poet's now aged muse and mistress and her niece, neither of whom, the narrator hints, is capable of fully appreciating the poet's work. The result is a curious and sometimes highly ambiguous portrait of a critic who sees himself charged with the responsibility of retrieving from the unworthy hands of unknowledgeable and untrained women a treasure that properly belongs in the literary realm—and by implication, of course, in the hands of someone who is indeed a trained literary professional.

However radically opposed the agendas of *St. Elmo* and *The Aspern Papers* are, then, the questions these two novels pose are unnervingly similar: who has the right to write and who does not, to whom should art be directed and why, and what ultimate effect should art bring about in its readers? Both novels also raise the question of the relationship between literature and money, whether a novel or a poem should be regarded as a commodity or as a carefully crafted artifact removed altogether from monetary considerations. This last question is particularly crucial because it foregrounds the growing division in the second half of the nineteenth century between self-consciously defined high culture—the kind of culture championed, for instance, by James himself and by implication removed from mundane monetary considerations—and popular culture, defined in part by its very complicity with those considerations, by the kind of financial success a writer like Augusta J. Evans was able to achieve with the best-selling *St. Elmo.*

These questions, then, specifically pondered what direction American fiction should take—the way it was to be written, by whom and for whom—and what control should be exerted over the literary marketplace emerging by the 1850s and 1860s. "One of the basic facts in American literary history," Alfred Habegger writes in *Gender, Fantasy, and Realism in American Literature,* "is that during the decade in which Howells and James came of age, the 1850s, the best-selling American works of fiction were written by, and probably consumed by, women."[5] Susan Coultrap-McQuin estimates that in the antebellum period 40 percent of novels reviewed in journals and newspapers were written by women. By the 1850s, she adds, women writers had produced nearly half the decade's best-sellers, and "by 1872 women wrote nearly three-quarters of all the novels published."[6]

Clearly, by midcentury the American novel had begun to emerge as a peculiarly feminine business, and what's more, increasing numbers of women made a living producing novels about and largely for women. For many of those women authors, writing novels was a matter of sheer financial survival, but producing fiction for and about women could be surprisingly profitable as well. Susan Warner's 1851 novel *The Wide, Wide World* sold more than 100,000 copies, and Harriet Beecher Stowe's *Uncle Tom's Cabin,* Coultrap-McQuin observes, "surpassed the 300,000 mark within the first year of publication."[7]

Most popular of all may well have been Evans's own *St. Elmo,* which probably sold more copies than any other single work about a woman by a woman novelist. The novel is still "ranked among the most successful works published in the nineteenth century," according to Nina Baym.[8] So quickly did the novel sell when it was first issued that its publisher, G. W. Carleton, found it necessary to run notices in the New York *Tribune* apologizing for falling behind with orders for the book. After just four months, the publisher noted, one million people had already read the novel—at a time when the national population was estimated at 36 million.[9] *St. Elmo* was to maintain its popularity for years and then decades, and would eventually inspire the naming of steamboats, railroads, towns, hotels, and even a host of assorted luxuries. "There was," Evans's biographer reports, "a 'St. Elmo' punch, a very strong 'St. Elmo' cigar, and several blue-ribboned dogs named 'St. Elmo.' "[10] On the strength of the popularity of *St. Elmo,* Evans was able to command a hefty $15,000 advance for her next novel, *Vashti,* published in 1869, and by 1884 she had reportedly earned approximately $100,000 from her best-selling novels.[11]

Interestingly enough, the novels written by women writers like Evans tended to fit a familiar pattern, as Baym notes in her study of women's fiction in the nineteenth century. It was, essentially, the same tale told over and over again, that of "a young girl who is deprived of the supports she rightly or wrongly depended on to sustain her through life and is faced with the necessity of winning her own way in the world." By the time she comes to an end of her trials and the novel's end as well, she has developed a sense of "her own worth as a result of which she does ask much from herself." Molding herself according to her own standards, she also changes the way her world perceives her, and the result, Baym concludes, "is a new woman, and by extension, the formation of the world immediately around her."[12]

The language and the plots used to evoke this transformation are frankly sentimental, a term that since the late nineteenth century has increasingly been associated with excessive appeals to emotion, idealization, evasion of reality, and calculating commercialism, not to mention clumsy and implausible plots and flat, stereotypical characters. But those associations were in part the formulation of writers like James and modernist novelists anxious to expel the sentimental from fiction altogether and thereby effecting, as Philip Fisher argues, a radical division by the early years of the twentieth century between the best-selling novel that appealed to sentiment and, by implication, to the lowest common denominator, and the novel of high art, defined in part by its rejection of the sentimental and the popular. Such wholesale dismissals, though, are in many respects highly misleading because they simply ignore or dismiss the explicitly political and often radical agenda often linked with the sentimental novel—that is, its appeal to readers for sympathy for those generally considered marginal in society—the slave, the child, the poor, the outcast, the elderly. It was through sentimental appeals and language, after all, that Harriet Beecher Stowe made her daring bid to attack slavery as an institution that directly threatened the American family itself.[13]

Perhaps even more to the point, sentimental novels ranging from Susan Warner's *The Wide, Wide World* and *Uncle Tom's Cabin* to *St. Elmo* contributed to the growing pluralization of the public arena at midcentury by extending within the realm of literature "a full and complete humanity," as Fisher astutely argues, "to classes of figures from whom it has been socially withheld." Those who are designated the proper objects of sentimental compassion, Fisher adds, "are the prisoner, the madman, the child, the very old, the animal, and the slave. Each achieves, or rather earns, the right to human regard by means of the reality of their suffering."[14] These are figures, sentimental novels argued, who deserve not only the compassion of novel readers but the right to be heard and to be recognized as fellow actors in the public sphere; hence sentimental novels in general tended to counsel their readers on the necessity of awarding recognition of the suffering and the identity of these figures commonly regarded as marginal and inconsequential.

Implicit in this insistence upon extending recognition to those who had generally been denied it was the assumption that the public sphere of American life could be reorganized according to the ideals of the home and domesticity—the priority of family well-being over the demands of competitive business, for instance, and the primacy of religious piety as well. Writing and reading a sentimental novel meant acting on the compassion generated by the depiction of the lowly and deserving and thus making that sense of compassion felt in the public sphere. In a word, the public sphere could be transformed through the power exerted by the sentimental novel upon its readers. To write a sentimental novel, as one critic has recently observed, was "to make a space for woman's voice" in the public arena of political and literary debate, and even more, to assume the possibility of remaking that arena according to the values associated with women and the home—in particular, the valuing of family integrity, the upholding of morality, and the championing of religious piety.[15]

This is the agenda that Edna explores almost from the very beginning of the novel, which opens with the 13-year-old girl happening upon a duel, fought by two men in the name of "honorable satisfaction," which results in the death of one of the participants. The duel evokes both the masculine nature of the public sphere upon which Edna has inadvertently stumbled and its impiety, for Edna immediately sees the reckless encounter as thoroughly irreligious and destructive and denounces it as murder. Early on, then, the duel impresses upon Edna the necessity of reforming the public sphere in the interest of family and religion, an agenda Edna explicitly articulates for herself when she begins to pursue the "daring scheme of authorship." All books, she maintained, "should be to a certain extent didactic, wandering like evangels among the people, and making some man, woman, or child happier, or wiser, or better, more patient or more hopeful by their utterances" (126).

Accordingly, her first novel, begun when she is merely 18, aims to offer "a vindication of the unity of mythologies"; finding it necessary "to popularize a subject bristling with recondite archaisms and philologic problems, she cast it in the mould of fiction" (126). The book becomes a best-seller, and Edna herself is lionized. As the narrator notes with no little satisfaction, "the blacksmith's grandchild had become a power in society" (346). Conscious of the influence she wields over the public, she then starts a new novel, which she titles "Shining Thrones of the Hearth" and envisions as an explicit defense of woman's domestic sphere and literary sentimentalism. Motivated by her distaste for and distrust of feminism and the women's suffrage movement, Edna nonetheless insists that women are "the real custodians of natural purity, and the sole agents who could successfully arrest the tide of demoralization breaking over the land" (358).

Still, Edna's agenda of transforming the public sphere through the power of sentiment is a precarious one at times, in part because of the "prejudice that exists against literary women," as the narrator notes (358). Indeed, Edna herself is repeatedly castigated for her boundless ambitions by everyone from her minister to St. Elmo, the rake whom she eventually reforms. She is told time and again that her literary designs are unwomanly and beyond her capacity, until she begins to wonder "whether all women were browbeaten for aspiring to literary honors" (177). So relentless is the criticism of her literary ambitions that she ponders the difficulty of entering "that arena, where fame adjudges laurel crowns, and reluctantly and sullenly drops one now and then on female brows" and puzzles over possible solutions "to baffle the dragon critics who jealously guard" the literary arena (177). Two particularly formidable guardians of that arena appear to be St. Elmo Murray, the beloved rake from whom she is estranged for so much of the novel, and his close friend Douglass Manning, who edits the learned periodical in which Edna first begins to publish. Both of them present initially fierce opposition to Edna's literary ambitions and her openly sentimental agenda. Manning even chastises her for indulging in "the rather extraordinary belief that all works of fiction should be eminently didactic, and inculcate not only sound morality but scientific theories" (281). Writers, Manning tells her, are not, as she says, "custodians" of an age's "tastes" and "morals"; rather, "they simply reflect, and do not mould public taste" (282). Critics who follow, responding to her first book, bombard her with denunciations:

Newspapers pronounced her book a failure. Some sneered in a gentlemanly manner, employing polite phraseology; others coarsely caricatured it. Many were insulted by its incomprehensible erudition; a few growled at its shallowness. To-day there was a hint of plagiarism; to-morrow an outright, wholesale theft was asserted. Now she was a pedant; and then a sciolist. Reviews poured in upon her thick and fast; all found grievous faults, but no two reviewers settled on the same error. (340)

Even Edna's body and its perceived weaknesses seem to conspire against her ambitions, for her own doctor warns her of the danger of "incessant mental labor" for a woman of her delicate health (334).

Yet Edna and her novels eventually triumph, for, as the narrator notes, "while the critics snarled, the mass of readers warmly approved; and many who did not fully appreciate all her arguments and illustrations, were at least clear-eyed enough to perceive that it was their misfortune, not her fault" (341). She wins "public favor" and becomes financially successful enough to anticipate writing full-time instead of working as a governess to earn her living, as she has up until her triumph. She succeeds, in short, in transforming the public sphere, and not the least impressive of her converts is the literary critic Douglass Manning, whose initial censure turns first to admiration and then to an offer of marriage. But the most telling example of her transformative powers is St. Elmo Murray himself, a man whose former dissipation has impelled her to reject his suit but whom her steady influence remakes. Once the proudest and most cynical of reprobates, St. Elmo eschews his cynicism and dissolute behavior, regains his lost religious faith, and is ordained as a minister. Edna in turn finally accepts his proposal of marriage and, in a reversal of everything she has worked for, suddenly gives up her ambitions. On their wedding day St. Elmo tells her: "To-day I snap the fetters of your literary bondage. There shall be no more books written! No more study, no more toil, no more anxiety, no more heart-aches! And that dear public you love so well, must even help itself, and whistle for a new pet. You belong solely to me now, and I shall take care of the life you have nearly destroyed, in your inordinate ambition" (437). In a sense, St. Elmo represents the greatest success of her project of reform and social reconstruction, but that success, curiously enough, comes at the cost of her career as a writer.

That ending in turn reminds us that women writers at midcentury found themselves pressed between the demands of participating in the public arena as authors and obeying at the same time the prescriptions of True Womanhood, which dictated that woman's place was truly in the home, where Edna Earl herself, once "a pet with the reading public," finally ends up (359). Perhaps it is not so surprising, after all, as Mary Kelley and Nina Baym have argued, that so many women writers of this period modestly refused the mantle of artist and instead described their literary pursuits, in Baym's words, "as work and not art."[16] But if sentimental novelists like Augusta Evans tended to define their own agendas in terms of reconstructing and reforming the public sphere, they did not necessarily see literature and money earned from its production as antithetical values. A good many successful women writers of the 1850s and 1860s, like Evans herself and the prolific E.D.E.N. Southworth, turned to writing novels precisely because it was one of the few respectable ways they could earn money when they and their families were financially pressed. As Kelley notes, "The need for income launched the professional careers of some of the literary domestics, careers that might otherwise never have been."[17]

Indeed, one of the most striking features of Evan's *St. Elmo* is the frankness with which both the narrator and Edna Earl acknowledge that money, in a sense, makes art possible. As the novel opens, there appears to be little opportunity to pursue learning and art in earnest in the impoverished household of Edna's grandfather, where books themselves are few and far between. But when Edna loses her grandfather and ends up in the household of St. Elmo Murray and his mother through an act of charity, broad vistas of learning, art, and literature suddenly open before her precisely because the Murray household is so wealthy. St. Elmo's own private rooms, a veritable museum of rare books and beautiful objects of art from all over the world, testify to the power of money to make art and literature accessible, and it is significant that Edna herself does a good deal of thinking, reading, learning, and writing in those rooms during St. Elmo's frequent absences. Accordingly, neither Edna nor Evans herself seems inclined to see art and money as separate and antithetical. The Murray money, after all, makes it possible for Edna to pursue every erudite project she desires, from learning Greek to pondering mystery religions of the East. And when Edna first begins to find success as a writer herself, that success is measured primarily by the best-selling status of her books and by the money that she anticipates will eventually make her financially independent.

In some respects, then, Augusta Evans anticipates postbellum definitions of authorship as tied to the marketplace and wedded to commercial values. Antebellum authorship, in contrast, tended to be associated with what Susan Coultrap-McQuin calls "genteel amateurism."[18] The slow growth of the publishing business, the lack of an international copyright agreement, and low pay scales for magazine contributions conspired to treat authorship in general as a leisured avocation rather than as a professional vocation in its own right.[19] This notion of authorship provided a toehold for women writers who tended to associate themselves with a sentimental ethos emphasizing emotion and intuition over reason, calculation, and self-advancement. As Christopher Wilson succinctly puts it, "it is a remarkable fact that perhaps our most potentially professional writers of the nineteenth century, those 'female scribblers' scorned by Hawthorne and others, were obliged . . . to masquerade as amateurs."[20]

In the 1860s, 1870s, and 1880s, though, the premium placed on leisurely amateurism began to give way to pressures exerted by the rise of a new mass market for publishing and writing. The Civil War and newspaper and periodical coverage of battles had increased both the number of periodicals in circulation and the public appetite for the written word, and audiences for printed material expanded with the increase in literacy in the second half of the nineteenth century. In 1867 the first federal Department of Education was created to foster the development of free schools, and by 1881, 19 states had passed compulsory education laws.[21] Accompanying the growth of reading audiences were several factors—the Postal Act of 1879 and technological improvements in printing, engraving, and paper-making—that laid the foundation for a mass magazine market.[22] Responding to those developments was a new breed of business-men publishers replacing the "gentleman publishers" of the ante-bellum period who stressed personal relations with their writers and resisted goals defined by commercialism. Men like George P. Putman, Charles Scribner, Daniel Appleton, William Ticknor, James T. Fields, Joshua Lippincott, and James Osgood were much more concerned with reaching a mass audience than with serving as custodi-ans of taste and morality, and accordingly, as Coultrap-McQuin argues, they "competed for authors, commissioned and planned authors' articles and books, then used expensive, modern advertis-ing to sell those works."[23] Similarly, magazine editors like S. S. McClure, Edward Bok, Cyrus Curtis, George Horace Lorimer, Frank Munsey, and Walter Hines Page would increasingly distance themselves from the aristocratic standard associated with mid-nineteenth-century editors like Bliss Perry, who tended to define his audience as "well-bred people listening to after-dinner conversation in public."[24] Younger editors frankly resorted to the language of business to define publishing concerns and the priorities of literati. "A successful magazine," Bok declared in his autobiography, "is exactly like a successful store: it must keep its wares constantly fresh and varied to attract the eye and hold the patronage of its cus-tomers."[25]

Like publishers, writers in this period were to become increas-ingly conscious of the power of the marketplace, and the ideal of the leisured writer pursuing his or her craft as an avocation began to give way to the reality of the author attuned to the necessity of mar-keting that craft. As Alexis de Tocqueville had prophesied early on in the century, "Democracy not only infused a taste for letters among the trading classes, but introduced a trading spirit into litera-ture. . . ."[26] By the end of the century, American writers were begin-ning to take their cue from English authors, who were signing royalty contracts as a matter of course for their books and sometimes receiving large monetary advances before publication. Some even relied on literary agents to negotiate the thickets of the marketplace.[27]

The result was what historian Robert G. Albion once called the "communications revolution," a veritable flood of words streaming into the latter half of the nineteenth century.[28] "Between 1880 and 1900," Burton Bledstein reports, "the number of new books and editions increased three fold; between 1870 and 1900 the number of copyright registrations increased eight fold, and the number of patents applied for and issued for inventions two fold."[29] Accompanying this revolution, though, was vast anxiety about the proper way to navigate one's course through that sea of words, and out of the crisis of cultural authority marking this period arose a new veneration for the expert and the professional—for, in short, the authoritative word. In his study of professionalism and higher education, Burton Bledstein notes that middle-class audiences responded to the "riot of words" defining their era by turning for guidance to educators like Charles William Eliot of Harvard, Alice Freeman Palmer of Wellesley, and G. Stanley Hall of Clark and to reassuring texts like Noah Porter's 1870 best-seller *Books and Reading: Or, What Books Shall I Read and How Shall I Read Them?* Such experts provided a soothing aura of knowledge, rationalization, and systematization in what Lawrence Levine calls "this new universe of strangers" where late-nineteenth-century Americans suddenly found themselves stranded.[30] Hence professional schools sprang up with impressive speed, increasing the number of institutions providing training for theology, law, medicine, dentistry, pharmacy, and veterinary science from 35 in the early nineteenth century to 283 in the period between 1875 and 1900. Not surprisingly, then, it was during this period, as Bledstein observes, that the term "amateur" began to take on pejorative connotations.[31]

The need for those experts, though, and the authority they represented by virtue of their training, knowledge, and credentials, also implicitly acknowledged the ever-present possibility of disorder and disruption in an emerging mass society. All the rules, regulations, and expertise associated with what Bledstein calls the culture of professionalism testified to the never-ending struggle to impose order on disorder, normality on abnormality, expertise upon amateurism. As Bledstein himself notes, "the culture of professionalism tended to cultivate an atmosphere of constant crisis—emergency—in which practitioners both created work for themselves and reinforced their authority by intimidating clients."[32]

Indeed, the term "culture" itself, as it emerged in this period, resonated with a barely contained sense of crisis about the difficulty of structuring the new urban world of strangers emerging in this period, a world often defined by unauthorized and unsupervised spaces, from music halls to public streets. Explicitly linked with European operas, museums, and literature, "culture" evolved as a serious business above and beyond the vitality of popular music, itinerant artists, and best-selling novels.[33] So serious was that business that it was necessary for the public to turn to the experts to be told what was culture and what was not, thereby embodying, as Alan Trachtenberg suggests, "a hierarchy of values corresponding to a social hierarchy of stations or classes." Quite simply that hierarchy of values involved "respecting one's 'betters,' . . . 'knowing one's place' "; these were ideas, Trachtenberg adds, that "filtered almost inconspicuously into public discourse especially in respectable journals."[34] The audiences for high culture envisioned by those journals, in short, were implicitly acquiescent, reverential, silent, willingly led by those knowledgeable enough to define "the distance between amateur and professional."[35]

Howells and James eagerly took the lead in defining that distance in literature, and no doubt contributing to the alacrity with which they rose to the task was their eagerness to draw a sharp line between their work and that of the best-selling female novelists of the 1850s and 1860s, especially sentimental novelists like Evans.[36] "It was on this line," Alfred Habegger flatly states, "that [James] had built his career."[37] In their fiction and in their literary criticism, Howells and James took careful aim at domestic novels and the women who wrote them; the gist of their critique, whether in Howells's denunciation of the dangers of sentimental fiction in *The Rise of Silas Lapham* (1885) or James's attack on a "feminized" age in *The Bostonians* (1886), was an assault on what they saw as the lack of art, skill, and knowledgeability—in a word, the lack of professionalism—characterizing novels written for and about women.

What was needed, they both argued, was the taste and fine sense of discrimination that could be offered by the true man of letters willing to guide an unknowledgeable public into the fold of high art and culture. But such guidance did not come easily or cheaply.

"Honest criticism," Howells observed in an early review, "is at once the attribute and the indication of an educated and refined literary taste." And rather pointedly he added, "It is the impulsive act of an accomplished man."[38] Henry James for his part lamented what he perceived to be "our huge Anglo-Saxon array of producers and readers" who write and read "production uncontrolled, production untouched by criticism, unguided, unlighted, uninstructed, unashamed, on a scale that is really a new thing in the world." What was lacking, he added, was precisely the sort of professional guidance that he himself sought to offer: "It is the biggest flock straying without shepherds, making its music without a sight of the classic crook, beribboned or other, without a sound of *the* sheepdog's bark—wholesome note, once in a way—that has ever found room for pasture."[39] Hence James's prefaces in the New York Edition of his collected works, published in 1905, were to function, he told Howells, as "a sort of plea for Criticism, for Discrimination, for Appreciation on other than infantile lines as against the so almost universal Anglo-Saxon absence of these things, which tends so, in our general trade, it seems to me, to break the heart."[40]

But if James pleaded the case for high culture and its proper custodianship, he could never quite forget that a new and profitable marketplace was opening up for writers, a marketplace, moreover, that he as a self-designated custodian of culture could never quite penetrate. He might insist in "The Art of Fiction" that writing was a vocation, not a business, and that a novel drew its value from the novelist's artistry and not from the buyer's degree of interest, but he could never quite reconcile himself, as Edith Wharton once suggested, to his own apparent lack of marketability in an age when selling books was becoming a big business. By the 1880s and 1890s a mass market for fiction had come into its own, made possible by the establishment of libraries, the introduction of wood-pulp paper and high-speed printing, and the availability of cheap reprints. But the world of the best-seller seems to have remained closed to James after his early success with *Daisy Miller* in 1878.[41]

A good deal of James's ambivalence about the emerging literary marketplace, as well as his gender anxieties about the literary profession, shapes the narrative of the 1888 novella *The Aspern Papers*, a text that suggests just how intertwined the battles between art and marketability and between male professionalism and female sentimentalism were in the second half of the nineteenth century. The first-person narrator of this short novel is by his own description one of the "ministers" of the temple of the poet Jeffrey Aspern, an early nineteenth-century American writer who evokes the shades of both Shelley and Hawthorne.[42] Self-defined as "a poor devil of a man of letters who lives from day to day," the narrator has traveled to Venice for the express purpose of prying away from Aspern's much-aged mistress, Juliana Bordereau, a supposed treasure-trove of the poet's papers (340). To acquire those papers, however, the narrator is forced to undergo an elaborate masquerade and a series of delicate negotiations requiring large expenditures of money as the price to be paid for the precious papers, and therein lies the curious hesitation in the novel between the language of money and the language of art, two idioms that the narrator initially assumes to be separate and opposing.

In the name of art, the narrator lands on the doorstep of Juliana Bordereau as a romantic traveler enchanted with her crumbling palace and determined to find temporary lodging there. "I can arrive at my spoils only by putting her off her guard," the narrator tells himself. "Hypocrisy, duplicity are my only chance. I'm sorry for it, but for Jeffrey Aspern's sake I would do worse still" (282). But the narrator has more in mind than enriching his own research and writing about the poet. He intends to wrest an inestimable prize away from improper and unworthy hands, from the unappreciative and unknowledgeable custodianship of women who have no sense of high art. Juliana herself might have served as the muse of Aspern's lyrics, but she lacks the expertise, the professionalism if you will, to understand the true value of her suspected possessions. "So little are women to be counted on," the narrator concludes (290). Indeed, the narrator worries that Aspern's relationships with women, at least those to be discerned from his correspondence, can best be compared to that of Orpheus and the Maenads. "All the Maenads were unreasonable and many of them insupportable," he decides (278).

The narrator's goal, then, is to retrieve the papers of Jeffrey Aspern and return them to their proper sphere, the world of letters and art that is implicitly understood to be male. Of that world the narrator declares, "I felt even a mystic companionship, a moral fraternity with all those who in the past had been in the service of art" (305). But to fulfill his task of rescuing art from improper hands, the narrator finds himself using a tool apparently at odds with the lofty nature of

Aspern's art—money. He pays an exorbitant amount of rent for his lodging in Juliana's palace, at her insistence, and discovers that Aspern's muse is oddly preoccupied with extorting as much money as possible from him, and that preoccupation increasingly disturbs him: "Juliana's desire to make our acquaintance lucrative had been, as I have sufficiently indicated, a false note in my image of the woman who had inspired a great poet with immortal lines; but I may say here definitely that I recognised after all that it behoved me to make a large allowance for her. It was I who had kindled the unholy flame; . . . it was I who had put into her head that she had the means of making money" (339). At one point the narrator nearly begs Juliana not to harp on money in their relationship, if only for Aspern's sake. As the narrator himself observes, ". . . it had begun to act on my nerves that with these women so associated with Aspern the pecuniary question should constantly come back" (299).

But the problem here is that it is the narrator whose view of art appears to be wholly utilitarian and profit-driven. However reverential he might be of Aspern's art, he is willing to commit any indiscretion—from gently wooing Juliana's simple niece Tita to violating the sanctity of Juliana's bedroom at night—to fulfill his "desire to possess myself of Jeffrey Aspern's papers" (360). He is, in fact, distressingly susceptible himself to defining Aspern's papers in monetary terms—like "spoils," "goods," and "treasure"—rather than in the high vocabulary of art, and those terms blur the boundaries that the narrator assumes exist between the world of art and the world of money. By the time that Miss Tita suggests the possibility of marriage in exchange for possession of the papers, the narrator has become quite used to the idea of defining his prized goal as what Pierre Bourdieu would call "cultural capital," a commodity whose worth is defined by its exchange value and by the difficulty of acquiring it.[43] In the end, when the narrator contemplates his lack of success in acquiring Aspern's papers, he mourns his "loss," and in that lone word can be detected just how completely the vocabularies of art and money have merged for him.

Just as problematic is the narrator's conviction that women have no real place in the realm of arts and letters. For however much he might proclaim Jeffrey Aspern "not a woman's poet" and however passionately he might pursue the acquisition of the poet's papers, he is left with the nagging impression that Juliana and Tita, by virtue of their femininity, possess knowledge about art that he does not (277). Indeed, Juliana as muse for Aspern's art seems to evoke the possibility of "esoteric knowledge" (306). She is in some respects "too strange, too literally resurgent," in part because the narrator suspects that she has a "fuller vision of me than I had of her" (291, 293). Behind his unease is the unsettling suspicion that she knows and recognizes the narrator for what he is, knows and understands the limits of his professionalism, which cannot in the end encompass or truly do justice to Aspern's greatness as a poet.

But it is when Juliana finally confronts the narrator in her rooms at night with the epithet "publishing scoundrel" that we learn just how limited his perceptions of art and knowledge are (363). Juliana comes upon the narrator while he is frantically rifling through her secretary searching for the coveted papers, and in that terrifying confrontation with the old lady he experiences something like a recognition that he himself has been seen for exactly what he is, that Juliana possesses the ability to look deep within his soul: ". . . for the first, the last, the only time I beheld her extraordinary eyes. They glared at me, they made me horribly ashamed" (362).

And if her glaring eyes suggest an unexpected but unmistakable recognition of all that the narrator is and plots, so too does the simple and direct accusation: "Ah, you publishing scoundrel!" That accusation links the narrator with the world of the marketplace, with the business of publishing and all the compromises it represents. He may be, as he asserts, one of the "ministers" of Aspern's temple and a jealous guardian of the poet's memory, but the dogged and methodical determination by which he pursues his plot to retrieve the Aspern papers from unworthy and unqualified hands underscores his own inadequacies. He has forgotten what it is to respond to Aspern's poetry with simple, direct, uncomplicated emotion, with the sort of empathy and passion generally associated with reading sentimental literature. This is the sort of emotional intensity, strangely enough, that the narrator associates with Juliana, whom he sees marked by "a perfume of reckless passion, an intimation that she had not been exactly as the respectable young person in general" (309). Long decades after her romance with Aspern, Juliana prizes his papers and keeps them in hiding because, as Miss Tita tells the narrator, "she loves them" (337) and "lived on them" (373). And it is precisely this sort of passionate and visceral response to Aspern's poetry that seems to elude the self-appointed "minister" of his temple. The very standards the narrator sets for the reading and understanding of Aspern's poetry, for designating those who are qualified to read that poetry and those who are not, have drained him of the capacity to feel the dead poet's art. He has, as he initially says, "the responsibilities of an editor," but hardly the emotional depth for responding to art (279).

Ultimately, it is the narrator's second confrontation, this time with Miss Tita after Juliana's death, that most fully underscores his own failings. For Miss Tita in an odd sort of way suggests precisely the sort of sentimentalism against which the narrator defines his own professional set of standards. She is utterly unknowledgeable about life in general, and it is entirely probable "that Miss Tita had not read a word of [Aspern's] poetry" (319). For a person of the narrator's learning and acuity, it is, accordingly, "impossible to overestimate her simplicity" (314), and at times the narrator tells himself that she behaves as only "a completely innocent woman" would (320). But it is Miss Tita who nonetheless undertakes the final custodianship of Aspern's papers after Juliana's death, and ill-read though she may be, she turns out to be the most zealous guardian of all Aspern's ministers against possible exploitation and commodification. Miss Tita initially offers the papers to the narrator in return for marriage, an offer that he refuses in mingled horror and confusion. And when the narrator, upon reconsideration, returns the next day with a renewed "passionate appreciation" of Juliana's papers (380), he is struck in particular by the wonderful transfiguration that Miss Tita has undergone by virtue of the simple and direct emotions of abandonment and loss that she feels: "She stood in the middle of the room with a face of mildness bent upon me, and her look of forgiveness, of absolution, made her angelic. It beautified her; she was younger; she was not a ridiculous old woman. This optical trick gave her a sort of phantasmagoric brightness . . ." (381). So transfigured is she that the narrator feels tempted by her offer, but then he learns that the papers are lost forever. She has burned them, she tells the narrator, and then she "turned her back" on him. The narrator in turn is left wondering, disoriented as he is by this unexpected turn of events, if the "loss" he feels is that of the papers or of Miss Tita herself (382).

Ultimately, the ending suggests, he is compromised, even damned, by his inability to feel the simple and direct emotions that Miss Tita does. He is, we as readers are left feeling, simply too much the professional, too much the critic and the editor. In the spirit of professionalism he succeeds in extricating himself at least from the entanglements represented by Miss Tita and sentimentalism in general, but it is, once again, at the cost of that "loss" that the narrator of *The Aspern Papers*, for all his self-described acuity, is finally unable to define. Therein lie some of James's own strangely ambivalent feelings about literary professionalism and its curiously symbiotic relationship with sentimentalism. The same novel that ostensibly tries to define and defend literary professionalism and its standards against the formlessness, commercialism, and emotion of sentimentalism nevertheless covertly acknowledges both the power of the sentimental agenda and perhaps even the shortcomings of professionalism defined in opposition to that agenda. Paired with *St. Elmo*, a novel embodying all the ills that James saw as constituting bestselling sentimental fiction, *The Aspern Papers* eerily and perhaps inadvertently reveals James's own reluctance to succumb to easy answers about literary standards and even the motivations prompting the articulation of those standards. He was, after all, too much the self-conscious artist to resort to easy categorizations and dismissals, and however much he might deplore what he saw as the lack of craft in so much sentimental fiction, he could not deny the dangers of imposing too rigid a formula of expectations on a genre he once pronounced "the most independent, most elastic, most prodigious of literary forms."[44] As a young aspiring novelist and critic, James happily and enthusiastically savaged sentimental fiction, but as the seasoned novelist he could not deny the power wielded by the sentimental—or by women, for that matter—in the halls of art.

It was, in fact, precisely that power that worried him—as even his early strident attacks on sentimentalism half-reluctantly revealed. By the 1860s women novelists had firmly lodged themselves in the world of American letters. Their presence meant that energetic debates between male and female writers would continue—on the shape, standards, and gender of the literary profession, on the form of the novel, and even on the very meaning and ownership of that hotly contested literary term, realism. Defining realism and its gendered associations, in fact, would occupy the energy of two writers as disparate as Rebecca Harding Davis in the 1860s and William Dean Howells in the 1880s, and the result would be no less contentious than the war between sentimentalism and professionalism waged by Evans and James—and no less inconclusive.

2

Contending Versions of Realism: Rebecca Harding Davis and William Dean Howells

The Aspern Papers might have inadvertently raised certain doubts that Henry James had about the worth and value of professionalism in relation to sentimentalism, but in his early years as a young and aspiring writer and critic, James was notably unequivocal in his assessment of sentimentalism: writing wedded to flagrant emotional appeals and bids for the reader's sympathy was disqualified as "serious," artistically informed literature. Never was James firmer on this issue than in his reviews in the late 1860s of pioneering realist Rebecca Harding Davis. Quite simply, James found Davis's reforming instincts overly "sentimental" and didactic and her writing insensitive to issues of craft and form, in marked contrast with what he referred to as "the other school of the novel," writers implicitly male and supposedly more attuned than Davis to issues of aesthetics. Davis, James declared in 1868, "takes life desperately hard and looks upon the world with a sentimental—we may even say, a tearful—eye. The other novel—the objective novel, as we call it for convenience—appeals to the reader's sense of beauty, his idea of form and proportion, his humanity in the broadest sense."[1]

More devastating still was James's assessment of Davis's 1868 novel, *Waiting for the Verdict*. "She drenches the whole field beforehand with a flood of lachrymose sentimentalism," the young reviewer proclaimed, "and riots in the murky vapors which rise in consequence of the act." Rather grudgingly, James noted that she had "made herself the poet of poor people—laborers, farmers, mechanics, and factory hands"—and that her intention of representing "their manners and habits and woes" was essentially "good." But the problem, he added, was that "the execution has, to our mind, always been monstrous."[2]

Davis, however, was hardly the excessive sentimentalist that James claimed her to be. Her path-breaking 1861 novella *Life in the Iron-Mills* had captured widespread attention for its graphic descriptions of poverty, class tensions, and industrial grime. Allied in part with women's sentimental writing by virtue of her reform sentiments and her overt appeals to readers' emotions, she nonetheless was as inclined to pepper her nonfiction and fiction with acerbic remarks on the dangers of excessive idealism as were James and William Dean Howells themselves.

But in the second half of the nineteenth century, condemnations of women's writing as sentimental—and implicitly unrealistic—had become a recurring, even obsessive motif in the essays of James, William Dean Howells, John W. De Forest, Mark Twain, and Frank Norris. Twain himself summed up this general assessment in devastatingly funny descriptions of Evangeline Grangerford's morbid, formulaic poetry and drawings in *Adventures of Huckleberry Finn*. Sentimentalism, with its stark good and evil characters, its didacticism, its celebration of free-flowing emotion, and its happy endings, emerged as a foil for literary realism, generally defined by its concern with objective narration, its close attention to the ordinary and the everyday, and its emphasis on ordinary language. Following the lead of these writers, critics like Alfred Habegger, Michael Davitt Bell, and David Shi have recently redefined American literary realism as an exercise in defending the boundaries of late-nineteenth-century masculinity. In Bell's words, "To claim to be a 'realist' in late nineteenth- and early twentieth-century America, was among other things to suppress worries about one's sexuality and sexual status and to proclaim oneself a man. . . ."[3] Similarly, Habegger has argued that realism "bore in part an adversary or corrective relation to a major type of novel, women's fiction."[4]

However illuminating and useful this critical approach has been for late-nineteenth-century literary studies, it tends to deemphasize the pioneering contributions of antebellum women writers to realism. Judith Fetterley, Sharon Harris, and Elizabeth Ammons, among others, have argued that a serious consideration of women realist writers would require rethinking our basic notions about literary realism—its beginnings, its major figures, and its major concerns.[5] For American realism is generally described as beginning in earnest in the mid-1880s, with the publication of William Dean Howells's *The Rise of Silas Lapham*, James's *The Bostonians*, and Twain's *Adven-*

tures of Huckleberry Finn.[6] These were the novels that appeared to exemplify the major tenets of realism—commonplace subject material, detailed observation, and objective narration.[7] But as Habegger, Shi, and Harris have suggested, long before those three supposedly seminal realist novels appeared, antebellum domestic novelists like Caroline Kirkland in *A New Home, or Who'll Follow?* (1839) and Susan Warner in *The Wide, Wide World* (1850) had experimented with techniques emphasizing close observation and a wide range of characters, including the lowly and the outcast.[8] And even as relentless an opponent of sentimental literature as William Dean Howells himself acknowledged that in late-nineteenth-century American literature, "the sketches and studies by the women seem faithfuler and more realistic than those of the men."[9]

More to the point, focusing on literary realism as an expression of besieged masculinity tends to downplay the multiple, heterogeneous nature of American realism—its wide-ranging manifestations from local color to impressionism—and the sometimes congenial, sometimes tense debate between late-nineteenth-century male and female writers on the definition and constitution of literary realism and by implication the nature of the "real."[10] Shifting our perspective to the heterogeneity of realism and its underlying debates helps us make sense, first of all, of what Amy Kaplan refers to as the "bellicose" nature of the vocabulary often defining realism—its positioning of idealism, romanticism, and sentimentalism as the opposition against which it defines itself, its preoccupation with the "war" to make a place for itself in the literary pantheon, and its belligerent engagement with putative opponents even on issues of style.[11] Twain was certainly not alone in his insistence that prose itself should be combative. "Style," he declared in "Cooper's Prose Style," his famous condemnation of "unrealistic" antebellum writing, "may be likened to an army, the author to its general, the book to the campaign."[12]

This sort of combative language and the issues involved become more understandable if we pair two novels about the Civil War and its aftermath, Rebecca Harding Davis's pioneering realist novel *Waiting for the Verdict* (1868) with a novel long acclaimed as a defining text in American realism—William Dean Howells's *The Rise of Silas Lapham* (1885). Such a pairing makes it easier for us to understand the conflicted, even ambiguous nature of American realism, the role literary realism was seen as playing in defining an American sense of shared culture, and the gender anxieties accompanying that role. Both novels position themselves as true-to-life representations of Civil War and postbellum America, and the realities the novels purport to represent are ambiguous and impenetrable enough to confound seeing, understanding, and interpretation. Both novels also define their own realism in contrast to mystifying sentimentalism. But they differ to a considerable extent on how realism and sentimentalism should be defined, how men and women are allied with realism and sentimentalism, and what role the domestic and the public play in creating realistic and sentimental perspectives. The result of this pairing is a picture of American literary realism, to borrow Sharon Harris's words, as "highly contested," one in which American writers, often male and female writers, differ sharply on how realism and by implication "the real" are to be determined, in part because of tensions and anxieties accompanying rapidly changing gender roles.[13]

If representations of the "real" did appear to be so problematic in the second half of the nineteenth century, it was because Americans in this period lived in a world marked by what historian John Kasson has called "a semiotic breakdown" in reading and understanding everyday life. "In the new urban centers of the Western capitalist democracies," Kasson notes, "traditional notions of social relations, manners, and appropriate behavior all appeared in disarray."[14] Buffeted by the impersonal forces of urbanization and industrialization, a growing number of Americans no longer lived in small, homogeneous, face-to-face communities structured by the traditions of religion and hierarchical deference. Throughout the second half of the century, religion experienced, in historian Anne C. Rose's words, "the quiet erosion of inherited patterns of feeling, belief, and practice," and in the new, impersonal, transient realm of the city, social background and position no longer seemed easily decipherable.[15] The public and the private appeared at least to move increasingly apart as white middle-class men and women allied themselves with the worlds of business and domesticity, respectively. While the family home presented itself in advice books, domestic manuals, and popular magazines as a haven from the world of business and economic competition, the public realm itself appeared inscrutable and fraught with peril. To navigate and read the public sphere, Americans turned increasingly to the growing number of practitioners skilled in "the semiotics of everyday life"—Kasson's apt phrase—including urban journalists, caricaturists, actors, performers, autobiographers, travelers, and writers of etiquette books and advice manuals.[16]

Literary critics and novelists were no less concerned with the issue of learning to read the world "out there," especially in the bewildering byways of post–Civil War America. In the long process of national healing and reconciliation after the war, the American novel was perceived as an especially useful tool for telling Americans who they were, for knitting together the separate strands of national identity, and for defining a common sense of culture. But as far as writers like John W. De Forest were concerned, the American novel of the 1860s fell short of that goal. "Is there, in other words," he asked in a now-famous essay, "The Great American Novel," "a single tale which paints American life so broadly, truly, and sympathetically that every American of feeling and culture is forced to acknowledge the picture as a likeness of something which he knows? Throwing out 'Uncle Tom's Cabin,' we must answer, Not one!" As a result, De Forest lamented, American identity was singularly fragmented and chaotic. "We are a nation of provinces," he concluded, "and each province claims to be the court."[17]

In the decades to follow, though, realism increasingly came to be perceived as the medium through which those provinces could indeed be unified into a genuine nation. Postbellum writers, Daniel Borus suggests, were acutely aware that authors and audiences in the bewildering new world of booming cities and industries no longer shared the common cultural assumptions characterizing the relationship between authors and audience in the antebellum period, assumptions ensured by the class restrictions generally defining both writers and readers. "One of the tasks that realists set for themselves," Borus notes, "was the construction of a common culture in which all classes could partake."[18] As Edward Ross was to argue in his 1923 volume *Social Psychology*, realism could forge bonds to weld together the country's increasingly fragmented mosaic of economic classes and ethnic groups. "By depicting how people of different regions, classes, races, and conditions lived," Ross declared, "the realistic writer or artist 'calls forth fellow feeling' and knits anew the ever-ravelling social web."[19]

Equally useful was the new emphasis upon empirical observation, as egalitarian in its implication as inclusive subject matter. For literary realism, as George Becker argued some thirty years ago, denied the existence of reality lying beyond the access of the senses and insisted instead upon the common experience of sensory perception shared by reader and writer. Indeed, Becker suggests that the realist writer by definition seeks to instill in his or her reader the same sensory impression by trying on the page "to retrace the steps by which he [or she] arrived inductively and empirically at certain generalizations."[20] Realism could, in short, imply equal "access to the real" for everyone.[21]

The problem was, of course, that realism by its very nature also suggested the uncertainty inherent in empirical observation. To a certain extent, as June Howard has argued, realism did indeed possess the sort of "prescriptive power" that made it difficult to envision alternatives to what was being represented.[22] But by emphasizing empirically observed details and muting authorial voice and perspective, realism also undercut the notion that everyday life could be summed up by a unitary, authoritative voice. Instead of a single perspective offered by the author and dictating the reader's response, realist novels more often than not left the task of making sense of that plethora of everyday details to the individual reader. Therein lay much of the epistemological uncertainty—the hesitancy about how to interpret those details—characterizing late-nineteenth-century American realism.[23] Novels from this period are replete with scenarios illustrating the difficulties of seeing, understanding, and interpreting anything under observation. Robert Shulman, for one, suggests that realists "often represent the epistemological consequences of the new America through images of impenetrable fog and darkness, from Twain's river through the house of darkness at the highest reaches of the class system in *Portrait of a Lady* to the dark cellar and fog in *Life in the Iron-Mills*."[24]

It was this uncertainty—and the inadequacy of sentimentalism in dealing with that uncertainty—that concerned both Rebecca Harding Davis in *Waiting for the Verdict* and William Dean Howells in *The Rise of Silas Lapham*. Significantly, both writers chose the Civil War and its aftermath—Howells less directly and immediately than Davis—as the setting of their tales to underscore the cultural disorientation of the postbellum period and the difficulty of navigating one's way through everyday life. No other event, their novels imply, could exemplify as well the chasm lying between a smaller, simpler, rural antebellum America and the postbellum America of bustling cities, population shifts, impersonal businesses, and incomprehensible market forces.

For Davis in particular, as her biographer Sharon Harris observes, seeing the war in all its brutality firsthand was one of the transformative experiences of her life. Davis herself took note of the disruptive impact of the war on individuals and on settled notions of tradition in her memoir, *Bits of Gossip.* "You cannot take a man away from his work in life," she noted caustically, "whether that be selling sugar, practicing law, or making shoes, and set him to march and fight for five years, without turning his ideas and himself topsy-turvy."[25] This is the lesson that Davis's large cast of characters—from a bookish Unionist white Southerner to a family of slaves escaping to the North—learn as the full extent of the war's upheaval reveals itself. The narrative of the novel basically traces the profound impact wrought by war upon a large cast of characters, northern and southern, white and black, elite and working-class, but what those changes would bring remained to be seen—even at the novel's end, which is strangely inconclusive and even resistant to resolution. Rather pointedly, Davis entitled her book *Waiting for the Verdict* to underscore the uncertainties awaiting blacks and whites living in a world in which slavery no longer existed.

As American consul in Venice during the war, Howells never encountered the war on the immediate level that Davis did—and he was to remain highly ambivalent about sitting out the war throughout his life—but his novel's protagonist, Silas Lapham, rose in the Union ranks from private to colonel and saw his world utterly changed in the postwar years.[26] Returning home, he tells the reporter interviewing him at the novel's outset, he found "that I had got back to another world. The day of small things was past, and I don't suppose it will ever come again in this country."[27] In a matter of a few short years, his painting business is transformed into an international concern, the Laphams find themselves living a life of wealth and leisure in Boston, and the unfamiliar reaches of Boston society appear open to them. But in this new world of money-making, speculation, buying and selling on margin, society dinners, and social calls, the naive, country-raised Laphams are cast adrift, and the bulk of the novel concerns their efforts to make sense of this unsettling and unfamiliar realm—of a world of subtly defined social distinctions, of suitors who may or may not be serious, and of ethical dilemmas in business that defy easy summary or even easy resolution.

In an increasingly materialistic world, both Davis and Howells insisted, ideals and plots lifted from romantic or sentimental novels were unlikely to provide any sort of guidance. If anything, relying on the romantic and the sentimental could be misleading at best and self-destructive at worst. Accordingly, both *Waiting for the Verdict* and *The Rise of Silas Lapham* devote a great deal of their narrative energy to the dangers awaiting those who rely on sentimental and romantic models to interpret their surroundings.

Nowhere were those dangers more pronounced, Davis and Howells implied, than in popular narratives of the Civil War in magazines in particular, for both writers were quick to voice their dismay with popular representations of the country's bloodiest conflict. "Novels and magazines," Davis observed in her early-twentieth-century memoir, "are filled nowadays with stories of gallant boys and noble old men from every free and every slave State dying for the cause they loved." It was appealing to think, she added, that only the best motives of patriotism and self-sacrifice characterized both sides, but any realistic account of war, she warned, must include the "sordid facts" of price-gouging, backroom deals, and confidence artists quick to take advantage.[28]

Davis took particular aim, though, at the lofty, abstract ideals that the Concord Transcendentalist circle saw distinguishing the Union cause. Visiting in Concord during the early 1860s, she was struck, she noted later, by the sheer irrelevance of the idealistic language they used to discuss the war. "Their theories," she said, "were like beautiful bubbles blown from a child's pipe, floating overhead, with queer reflections on them of sky and earth and human beings, all in a glow of fairy color and all a little distorted." In contrast, Davis herself, fresh from firsthand encounters with wartime encampments and military occupation, was all too aware of the conflict's tragic complexity:

I had just come up from the border when I had seen the actual war; the filthy spewings of it; the political jobbery in Union and Confederate camps; the malignant personal hatreds wearing patriotic masks, and glutted by burning homes and outraged women; the chances in it, well improved on both sides, for brutish men to grow more brutish, and for honorable gentlemen to degenerate to thieves and sots. War may be an armed angel with a mission, but she had the personal habits of the slums.[29]

As if to underscore the pitfalls to be found in the distance between lofty ideals and the realities of war, Davis does her best in *Waiting for the Verdict* to evoke something of the war's enormous complexity

by creating a wide-ranging, multiple narrative of the war's impact
on scenes ranging from New Jersey farmhouses to Union encampments and on characters from abolitionists to Kentucky aristocrats
and their slaves. Nothing and no one will be the same after this conflict, the narrative repeatedly emphasizes, from runaway slaves to
white Northerners who must confront the issue of racial bigotry.
Into this upheaval is cast one of Davis's central characters, an aristocratic Kentuckian with Unionist sentiments named Garrick Randolph, who is distinguished by an almost comical devotion to the
bookish, the sentimental, the chivalric, and the romantic. That
dreamy affiliation turns out to be his undoing for nearly the whole
of the novel since he struggles, largely without success until the
very end, to discover a role in the war to fit his Unionist sympathies,
an occupation to support his new family, and a way of coming to
terms with a disturbing family secret. Randolph's romanticism and
his "book-notion of marriage," his wife, his own identity, and nearly
everything else, for that matter, trip him up at nearly every narrative turn, and nowhere more so than when he is trying to understand his practical, abolitionist-minded wife Rosslyn, who has little
use for his sentimental inclinations.[30] "He did not even know what
meaning the day had for her," the narrator tells us. "Inside of the
cordial laugh, the affectionate, helpful look, Ross' brown eyes kept
their own secret" (245). Rosslyn's father Joe Burley tells Randolph
with a laugh that the latter is unable to "see" anything that contra-
dicts his ethereal ideals of gallant, chivalric men and distant, pristine ladies, and this incapacity turns out to be a major handicap in a
novel where nearly every character has something to hide and thus
requires careful scrutiny and "reading" for full comprehension.

In a like vein, Howells takes as a major concern in *The Rise of Silas
Lapham* the dangers of sentimentalism in a world made perilous and
unfamiliar by the aftermath of war and the momentous changes it
has brought about. Like Davis, he was horrified by romantic representations of the war appearing the first few years after Appomattox
and distinctly relieved by the appearance of John W. De Forest's
1867 novel *Miss Ravenel's Conversion from Secession to Loyalty*, often
described as the opening shot of realism's war on sentimentalism.
". . . [T]he heroes of young-lady writers in the magazines," Howells
lamented in a review of De Forest's book, "have been everywhere
fighting the late campaigns over again, as young ladies would have
fought them." De Forest, though, wrote about the war from his own

experience as a soldier. "His campaigns," Howells asserted, "do not try the reader's constitution, his battles are not bores. His soldiers are the soldiers we actually know. . . ."[31]

And like Davis again, Howells was so utterly convinced of the difficulties sentimentalism posed for reading and comprehending reality that a good deal of his story about the rise and fall of Silas Lapham's fortunes in postbellum Boston concentrates on the misunderstandings arising from depending too heavily upon the romantic plots of sentimental novels. Guided by his wife Persis, Silas comes to believe, like his entire family, that the Brahmin Tom Corey is courting his strikingly beautiful younger daughter Irene, who has few gifts as a conversationalist, whereas the truth is that Tom is taken with Penelope, the older, clever daughter who appears to be defined largely by her wit and by her extensive but haphazard reading. It is all too easy, as the Corey family minister Reverend Sewell declares, for people to follow the lead of romantic plots of beautiful heroines and gallant suitors since sentimental novels absorbed with love and marriage appear to form "the whole intellectual experience of more people" (1044). Readers are too easily influenced, Sewell adds, by the "whole business of love, and love-making and marrying," which novelists portray "in a monstrous disproportion to the other relations of life" (1044).

Even the most avid readers in Howells's novel, Penelope herself and Tom's sister Nanny, feel compelled at times to denounce popular novels for their idealistic posturing and their celebration of flamboyant self-sacrifice. One novel in particular that those readers discuss, *Tears, Idle Tears,* focuses on a love triangle eventually resolved by the refusal of a young woman to accept the man who loves her in order to spare the unrequited feelings of a friend in love with the man. The plot is initially disparaged by Penelope and pronounced "'Slop, Silly Slop'" by Nanny (1043), but its momentum seems to sweep up Penelope and the other characters, who find themselves reenacting the novel's plot of self-sacrifice when Tom's love for Penelope is revealed. "It's the end of life for me," Penelope dramatically tells Tom, "because I know now that I must have been playing false from the beginning" (1067). Determined to be noble and to save her sister's feelings, she resolutely renounces Tom, only to create chaos in both households—the Coreys are thoroughly disoriented by this development, and the family peace of the Lapham household is disrupted. Not until Penelope in particular is weaned

from the sentimental plots she has read, Howells suggests, can her
own narrative be set aright to run smoothly.

Sentimentalism, then, served to define everything that realism
was not, as far as both Howells and Davis were concerned, but just
how one was to define realism and the real was another matter altogether, one on which the two writers differed sharply. The "real"
that Davis paints is considerably more ambiguous and heterogeneous than the one created by Howells. Davis's characters include a
far greater range—from aristocrats to slaves and laborers—than
Howells's slice-of-life in genteel, upper-class Boston. But perhaps
even more disconcerting is the way two aspects of the "real," the
domestic and the public, are represented in each novel and the
implications those representations hold for the writers' respective
notions of the "real." Davis portrays a setting in which the boundaries between the private and the public have been unsettled to a
considerable degree by the war, and those blurred boundaries in
turn suggest in general a fluid, unstable notion of reality and in particular new roles for men and women and an implicitly egalitarian
view of marriage. Howells, in contrast, evokes a postbellum world
rigidly divided between the domestic and the public, between the
world of women and the world of men, and his solution to this
demarcation is to return to a more straightforwardly patriarchal era
predating the emergence of domesticity.

From the beginning, Davis questions conventional boundaries supposedly separating the public from the private by choosing as one of
her central characters Rosslyn Burley, introduced as an herb girl who
regularly plies her wares in Philadelphia's marketplace among the
roughest of associates. Rosslyn is also the illegitimate daughter of
James Strebling, a Kentucky aristocrat, who apparently abandoned her
pregnant mother. Significantly, the weak-willed and morally obtuse
Strebling, who first meets his daughter as a small child, takes for
granted Rosslyn's "outcast" status in polite society and tells an
acquaintance, a young woman named Margaret Conrad, that any
meeting between the two women in Philadelphia would be inconceiv-
able. Rosslyn, he tells Margaret quite firmly, lives in a world of the
marketplace and hence by definition would be barred from polite society and the private sphere of middle-class and upper-class women.
But Margaret does come to meet Rosslyn, simply because they both
cross the boundaries between public and private with an ease that
tends to horrify the more conventional characters in the novel.

Rosslyn, we learn, defies convention by working as an operative for the last stop of the Underground Railroad and has opened her New Jersey farmhouse to an odd assortment of runaway slaves and social outcasts. She is, moreover, an artist who specializes in drawing scenes and people lying far outside the purview of the conventional middle-class home, from runaway slaves to hucksters in the marketplace. Margaret Conrad, in turn, the daughter of a blind Methodist preacher, demonstrates her own unconventionality by taking it upon herself to manage her father's mule-selling business, even to the extent of crossing the lines between Federal and Confederate forces in Kentucky. Both young women, in short, seem to illustrate the shifting status of women during the Civil War who felt compelled to take on occupations conventionally associated with the male public sphere. The alarm that they provoke among the novel's more traditionally oriented characters, like Garrick Randolph's imperious, aristocratic-minded aunt, is portrayed with a certain malicious relish on Davis's part. "Young women of the present day were different from those she knew," the narrator notes pointedly of the aunt.

It was owing to the "march of mind," perhaps, or transcendentalism, which was the same thing, she believed; they had not penetrated into the old Virginia houses in which she had lived; among the light-hearted, clear-eyed young girls there; girls whose literary taste were formed on the Spectator, and Scott's novels. . . . Perhaps they did not keep up with the run of current books, but they were tainted with no vulgar radicalism about slavery or spirit rapping. . . . (37)

After the fashion of Harriet Beecher Stowe, whom Davis admired, the novel also underscores the intrusion of the public sphere into the private realm by the great issue of the day—slavery. In a world in which slavery continues to exist, Davis insists, no home, no private life, can be left secure and intact. Hence character after character reveals that at the heart of the private and the domestic lies the corrosive impact of slavery. Garrick Randolph's pride in his aristocratic lineage is considerably shaken when he learns that his father may have been disinherited by his grandfather and that the will documenting that move may have been guarded all these years by a family slave who literally and figuratively holds the fate of the Randolph home in his hands. John Broderip, a Philadelphia physician famed for his elegant home and aristocratic taste, harbors his own secret: his true identity as the slave boy who appears briefly at the very beginning of the novel and then seemingly disappears. Once he reveals that identity to the world at large, significantly enough, his richly furnished home is dismantled and summarily invaded by white Philadelphians who regard his revelation with contempt. Nowhere, though, is the intrusion of slavery into the home more pronounced than in the portrayal of the slaves Nathan and Anny, whose family has been scattered by the unthinking and arbitrary actions of their owners and whose dreams of freedom, like those of George and Eliza Harris in *Uncle Tom's Cabin*, are summed up in the vision of a small modest home safe from harm.

If Davis questions the traditional division between domesticity and the public realm, she also, with a certain caustic pleasure, interrogates conventional associations of the sentimental with the feminine and the realistic with the masculine—most prominently in her portrayal of the romance and marriage between Garrick Randolph, the Kentucky aristocrat, and Rosslyn Burley, the abolitionist and artist fiercely loyal to her rough wagoner grandfather and her own humble background. Theirs is a romance, the novel suggests with a touch of acidity, that begins with the reversal of romance and its expectations for heroes and heroines. "In the old romances . . . ," Randolph himself notes, "the adventure always begins by the rescue of the maiden's life by the knight," but he himself, he acknowledges with chagrin, has been the rescued, not the rescuer (89). Long dissatisfied with his bookishness and his distance from what seems to be "real" life, Garrick takes on the mission of a dead Union soldier to relay important information to the Federals, but in the course of that mission he is nearly captured by Confederate troops, only to be saved by Rosslyn, who makes him masquerade as her mulatto driver and who directs him safely to Federal lines.

That reversal of traditional gender roles seems to distinguish their relationship as a whole. From the beginning Garrick is defined as the dreamy sentimentalist unfamiliar with "real" life, unused to action, and thoroughly convinced that old romantic books provide the best guide to life. "All of Randolph's thoughts," the narrator observes, "ran formally like sentences in books, and sounded to him generally, as if some one else had spoken them, there had been, so far, so little live pleasure and pain in them" (42). Rosslyn, in contrast, is distinguished by her capacity to take charge and for her "blunt words" (91). She is, we are told, "as headlong as her blundering old grandfather in putting out her hands to anybody who was in the mire; whether man, woman or beast, mattered nothing to her" (52).

Their courtship and marriage is a study in opposites, and the narrator spares no effort in telling us how thoroughly "unrealistic" Randolph is in comparison with Rosslyn's sturdy earthiness: "Now Ross had always been content to shoulder the circumstances of her life as they were, but ten minutes after Randolph heard them, and while he was telling her his love, he was smothering and clothing them in a mist of poetic fancies" (232). Randolph dreamily envisions Rosslyn as a heroine awaiting a prince charming and dismisses her abolitionist beliefs and those of her guardian Friend Blanchard as "a woman's puny view . . . of a great political controversy" (56). Rosslyn in turn responds with anger to Randolph's remarks about the degrading nature of physical labor and with impatience to his unworldliness. "In the market and alley where she had lived, she had known sights and sounds which would bring a blush to this young man's cheek," the narrator observes (83). Moreover, she finds his pride in "blood" absurd and his notions of the paternalistic nature of slavery fanciful at best. Having helped many an escaped slave on the last stop of the Underground Railroad, she is the one, she tells him pointedly, who has "the ugly fact [of slavery] in my hands" (57).

Their opposing traits of sentimentalism and realism eventually create a gulf between them after their marriage. Randolph remains mired in his romantic notions of men and women and in his conviction about the rightness of slavery and his place as a slaveowning aristocrat. Rosslyn, in contrast, comes to see her husband with all his failings, "coolly, critically, apart from all glamour of love" (245).

Davis is not content, though, with reversing the association of masculinity with realism and femininity with dreamy idealism. Garrick's airy notion of chivalry and family honor, she suggests, is dangerous precisely because it prohibits a clear-eyed view of the nefarious institution of slavery. Blinded by his determination to maintain his sense of self as an aristocrat, Garrick even goes as far as to sell the slave guarding the ugly secret of his inheritance to Confederate troops in Georgia. Not until he resolves to rectify that act and find the slave does he come to see slavery—and its aftermath of lynching, brutality, and poverty—for what it truly is. Opening his eyes to the institution's abuses, he thereby acknowledges the rightness of Rosslyn's views, on everything from slavery to the dangers of romanticism.

Having been converted to Rosslyn's realism, Garrick Randolph finally sheds his southern romanticism, rectifies the wrong done to the family of slaves the Randolphs have owned, and achieves his "true" manhood in a turn of plot offering nothing so much as a sly dig at the plot of John W. De Forest's novel *Miss Ravenel's Conversion from Secession to Loyalty*, which forthrightly insists upon the necessity of converting feminine sentimentalism and romanticism to masculine realism. For in De Forest's novel, much praised by Howells for its realism, a young Louisiana belle named Lillie Ravenel makes a journey from starry-eyed, unthinking loyalty to the South to a somber affiliation with the Union cause and is able to do so in part because she finally marries the right man. Initially a southern partisan "strictly local, narrowly geographical" in her feelings and opinions, Lillie eventually comes to eschew all things glamorous, romantic, and southern in favor of the Union and antislavery.[32] Guiding her way in part is the right-thinking, right-living New Englander Captain Colbourne, who, significantly enough, sees the war as a lesson in acquiring true manhood. "I believe," Colbourne tells her, "the War will give a manlier, nobler tone to the character of our nation" (453). The implication here, of course, is that the nation needs a good dose of masculine realism to rid itself of the deadly effects of feminine romanticism—partly responsible, the novel pointedly suggests, for the country's worst conflict. This is the assumption, though, that Davis questions and gently lampoons. Her particular convert to the northern cause can only gain true manhood once he heeds his wife's more realistic perspective.

The tale of how Garrick Randolph does find his manhood is only one of several story lines in the novel. Like so many other writers of her age, Davis tended to see the Civil War as a supreme test in manhood, but masculinity, the novel repeatedly suggests, comes in many forms, and therein lies a good deal of the complexity and open-endedness puzzling and even exasperating the novel's contemporary reviewers. There is the "true manhood," for instance, that the runaway slave Nathan finds in joining the Union army at great personal risk (303). There is also the yearning for manhood that Dr. John Broderip feels impelling him to reveal his race to the world and to throw in his lot with black Union troops. "How to be a man—," he wanly tells a friend appalled by the doctor's self-sacrifice; "that's what we want to know—not how to be a God" (320). To achieve these versions of manhood, the novel implies, one must reveal a hidden self, a true reality—whether the "secret self" that Nathan reveals when he drops the fawning mask of the slave and aids Federal soldiers or the true identity that Broderip has long guarded. And to reveal that hidden self, disconcertingly enough, means uncovering not a shared experience of reality but a multileveled, heterogeneous reality, one that shifts from perspective to perspective—from abolitionist to slaveowner to slave. A Union soldier discovers something of that multiple truth when he suddenly realizes that Nathan as runaway slave embodies not just untapped potential but an alternative sense of reality: ". . . here was a call for strength outside of his world: a man sinking into a slough which would be death to body and soul, and be inefficient on the brink" (169).

The result is a novel of multiple revelations and plots not unlike the odd household that Rosslyn gathers about her of society's odds and ends—or, for that matter, her drawings of everyday life. "They are studies of nature," she tells Randolph, "which no book can furnish me" (97). Accompanying the story of Rosslyn and Garrick Randolph are those of Nathan and his family, John Broderip and his growing love for Margaret Conrad, the Methodist preacher's daughter, Margaret's own struggle with her instinctive dislike of anyone black, and Joe Burley's long-simmering feud with James Strebling, the man who abandoned his daughter.

Together those plots resist easy summary or the evocation of a unified sense of reality, and it was precisely that difficulty, oddly enough, that irritated the young Henry James reviewing the novel. The general idea of opposing northern and southern character in the novel, James suggested, was praiseworthy, but he added: "The chief fault, artistically, in working out this idea is that she has made two complete plots with no mutual connection. The story balances in an arbitrary manner from Ross Burley to Margaret Conrad and from Randolph to Dr. Broderip."[33] Sixteen years later, though, in his famous essay "The Art of Fiction," James himself would underscore the necessity of resisting easy categorizations of the real. "It goes without saying," he observed, "that you will not write a good novel unless you possess the sense of reality; but it will be difficult to give you a recipe for calling that sense into being. Humanity is immense, and reality has myriad forms. . . ."[34] One could argue, then, that Davis's novel anticipated certain aspects of James's own theory of literary realism by a decade and a half.

Howells, in contrast, was far more inclined to give something that did indeed resemble a recipe for reality in his essays and his novels.

A year after the publication of *The Rise of Silas Lapham*, he quite explicitly suggested that American realism required by its very definition the omission of the unpleasant and the disturbing. "In a land," he observed, "where journeymen carpenters and plumbers strike for four dollars a day the sum of hunger and cold is certainly very small, and the wrong from class to class is also almost inappreciable." Hence he added, "We invite our novelists . . . to concern themselves with the more smiling aspects of life, which are the more American."[35] And in striking contrast to Davis, Howells tended to see the world he represented in his fiction as far less fluid and susceptible to change, particularly in regard to the boundaries separating the private from the public.

The postwar Boston represented in *The Rise of Silas Lapham*, in fact, is one rigidly divided between the feminine realm of the domestic and the masculine realm of business, and therein, the novel suggests, lies the origin of the mishaps befalling the Laphams.[36] Reaping the benefits of his successful paint business, Silas Lapham appears to live in a world almost wholly limited to business, money, and the buying and selling of commodities. "Besides himself and his paint Lapham had not many other topics" of conversation, the narrator tells us quite explicitly (961). The house he decides to build on the Back Bay becomes in many respects his most conspicuous commodity, the most distinctive badge of his business success, and even the books he purposes to buy for his new library are viewed as mere badges of his wealth.

Immersed in the business of making money, Silas leads an inner life that has drifted apart from that of his wife Persis, once his closest confidante and adviser in the paint business but now lodged in a new feminine world of parlors, leisure, and shopping. The energetic and sensible Persis, the novel makes clear, is clearly wasted in this world, but the momentum of Lapham's business success seems to have made relegation of husband and wife to separate spheres all but inevitable:

She was a woman who had been used to seek the light by striving; she had hitherto literally worked to it. But it is the curse of prosperity that it takes work away from us, and shuts that door to hope and health of spirit. In this house, where everything had come to be done for her, she had no tasks to interpose between herself and her despair. She sat in her own room and let her hands fall in her lap,—the hands that had once been so helpful and busy,—and tried to think it all out. (1076)

Traditionally, Persis Lapham has been viewed as the conscience of the novel, the warning voice that Lapham fails to heed as he tries "to get in" with the Brahmin Coreys, acquire an aristocratic son-in-law and a new social standing, and indulge in the reckless practice of buying and selling on margin. But as John W. Crowley argues, Howells was clearly disturbed by the world of domesticity that seemed in many respects to define white middle-class women apart from the realm of men and business. To Howells, separating the private from the public created, in Crowley's words, "a gap between men's and women's lives that was potentially destructive to American society." Preoccupied with business, men had no time for art or manners, and women isolated in the domestic realm had little worthwhile with which to occupy their time. As Penelope Lapham asserts, girls and women "haven't got to do *any*thing" (972). Worst yet, Crowley suggests, women's instincts in the closeted world of the middle-class home by Howells's lights "were given either to atrophy or . . . hyperdevelopment."[37]

Persis, the novel implies, discovers something of this truth when she learns how little she now knows about her husband's business. Once the driving force behind Silas's success, Persis has increasingly become barricaded within her parlor, her shopping, and her charity work, and as a result, she no longer provides her husband with the moral compass he once required. "Up to a certain point in their prosperity," the narrator says, "Mrs. Lapham had kept strict account of all her husband's affairs; but as they expanded, and ceased to be of the retail nature with which women successfully grapple, the intimate knowledge of them made her nervous." Once Silas became financially successful, she "abandoned herself to a blind confidence in her husband's judgment, which she had hitherto felt needed her revision. He came and went, day by day, unquestioned" (888).

Though Persis continues to caution her husband about his past dealings with his former partner Milton K. Rogers, worries about the extravagant cost of their new house, and warns Silas of the dangers of speculation, she is considerably less certain of her ability to guide her husband and daughters through the new, inscrutable world of upper-class Boston society. Every new encounter with the aristocratic Coreys, in fact, makes Persis falter, from deciphering the implicit rules of social calls to navigating through the shoals of a dinner invitation. "*I* don't know what it all means," Persis says despairingly after she receives a dinner invitation from the Coreys hard on the heels of an uncomfortable call by Mrs. Corey (1025). Indeed, what the novel implies again and again is that Persis, with the best of intentions, is a singularly bad reader of that new world and the Laphams' place in it. Admittedly not much of a book reader in her new domestic stronghold, she nonetheless seems to have imbibed enough of the plots from sentimental novels to misinterpret nearly every encounter involving the Coreys and a good many of her husband's actions as well.

It is Persis, after all, who first decides that Tom is "after Irene" and who tentatively plants in her husband's mind the vague but golden possibilities awaiting an ascent into the upper reaches of Boston society (941). Their house, she hesitantly suggests, is not in the "right" neighborhood, and their daughters have probably not received the sort of education required for entrance into Boston society. It is also Persis who is thoroughly flummoxed when she learns that Tom loves not the lovely Irene but the plain Penelope. ". . . [W]e've taken up with a notion," she tells Silas, "and blinded ourselves with it. . . . I declare to goodness, when he kept coming, I never hardly thought of Pen, and I couldn't help believing at last he *did* care for Irene" (1080). Worse yet, Persis seriously misreads the presence of a secretary in Silas's office as a romantic rival and fails to offer Silas the moral guidance he needs in his final encounter with his former partner Milton K. Rogers, who tries to draw him into an underhanded real estate deal. Silas himself realizes that she is so absorbed in an earlier wrong done to Rogers "that she was helpless, now, in the crucial moment, when he had the utmost need of her insight" (1168).

Left to his own devices, Silas himself goes astray by indulging in stock speculation and by miscalculating the workings of the baffling new market forces pitting his business against a sturdier West Virginia painting firm. And though he eventually resists Rogers's enticements, he realizes that his former partner's machinations constitute "a deeper game than . . . [he] was used to" (1164). Alone in the realm of business, the narrative implies, he is all too vulnerable to forces far beyond his control.

Rather pointedly, Persis blames herself for that vulnerability and in part for Silas's financial downfall. Realizing at one point that she has not visited her husband's office in nearly a year, she acknowledges "how much she had left herself out of his business life." The distance between their respective worlds, she tells herself, "was another curse of their prosperity." Now that their prosperity was ebbing away, she "was going to know everything as she used" (1175).

Persis yearns, in short, for a time before the public and the private parted ways, before domesticity diverged sharply from business. Strikingly enough, the ending of the novel seems to confirm the rightness of that yearning. Having acknowledged financial failure and bowed to Corey family member James Bellingham's sage advice, Silas gives up the bulk of his business, leaves Boston, and returns with his family to the old Lapham farm in upstate Vermont, where he and Persis once worked side by side. In this older, more familiar environment, no distance seems to lie between the masculine and the feminine, between business and domesticity.

Such an ending seems on the face of things to evoke Howells's own yearnings for a simpler, less stratified existence, one revealing what Walter Benn Michaels calls "a fundamentally agrarian, anti-capitalist vision of the world."[38] Michaels sees the ending as repudiating the "excessiveness" of sentimental novels and of financial speculation in freewheeling, capitalistic Boston and argues that our last picture of Lapham back in Vermont, once more the country squire, implicitly confirms the rightness of the "precapitalist domestic economy" of the antebellum era. "Thus the novel ends," he says, "with a vindication of realism and domesticity both, at the expense of speculation."[39]

Michaels's reading, though, overlooks the novel's persistent condemnation of domesticity and the ills it breeds as well as the ending's implication that Silas has in the backcountry of Vermont at last found his true manhood and sense of authority. He was, the narrative tells us, "more the Colonel in those hills than he could ever have been on the Back Bay" (1200). Having lost his money, Silas has in a manner of speaking regained his family and his authoritative place within it. "In the shadow of his disaster," the narrator says, "they returned to something like their old, united life; they were at least all together again . . ." (1189). Perhaps more pointedly, the narrator adds that adversity has "restored him, through failure and doubt and heartache, the manhood which his prosperity had so nearly stolen from him" (1196). In this respect, it might be more accurate to characterize the ending as celebrating an earlier, more distinctly patriarchal notion of manhood and family innocent of the separate spheres seemingly characteristic of urban middle-class white families. Back in Vermont, away from the vicissitudes of business and the bewildering etiquette of the newly emerged domestic realm, Silas is once again the family patriarch, authoritative and unconflicted. And significantly, there is not a sign of Persis or her daughters in the last scene in which he discusses the choices he has made with the visiting Reverend Sewell.

If the ending implicitly celebrates a return to earlier, more traditional notions of manhood, it also reveals a yearning for consensus, for a single, defining story and reality rising above class tensions and antagonisms. One could argue, in fact, that the move toward consensus in the end oddly resembles the narrative structure of 1850s domestic novels, which, Amy Schrager Lang argues, "depend on a strategy of displacement in which the language of class yields to the language of gender."[40] For the class tensions between the Laphams and the Coreys eventually give way to the Laphams' withdrawal from the scene of battle and what appears to be the restoration of Silas's antebellum sense of manhood.

On the issue of closure and resolution, too, then, Howells parts company with Davis, whose novel in contrast appears to experiment with the fragmenting of narrative into multiple stories and realities. Davis's characters are by no means reconciled in the end. Garrick Randolph and his wife Rosslyn have come to terms, but the other main female character, Margaret Conrad, remains restless and unhappy, now dedicated to the teaching of black children to compensate in part for her own racism. Even more pointedly, the runaway slave Anny remains apprehensive about the future of her bright young son, who is, she says, like millions of other ex-slaves, "waitin' for the verdict" of whites hesitating between bigotry and enlightenment (354). Howells, in contrast, ends his story by resolving the thorny class tensions between the newly rich Laphams and the aristocratic Coreys shaping most of the narrative of *The Rise of Silas Lapham*. He does so, one could argue, by simply sending the Laphams back to their past, and by implication the nation's past as well, thereby removing the potential of conflict from the present.

Silas and his family, after all, have been a source of unending discomfort to the Coreys, who are dismayed by the Laphams' lack of breeding and cultural sophistication and by the prospect of a family alliance. But even though Penelope Lapham does marry Tom Corey in the end, their marriage fails to have a significant impact upon the Coreys and their small, select society. If anything, the world of the Coreys—Brahmin, aloof, disdainful of money-making—has been left intact by Silas's financial downfall and departure from Boston. And though the narrative reveals sympathy alternately for both the Laphams and the Coreys, the scales eventually weigh on the side of the Coreys when Silas meekly seeks the advice of two Corey cohorts—Reverend Sewell and family relative James Bellingham. Our last view of Silas is through the eyes of the Corey family minister, and however sympathetic the latter may be, his perspective nonetheless serves to contain the disruptive potential of Silas's character. There is, then, a good deal of justification to be found in the perspectives of critics like Amy Kaplan and John Seelye, who lament the expulsion of the Laphams from Boston and castigate Howells for what Kaplan refers to in general as narrative strategies "for imagining and managing the threats of social change."[41]

That the Laphams finally retreat to the backcountry of New England, toward their reassuring past and away from the bustling, urban, baffling present, also says a good deal about the attractions and pitfalls of local color writing in this period. Rebecca Harding Davis's characters still appear all too vulnerable on the New Jersey farmstead where they gather at the novel's conclusion and await "the verdict" of history on the outcome of the war and emancipation, but the Laphams have found shelter seemingly beyond the reach of history, change, and bewildering market forces. The shelter they find offers in many respects a pointed commentary on the shortcomings of the present—the frenzied pace of urban life, the ever-increasing demands of business, the potentially destructive nature of impersonal market forces, and the suffocating requirements of domesticity. From this perspective, the ending of *The Rise of Silas Lapham*, like a good deal of local color writing exploring backcountry life in New England, the Midwest, and the South, can be read as exemplifying the best tradition of pastoralism, contrasting the past with the present and the country with the city.

As commentators like Raymond Williams are quick to warn, though, pastoralism is always double-edged, as susceptible to confirming the status quo as it is to criticizing it.[42] And in the ending of *The Rise of Silas Lapham*, in the fate of Silas himself, we can perceive something of the double-edged quality of late-nineteenth-century American local color writing. If Silas's fate implicitly offers a critique of the urban present and its failings, the outcome of the novel also serves to affirm the present as well. Silas represents not just a reproach to that present but all that it no longer is—an old-fashioned, principled, colorful past that by its very existence as a curiosity no longer really exists in the realm of the present-day. And it is as a curiosity that the Reverend Sewell carefully scrutinizes him in the very end, stopping off to see Lapham briefly as though the latter were nothing so much as a tourist attraction to be viewed for edification and reassurance. This double-edged quality would distinguish the best local color writing as well, by practitioners as varied as Sarah Orne Jewett, Charles W. Chesnutt, and Abraham Cahan. As different as the worlds they all three celebrated and mourned, their writing nonetheless revealed the same hesitation between critique and affirmation, between lamentation for the past and commodification of its attractions.

3

Local Color and the Ethnographic Gaze: Sarah Orne Jewett, Abraham Cahan, and Charles W. Chesnutt

Country refuges, quaint villages, and the lures of tradition, community, and authenticity extended their attractions far beyond the story of Silas Lapham told by William Dean Howells. In an age of rapid industrialization, urbanization, and new surges of immigration from eastern and southeastern Europe and from Asia, stories of the country's older regions, usually referred to as local color fiction and first appearing in influential magazines like *Century, Harper's,* and the *Atlantic Monthly,* found a ready audience in the emerging white middle class. Among readers much like Silas Lapham himself, uncertain of their newly acquired status as middle class and bewildered by a new and often incomprehensible urban environment, tales of tradition-bound small communities in old New England, the Midwest, the South, and even urban immigrant enclaves appeared to offer the solace of continuity and cultural stability. In those local worlds ambition, money-making, and impersonal market forces seemed on the face of things to be reassuringly absent, and therein lay the means of contrasting the complexities of the present with the simplicities of the past.

The nostalgia implicit in late-nineteenth-century local color fiction, though, was nothing if not double edged, as recent commentators like Susan Gillman, Amy Kaplan, and Richard Brodhead have argued.[1] Local color writing might have appeared to flee the present as readily as Lapham does, but ultimately tales of quaint and picturesque localities served in many respects to reinforce middle-class readers' sense of the rightness of the present. Indeed, local color fiction resembled nothing so much as the ethnological collections and exhibits of artifacts that proliferated in the second half of the nineteenth century and appeared to confirm the triumph of industrialized Western culture. Like exhibitions of "primitive" and "quaint" peoples, from Bushmen to South Sea Islanders, local color narratives focused on subjects assumed to be marginal to the norm—New England spinsters and widows, ex-slaves, and newly arrived immigrants. And like ethnological collections, based on the artifact extracted from its original culture, local color fiction was often published in the fragmentary form of novellas, short story collections, and short story sequences, thereby situating the genre as marginal and other to the era's quest for "the Great American Novel."

In particular, what both ethnological collections and local color fiction shared was a dynamic demarcating the boundaries between the ordinary and the strange, the normative and the eccentric, and above all, spectators and spectacles. These sets of symbiotic relationships implicitly situated both the viewer of the ethnological collection and the reader of local color fiction as members of the emerging white urban middle class. By definition the artifacts on display and the local color stories being read represented everything that the audience was not, whether regional, traditional, quaint, foreign, or ethnic. For the era's emerging middle class, whose boundaries and self-definition remained far from certain, that sense of difference, figured in the content and form of both ethnological collections and local color fiction, was distinctly reassuring.

Local color fiction, in short, owed as much to the century's newly formulated ethnographic gaze, defining the boundaries between the norm of Western self and non-Western Other, as did those popular exhibitions of Laplanders and Native Americans in industrial fairs and expositions. For writers of local color fiction like Sarah Orne Jewett, Abraham Cahan, and Charles W. Chesnutt, the ethnographic gaze, defined by the distance between the Western spectator and the spectacle of an exotic, primitive figure, emerged as a central trope and thus revealed local color fiction's affiliation with the emerging middle-class status quo and at the same time the genre's possibilities for disruption. Like collections of exotic and/or primitive art and artifacts, Jewett's *The Country of the Pointed Firs*, Cahan's *Yekl*, and Chesnutt's *The Conjure Woman* offered spectacles of the quaint and the curious for middle-class consumption, but the glimpses these narratives offered of life on the nation's margins, of New England fisher folk, Russian Jewish immigrants, and ex-slaves, could sometimes be unnervingly ambiguous and chameleonlike, as could, for that matter, the position of the spectator-reader in relation to those spectacles. Ultimately, local color narratives by Jewett, Cahan, and Chesnutt simultaneously situated their audience as the middle-class norm and questioned the rightness of that designation—as they implicitly questioned the conventional distinction between novels of mainstream America and short fiction collections and sequences of the curious and the exotic.

Local color's fascination with the backwoods of the South and New England and with emerging ethnic neighborhoods in cities appeared to be an inevitable offshoot of the forces of moderniza-tion—a sort of literary tourism, as Amy Kaplan and Richard Brod-head have suggested, attracting a newly emerging middle class struggling to understand its new social and economic status in a rapidly changing world.[2] Indeed, for Americans in the late nine-teenth century, a general yearning for authenticity, for a simpler and purer life, no doubt had a good deal to do with those impersonal market forces that turn out to be so baffling to Silas Lapham and as such raise serious questions about individual autonomy and con-trol. "For entrepreneurs as well as wageworkers," T. J. Jackson Lears notes, "financial rise or ruin came to depend on policies formulated far away, on situations beyond the individual's control." The result, Lears adds, was a pronounced sense of unreality, a fear that "real life," authenticity, emotional vitality, lay elsewhere, beyond the boundaries of middle-class neighborhoods and the workings of business. Even the notion of individual selfhood seemed open to question as writers of rags-to-riches tales, like Horatio Alger, and philosophers like William James speculated on the possibility that selfhood, in Lears's words, "was neither simple nor genuine, but fragmented and socially constructed." It was that possibility above all, Lears concludes, that gave rise to a pervasive feeling of unreality among late-nineteenth-century middle-class Americans: "Without a solid sense of self to deny or control, standards blurred and Victo-rian moral boundaries grew indistinct."[3]

Almost as though to illustrate that curious twinning of nostalgic unease and celebration of progress, the industrial expositions so popu-lar in nations of the North Atlantic nearly always included two prime features: displays of "primitive" and "exotic" people drawn from the margins of nations and empires, and celebratory exhibits of industrial wonders. These were features, Curtis M. Hinsley says, that characterized nearly all large expositions following the London Crystal Palace of 1851 and the Paris Exposition of 1867—in industrial fairs held in Chicago, St. Louis, Buffalo, San Francisco, Seattle, Atlanta, New Orleans, and Nashville. Alongside the latest technological marvel could be found live groups of "exotics" ranging from Native Americans to Buddhist priests and even whole reconstructed villages.[4]

Such displays of the industrial West's Others were made possible in part by what Virginia Domínguez calls "the Euro-American scramble for [ethnographic] artifacts" in the second half of the nineteenth century, a period aptly labeled the "Museum Age."[5] In this period, well-funded foundations concerned with ethnological collecting were first established—in Leipzig, Rome, Bremen, Hamburg, and Dresden—and leaders in the "Museum Movement" found prominence, men like Spencer Baird at the Smithsonian, Adolf Bastian at the Berlin Museum für Völkerkunde, Frederick Ward Putnam at Harvard's Peabody Museum, Franz Boas at the American Museum of Natural History, and George Dorsey at Chicago's Field Columbian Museum. Providing fuel for these developments were the new concepts of "artifact" and "specimen," the former evoking relics from the distant past and the latter suggesting "examples or illustrations of 'kinds.' "[6] Therein, Domínguez argues,

lie three of the paradoxes of ethnological collecting—that in intending to depict other cultures it is seeking a depiction of our own, that it rests on a strong historical consciousness but concentrates its work on peoples perceived to be without history . . . , and that it continually depicts "man" as subject—objectifier, creator, producer—but transforms him into an object and vehicle of knowledge.[7]

In short, ethnological collections exerted a strong appeal in the nineteenth century because those exhibits of "primitive" and "exotic" peoples supposedly offered portraits of the earliest antecedents of the present. Tutored by Charles Darwin and Herbert Spencer, ethnographers and casual museum-goers alike were taught to see "savage" societies through the lens of cultural evolution. However distant and exotic a "primitive" culture might be, it was nonetheless bound to the industrial, urban West by the chain of evolutionary progress. In the West lay that "early" society's future, just as the past of the West lay in the "primitive" and the "savage."[8]

To read the past in such explicitly ethnocentric terms had disturbing consequences, particularly when it came to live exhibitions of

Laplanders and Bushmen. Looking at ethnological collections implied a certain distance between the spectator and the spectacle and inevitably a demarcation between subject and object—with all the unequal distribution of power inherent in such a delineation. Barbara Kirshenblatt-Gimblett suggests that this mode of looking is akin to the panoptic mode that Michel Foucault sees as representative of the modern age. Such a mode, Kirshenblatt-Gimblett says, "offers the chance to see without being seen, to penetrate interior recesses, to violate intimacy. In its more problematic manifestations, the panoptic mode had the quality of peep show and surveillance— the viewer is in control." Not without reason, then, Kirshenblatt-Gimblett concludes, ". . . the ethnographic gaze objectifies."[9]

To a startling degree, then, ethnological collections had a good deal in common with the abundant displays of commodities that were beginning to appear in newly established department stores.[10] Both forms of display took for granted the viewer's status as consumer of objects. One museum pioneer in the period even went so far as to suggest that museums would do well to pattern themselves on the systematic display of consumer goods in department stores rather than the catch-all repositories and curio cabinets characterizing late-eighteenth- and early-nineteenth-century museums.[11] Assertions of this sort reveal, among other things, the homogenizing impetus created by store window displays and exhibitions of aboriginal life. Both forms of spectacle provided a unifying experience for their consumers, for all intents and purposes situating viewers as members of an undifferentiated middle class with similar likes and desires. Hence store window displays and museum exhibitions alike served as mediated forms of unity, creating, in Benedict Anderson's words, "an imagined community" replacing the local, face-to-face connected communities of past cultures.[12]

Both ethnological collections and department store displays in turn offer disconcertingly apt analogies for the central concerns and indeed the narrative structure of local color fiction in this same period. Consumer goods in store windows and ethnographic artifacts in museum and exposition exhibits focused on the object as their organizing motif, an excised fragment that, in Kirshenblatt-Gimblett's words, "stands in a contiguous relation to an absent whole that may or may not be recreated."[13] In a like vein, short story collections, novellas, and short story sequences offered only fragmentary glimpses of traditional or exotic worlds once assumed to be whole in New England, the Midwest, the South, and immigrant communities. To be sure, a good deal of local color fiction first appeared as separate short stories in magazines like *Century* and the *Atlantic Monthly,* and hence publishers tended to issue subsequent book versions in the form of collections, sequences, and novellas, rather than as novels.[14] But shorter or more discontinuous fictional forms also seemed more peculiarly suited to local color fiction than the conventional long novel because of the commodified nature of those brief glimpses of worlds in decline, and because of the special role played by local color fiction in situating readers as members of the white middle class.

Local color fiction itself, after all, was a product of an impersonal marketplace and accordingly offered easily consumable fragments of tradition for readers worried about permanence and continuity in a rapidly changing world. Packaged in short, discontinuous narratives, local color fiction, like ethnographic collections in museums and industrial expositions, tended to substitute, in Susan Stewart's words, "an illusion of a relation between things" for "a social relation."[15] If anything, the narrative form of local color fiction, departing from novelistic expectations, confirmed the decline of tradition and the commodification of nostalgia. Stories of Old New England, of the Old South, even of Old World Jewry in the New World, portrayed tradition- and past-bound localities in the process of breaking up, implicitly giving way to the unified present. What better way to underscore that process of fragmentation than in short, discontinuous narratives whose very form simulated that process?

Indeed, the short story itself, as J. Gerald Kennedy has argued, has long been haunted by a "nostalgia for community" precisely because its truncated form necessarily "isolates characters from a larger social order," for which they yearn. Much the same thing can be said about the novella by virtue of the brevity of its form. One can also argue that the short story sequence, with its threads of continuity linking separate stories and its discontinuities created by the breaks between the stories, is shaped as much by the short story's nostalgia for community as it is by a resigned recognition of communal decline and fragmentation. The very form of the short story sequence, simultaneously straining toward and drawing back from a unified story, hesitating precariously between one single narrative and smaller, multiple stories, resists, in Kennedy's words, "the novelistic illusion of a continuous experiential world."[16]

In this respect, local color short fiction functions in a peculiarly symbiotic relationship with the long realist novel so popular in this period and closely bound in turn to national identity. Like ethnographic artifacts displayed to a homogeneous middle-class audience, local color fiction offered an obverse reflection of everything the big novel of the late nineteenth century supposedly was not—fragmentation, discontinuity, a preoccupation with the peripheral, the colorful, and the foreign.[17] An ambitious big novel, for instance, like John W. De Forest's *Miss Ravenel's Conversion from Secession to Loyalty* (1867), stresses the importance of national reunion by tracing the journey of the title character, an ardent Confederate, from regional loyalties toward a new national affiliation.[18] De Forest's novel, in short, subordinates region to nation, and not surprisingly, De Forest himself made a famous early call for a "Great American Novel" weaving the nation's disparate parts together.[19] But local color fiction by figures as wide-ranging as Kate Chopin and Sarah Orne Jewett remains stubbornly rooted in the nation's regions. In this respect, local color short fiction, particularly in the form of short story sequences becoming increasingly popular in this period, tended to serve as something like the novel's Other, representing anomalies expelled to the margins to ensure the "major" and weighty status of the novel, devoted to the principles of unity and coherence and to characters and themes of acknowledged significance such as, for instance, the sort of moral dilemma that Silas Lapham faces in William Dean Howells's novel.

Inherent in that subordinate status, though, was also the potential to disrupt and to blur boundaries between center and margin. Figuring otherness in form and content, local color short story collections and sequences offered potent reminders of multiple identities and multiple ways to construct narratives—of alternatives, in short, to novelistic principles of unity, continuity, and community. By virtue of its concern with the marginal and the exotic, local color fiction implicitly questioned the "imagined community" of middle-class readers even as it helped bring that community into being; and the genre's fragmentary, discontinuous narratives hinted that the aim of "the Great American Novel" to tell a single national story was largely illusion, created by the anxious need to draw distinctions between novels of mainstream America and short fiction of the nation's periphery.

It was no wonder, then, that tales of the picturesque, the quaint, and the foreign by writers as far-ranging as Mary E. Wilkins Freeman, Rose Terry Cooke, Sarah Orne Jewett, Kate Chopin, Thomas Nelson Page, George Washington Cable, Charles Chesnutt, and Edward Eggleston tended to attract such attentive—and perhaps even worried—scrutiny on the part of literary critics and middle-class readers. Potentially unsettling—as were encounters with other cultures, for that matter—local color fiction appeared to be most reassuring when lines were carefully drawn between major and minor narratives and when local color narratives themselves were safely confined as ethnographic objects on display under the gaze of their audience.

Constructed by the ethnographic gaze, local color narratives ultimately revealed more about their viewers and the way they saw themselves than about those fragments of "traditions" under survey. Regionalist writing, as Richard Brodhead argues, might have "created literary opportunities for marginal groups"—like women, African Americans, and immigrants—but it also undertook the cultural work of defining the boundaries between American self and American Other—between white urban middle-class readers assumed to be the norm and those marginal figures under surveillance assumed to be everything that was not the norm—locality, regionalism, tradition, race, and ethnicity. Local color tales of the quaint and the foreign, ironically, helped tell white middle-class Americans who and what they were by presenting them with spectacles of what they were not.[20]

Resorting to others to define the self was a particularly important strategy in this cultural work because middle-class identity, as historian Stuart Blumin argues, was still in the process of emerging in the late nineteenth century and subject to unsettling blurring of class boundaries. Blumin suggests that visible distinctions "in daily routines and social networks"—particularly the differences between low and rising incomes, manual and nonmanual jobs, urban and suburban neighborhoods, tenements and detached houses—played important roles in defining the middle class apart. Increasingly, to be middle class came to be associated with working in certain nonmanual jobs that offered the possibility for advancement and with living in homogeneous suburban neighborhoods. But those distinctions, he adds, could at times be ambiguous enough to "confuse and erode class boundaries and alter the meaning of class." Differences between jobs and incomes at the "lower boundary of the middle class" more often than not appeared less than discernible.[21] Hence other visible distinctions—like those, for instance, offered by local color narratives—took on a special importance for middle-class audiences.

By the time Jewett, Cahan, and Chesnutt began publishing in the 1880s, local color fiction had firmly established the convention of offering the middle-class reader a reassuring self-reflection in the figure of the narrator, sometimes cast in the first person and sometimes in the third person but always implicitly white, urban, and thus allied with the norm. All three writers might have proffered strange and exotic portraits of region and locality, but they nonetheless ensured that those portraits were viewed through the lens of mainstream American culture—thanks in part, no doubt, to mentors who also served as molders and gatekeepers of middle-class culture. William Dean Howells himself was responsible for championing the work of both Jewett and Cahan and also for recognizing the implicit connections to be made between Cahan's vignettes of the urban ghetto and regionalist fiction about New England. And as significant as Howells's sponsorship was his declaration that Cahan's work in particular was "foreign to our race and civilization."[22]

In a like vein, the aspiring African American writer Charles Chesnutt was warned in 1889 by an early mentor, white novelist George W. Cable, to "remember that you are writing for white Americans and English" and accordingly "to yield all the ground you honestly can to the possible prejudices of your reader."[23] A decade later Chesnutt bowed to those prejudices by producing *The Conjure Woman*, a short story sequence of dialect tales about conjure written at the behest of his Houghton Mifflin editor, Walter Hines Page, who told him quite bluntly that the conjure tales, the most exotic of the stories Chesnutt submitted, were the only ones that the firm was interested in publishing.[24]

The narrator who introduces those quaint tales of conjure, that is, traditional African American magic, is accordingly an urbane, educated white entrepreneur named John who has moved from Ohio to the sandhills of North Carolina for his wife's health and for the lucrative prospect of establishing a vineyard. It is an area, he is assured, where ". . . labor was cheap, and land could be bought for a mere song"—attractions that signal as well as any other his middle-class affiliation.[25] John is a man who has a quick eye for a potential profit, and he rather enjoys matching wits with ex-slave Uncle Julius

McAdoo, who entertains the northern businessman and his frail wife with curious tales of the slave past and superstitions about conjure and ghosts. These superstitions John generally dismisses as quaint nonsense that hinders his plans to turn a profit—as indeed they sometimes do. For by and large Julius tells his stories to protect his own interests, whether a small revenue garnered from neglected scuppernong vines or a bee tree providing a personal source of honey. It is to his own credit, John periodically congratulates himself, that his business eye can perceive the economic motive lying behind Julius's stories of specters and magical transformations, but often we as readers discover that there is more to Julius's tales than meets John's eye.

Not so easily recognizable is the impersonal third-person narrator that Abraham Cahan uses in *Yekl*, an 1896 novella of Jewish immigrant life on the Lower East Side of New York.[26] This narrator has a far less pronounced presence than John does in *The Conjure Woman*, but what voice there is speaks with the accents of mainstream, middle-class culture by and large unfamiliar with life in the ghetto.[27] As Jules Chametzky observes, Cahan saw himself "as an interpretor to the broader English-reading public of the materials of his radical, Russian-Jewish world," in part because his "stories of the New York Ghetto" appeared in leading English-speaking magazines of the day.[28] Dazzled by the "aristocratic" world of letters that his sponsor William Dean Howells represented, Cahan implicitly allied the narrator of *Yekl* with the values of the mainstream, with the assumption that the world of the Lower East Side did indeed constitute a spectacle of exotica and squalor for curious middle-class onlookers. Thus early on the narrator feels compelled to take the reader on a tour of the New York ghetto with its "teeming populations of the cyclopic tenement houses."[29] This is an exotic world, the narrator obligingly informs the unknowledgeable reader, that

shelters Jews from every nook and corner of Russia, Poland, Galicia, Hungary, Roumania; Lithuanian Jews, Volhynian Jews, south Russian Jews, Bessarabian Jews; Jews crowded out of the "pale of Jewish settlement"; Russified Jews expelled from Moscow, St. Petersburg, Kieff, or Saratoff; Jewish runaways from justice; Jewish refugees from crying political and economic injustice; people torn from a hard-gained foothold in life and from deep-rooted attachments by the caprices of intolerance or wiles of demagoguery—innocent scapegoats of a guilty Government for its outraged populace to misspend its fury upon; students shut out of the Russian universities, and come to these shores in quest of learning; artisans, merchants, teachers, rabbis, artists, beggars—all come in search of fortune. (13–14)

However sympathetically the narrator describes the oppressive forces drawing Jewish immigrants to New York, he is nonetheless acutely aware that those "dense swarms of bedraggled half-naked humanity" and "garbage barrels rearing their overflowing contents in sickening piles" can appear strange and frightening to the Anglo-Saxon middle-class reader who might indeed feel that the "pent-in sultry atmosphere was laden with nausea" (13). Hence the narrator strives to render those scenes less potentially threatening by underscoring the lines between the "spectacle" and the onlooker (15). These are sights to be pondered as ethnological displays in museums are to be viewed, evoking in the spectator, Kirshenblatt-Gimblett tells us, a mixture "of repulsion and attraction, condemnation and celebration," but nonetheless safely confined as objects under scrutiny.[30]

In a like vein, Sarah Orne Jewett squarely allies her nameless first-person narrator in the short story sequence *The Country of the Pointed Firs*, published, like *Yekl*, in 1896, with a sensibility that by implication is everything that the Maine fishing village of Dunnet Landing is not—urban, up-to-date, cosmopolitan, defined by the industrial rhythms of labor and leisure. Far more so than either Cahan or Chesnutt, Jewett took for granted in her work and her outlook a perspective that Sandra A. Zagarell, among others, sees defined by a "genteel elitism."[31] Her narrator is a summer visitor in Dunnet Landing, a professional writer from an unnamed city who is enchanted with the village's "quaintness" and "elaborate conventionalities; all that mixture of remoteness, and childish certainty of being the centre of civilization."[32] This is a world that Jewett, like Cahan and Chesnutt, felt compelled to explain to readers rooted in an urban, industrial, middle-class world. As Jewett herself recalled,

When I was perhaps fifteen, the first city boarders began to make their appearance near Berwick, and the way they misconstrued the country people and made game of their peculiarities fired me with indignation. I determined to teach the world that country people were not the awkward, ignorant set those people seemed to think. I wanted the world to know their grand simple lives; and, so far as I had a mission, when I first began to write, I think that was it.[33]

Nevertheless, Jewett, even more so than Cahan, maintains a certain distance between her narrator and the Dunnet Landing folk and by implication between the spectacle of fishing village life and the middle-class reader. Indeed, the narrator at times explicitly allies herself with the reader—and defines both self and addressee apart from the village inhabitants—by using the second-person pronoun to describe her own experiences. Charmed by the quaintness and idiosyncrasies of seaport life, the narrator flirts with the idea of truly "belonging" but never really becomes a full-fledged citizen of Dunnet Landing. Eventually, at summer's end, she returns to her life—and by association the present—in the unnamed metropolis.

Still, that sense of distance between spectacle and spectator created by the era's ethnographic gaze was susceptible to disruption, and therein lay the possibility of creating alternative ways of seeing and alternative voices and identities. If all three writers, like so many local color authors of the period, ranging from Midwesterners like Edward Eggleston to Southerners like Ruth McEnery Stuart, found it necessary to abide by the dictates of publishers and the literary marketplace and to write for a white, native-born middle-class audience, they also consciously defined themselves and their writing as peripheral to the nation's center and to "the Great American Novel" that was supposed to give voice to that center. As a woman, a Jewish immigrant, and an African American, Jewett, Cahan, and Chesnutt were granted literary access through the genre of local color—minor figures writing in a minor vein.

They nonetheless brought that status into question by taking as their primary concern the politics of the ethnographic gaze. Just who is the spectator and who is the spectacle, their fiction asked over and over again, and what were the human costs of defining that demarcation? These were questions, ultimately, that unsettled the boundaries and stability of their middle-class audience and by implication pointed to the uncertainty of middle-class identity itself.

Of the three writers, Jewett was by far the most conservative and the most wedded to the social and economic status quo. As a famous writer in her own right and as a close friend of Annie Fields, the widow of the celebrated publisher James T. Fields, Jewett moved in the highest literary circles of Boston and Cambridge and counted among her friends Howells himself, Charles Eliot Norton and his family, author Harriet Waters Preston, Ralph Waldo Emerson, Harriet Beecher Stowe, John Greenleaf Whittier, and Julia Ward Howe, "the grand old lady of Boston." The publication of her first book, *Deephaven*, earned her a seat at the famous 1879 Oliver Wendell Holmes birthday party given by the *Atlantic Monthly*.[34]

Certainly a good deal of Jewett's own sense of entitlement and security can be detected in the sense of detachment characterizing the narrator of *The Country of the Pointed Firs*. The nameless writer who tells the stories of life in Dunnet Landing describes herself on the first page as an ardent "lover of Dunnet Landing," but one of the most striking features of her sketches is the ethnographic gaze that she turns on her surroundings, rendering everything around her picturesque, exotic, and ultimately objectified (377). Nearly anything she sees around her is a curiosity to watch and ponder, from the vague and elderly Captain Littlepage to the neatly arranged, old-fashioned houses crowded near the shore, and implicit in her never-ending gaze is the self-confident assumption that a great distance yawns between her and those she gazes upon. Each sketch in the sequence is organized around a different set of sights to be watched, from the schoolhouse view in which the narrator delights to that last glimpse of Dunnet Landing caught from the boat departing for the city.

Nowhere is this tendency to look at and to diminish accordingly more pronounced than in the narrator's persistence in reducing her landlady, Mrs. Todd, to the status of object on display. Repeatedly, she insists that Mrs. Todd has "the look of a huge sibyl" (381), deserves the descriptive adjectives "grand and architectural, like a *caryatide*" (401), stands before others "like a large figure of Victory" (408), evokes the presence of "Antigone alone on the Theban plain" (417), suggests "the renewal of some historic soul, with her sorrows and the remoteness of a daily life buried with rustic simplicities and the scents of primeval herbs" (417). These are terms, admittedly, of admiration and even awe, but the frequency with which Mrs. Todd is likened to myths and museum artifacts ultimately undermines the narrator's insistence that the two women acquire emotional intimacy as the summer progresses. Instead, Mrs. Todd emerges as something like the village's chief curiosity, at least from the perspective of the narrator.

The most curious thing about *The Country of the Pointed Firs*, though, is that the narrator is not the only watcher and connoisseur of strange and enticing objects. The village houses, like that of the late Mrs. Begg, are "decorated with West Indian curiosities, speci-

mens of conch shells and fine coral" brought back on the long sea
voyages that characterized Dunnet Landing's heyday as a bustling
seaport (384). These souvenirs and curios are reminders that Dunnet
Landing was once part of a wide-ranging international market, one
linking the North Atlantic, Latin America, and Asia, and that the
seaside village's few elderly men were once active participants in an
era of international discovery and trade. Elizabeth Ammons rightly
calls these artifacts "traces of empire—tiny trophies from 'exotic'
foreign ports and colonies" that served as reminders that Dunnet
Landing was not always a backwater village offering living rem-
nants of tradition and quaintness.[35]

Perhaps more to the point, the villagers themselves, like Mrs.
Todd and her visiting friend Mrs. Fosdick, are as prone as the narrator herself to ponder the odd quirks and quaint features of what
Mrs. Fosdick calls those "strange straying creatur's that used to rove
the country" (429). Indeed, those "curiosities of human natur' "—to
borrow Mrs. Todd's words—impel both Mrs. Todd and Mrs. Fosdick to tell stories of the strange and the curious, like the tale of
Joanna Todd's self-imposed isolation on Shell-heap Island (429). In
this respect, the two inhabitants of the quaint village resemble no
one as much as the narrator herself, who feels compelled to tell stories about Dunnet Landing precisely because the community seems
so different from the world she ordinarily inhabits. And like the narrator again, Mrs. Todd and Mrs. Fosdick mourn what they see as the
demise of the quaint and the curious. "There, how times have
changed," Mrs. Fosdick observes; "how few seafarin' families there
are left! What a lot o' queer folks there used to be about here, anyway, when we were young, Almiry. Everybody's just like everybody
else, now; nobody to laugh about, and nobody to cry about" (428).
Mrs. Todd agrees with those sentiments and observes that ". . . these
days the young folks is all copy-cats, 'fraid to death they won't be
all just alike . . ." (429).

The world of the present, in short, appears as homogeneous to the
two elderly women as it does to the narrator herself, and the effect
of this realization on the narrator is decidedly disorienting. Pondering the villagers and islanders she has already met, the narrator
uneasily tells herself: "It seemed to me that there were peculiarities
of character in the region of Dunnet Landing yet, but I did not like
to interrupt" (428). Suddenly, the line between the ordinary and the
extraordinary, the modern and the traditional, the spectator and the

spectacle, does not seem to be so firmly drawn, and the narrator falters in her confident assumption that life in Dunnet Landing is picturesque and entertaining precisely because it is everything that she and her world are not. Equally unsettling is the sudden change of perspective that descends upon the narrator when she returns to Dunnet Landing from a day trip to Green Island with Mrs. Todd to visit the latter's mother. Having enjoyed the stillness and solitude of the island, the narrator abruptly views Dunnet Landing in a distinctly different light: "The town of Dunnet Landing seemed large and noisy and oppressive as we came ashore. Such is the power of contrast; for the village was so still that I could hear the shy whippoorwills singing that night . . ." (420).

If there is any episode, though, that most sharply evokes the politics of spectator and spectacle in *The Country of the Pointed Firs*, it is in the tale told to the narrator by the elderly Captain Littlepage, once a daring seafarer eager to explore the realm of the strange and foreign and now merely a village curiosity whose stories of the exotic are generally dismissed by Mrs. Todd and her friends. This is a tale, first of all, that brings attention to the strangely gendered nature of the past in Dunnet Landing. In a village whose social life appears to be heavily dominated by elderly women like Mrs. Todd, heroic figures from the village's seafaring past, like Captain Littlepage, are decidedly peripheral and very nearly without a voice. Littlepage and fisherman Elijah Tilley do indeed tell their stories to the narrator, but by and large these elderly men, who represent a more cosmopolitan, prosperous time for the village, are curiously almost mute. "As you came to know them," the narrator notes, once again implicitly linking herself to the reader, "you wondered more and more that they should talk at all" (473). Elizabeth Ammons suggests that the marginalization of these once-heroic figures situates the volume as radically feminist precisely because this narrative move reverses the usual relationship between masculine center and feminine periphery.[36]

One can argue as well that this reversal of the heroic and the domestic, the masculine and the feminine, underscores the dehumanizing costs of turning a coldly objectifying eye upon other cultures. For the story that Captain Littlepage tells is from an earlier period of exploration and discovery, of journeys into the realm of otherness. Once shipwrecked in the far North, Littlepage tells a story of "a voyage of discovery" related to him on a near-barren island of "a country 'way up north beyond the ice' " (395). There the explorers found a great town populated by "fog-shaped men" who seemed to be in "a kind of waiting-place between this world an' the next" (396, 397). Eventually, the explorers are driven away by "the human-shaped creatures of fog and cobweb" (399). Despite their eagerness to tell the world of their discovery, "the ship was lost on its return"—all but the sole survivor who tells the story to Littlepage (395). Venturing too far and recklessly into the unknown, then, clearly has its costs, as does, for that matter, the inclination to see all that is unfamiliar with the calculating eye of the ethnographic gaze. For the lost explorers the "fog-shaped men" are merely curiosities, prizes to be seized as trophies of discovery. Those trophies ultimately elude the explorers, as, for that matter, they elude Captain Littlepage, now himself a shadow of a man, a village curiosity ruined by his own ventures into the unknown and utterly unable to persuade his neighbors that his fabulous stories of the "fog-shaped men" are actually true.

The narrator in turn is struck as much by the abrupt change in the former sea captain's gaze as she is by the story itself. Telling the story, the captain is marked by an "alert, determined look and the seafaring, ready aspect that had come to his face." But as soon as he ends his story, "there fell a sudden change, and the old pathetic, scholarly look returned." The narrator concludes the sketch by noting: "Behind me hung a map of North America, and I saw, as I turned a little, that his eyes were fixed upon the northernmost regions and their careful recent outlines with a look of bewilderment" (398).

Littlepage's oscillating gaze, hesitating between certainty and disorientation, becomes the narrator's as well. Determined as she might be to relegate the sights of Dunnet Landing to the status of quaintness and tradition, the narrator becomes increasingly unsteady in her own gaze. The views she ponders—of the village inhabitants, of the town, of the islands—are too susceptible to abrupt shifts in perspective, underscored by the breaks between the individual sketches themselves. What initially appears curious and homogeneous, like Dunnet Landing itself, suddenly becomes both familiar and open to multiple views and interpretations.

And as the narrator's gaze shifts uncertainly from the perspective of the city to that of Dunnet Landing, so too, implicitly, does her very sense of self. She leaves the village apprehensive that she will find herself "a foreigner" in the world to which she returns (484). Indeed, she even feels a certain sense of estrangement from the self that she briefly became during her summer stay in Dunnet Landing. Returning to her room at Mrs. Todd's house just before her departure, she sees the setting with the new eyes of a stranger. "So we die before our own eyes," she concludes; "so we see some chapters of our lives come to their natural end" (485). It is no wonder, then, that her gaze backward at Dunnet Landing from her position on the departing steamer suggests a certain amount of relief as well as nostalgia. For the time being, at least, the disconcerting oscillation that has come to define her view of Dunnet Landing—and by implication her sense of self as well—has come to an end. The disturbing shifts in perspective that she experiences, though, tend to dislodge her early sense of certainty and confidence and her never-articulated but unmistakeable assumption that she herself, a denizen of the city, is more "advanced" than the inhabitants of Dunnet Landing.

Abraham Cahan's third-person narrator does not undergo this sort of oscillation in *Yekl*, but the title character, known as Yekl in the Old World and Jake in the New, certainly does. Jake's double name signifies just how torn he is between two worlds, between the tradition-bound, devoutly religious family and shtetl in which he was raised and the fast-paced, pleasure-seeking, money-oriented life he finds for himself in the New York ghetto. Jake's sense of self is peculiarly doubled precisely because the protagonist feels such an abrupt break between his first 22 years in Russia and his three years in the New World. Indeed, the narrator tells us that after those three years, ". . . the thought of ever having been a Yekl would bring to Jake's lips a smile of patronizing commiseration for his former self" (12).

In New York, Jake finds himself less and less inclined to abide by religious observances—to pray and to observe the Sabbath—and even to recall his "antecedents" (24). Instead, he increasingly finds "vent in dancing and in a general life of gallantry" (25). Pronounced "a *regely* Yankee" by his half-admiring, half-jeering fellow cloak-shop workers, Jake takes pride in the English words that sprinkle his version of Yiddish and harangues his fellow workers about the necessity of assimilating to American culture (8). "Once I live in America . . . I want to know that I live in America," he tells his audience. "*Dot'sh a' kin' a man I am!* One must not be a *greenhorn*. Here a Jew is as good as a Gentile" (5).

Yet Jake also periodically gives way to nostalgic and guilt-ridden meditations on his wife and child, still in Russia and awaiting travel funds to come to New York. From time to time he feels, as one chapter title indicates, "the grip of the past," particularly when he learns of his father's death (24). Then he is quickly transported to the scenes of his past, to memories of the family's observance of the Sabbath and of his wife and child. "And thereupon everything round him," the narrator notes, "—the rows of gigantic tenement houses, the hum and buzz of the scurrying pedestrians, the jingling horse cars—all suddenly grew alien and incomprehensible to Jake" (31).

Even the language Jake uses bears witness to his double consciousness. We are told by the narrator that Jake speaks a peculiar kind of Boston Yiddish "more copiously spiced with mutilated English than is the language of the metropolitan Ghetto in which our story lies" (2). The dialogue itself captures the doubleness of his language—and by implication his identity—since it highlights in italics English words incorporated in Yiddish, strives to replicate the accented nature of the speakers' fragmentary English in dialect, and offers fluent and melodious versions of Yiddish in English translation.

This sort of doubleness no doubt characterized Abraham Cahan himself, who, like Jake, left Russia as a youth, fleeing the repressions following the assassination of Tsar Alexander II.[37] Once he arrived in New York, Cahan immersed himself in the world of the New York ghetto, finding a place for himself in trade-union activism, radical politics, and Yiddish journalism. By the late 1880s Cahan was also submitting English stories and sketches to Charles A. Dana's *New York Sun*.[38] And by the time he began writing fiction in the early 1890s, first in Yiddish and then in English, Cahan found himself straddling immigrant life and mainstream American literary culture. An admirer of William Dean Howells, the crusading journalist-activist told the influential critic and author when they first met in 1892 that he had read "every line" Howells had ever written.[39] It was, in fact, under Howells's urging that Cahan began writing tales of immigrant life for English publication, and those stories implicitly situated the author in an ambiguous zone lying somewhere between the familiar environs of the ghetto and the American literary scene that he admired. Cahan came to see himself as an interpreter of American culture to the immigrant community and as a translator of immigrant Jewish culture for a mainstream American audience.[40]

Hesitating between two cultures, Cahan and his protagonist Jake suggest the interaction and interdependence of nationalism and ethnicity and their constant reinvention of and renegotiation with one another. Both nationalism and ethnicity, Werner Sollers suggests, taking heed of the work of Benedict Anderson, emerged in the eighteenth and nineteenth centuries in response to the replacement of older, face-to-face communities with imagined communities. With the new advancements in printing, transportation, and communication, as Anderson has argued, communities could be invented and consolidated based not on kinship bonds and aristocratic systems but on "texts and words." By Sollers's lights, then, ethnicity serves "not so much as an ancient and deep-seated force surviving from the historical past but rather the modern and modernizing feature of a contrasting strategy that may be shared far beyond the boundaries within which it is claimed." In short, ethnicity "is not a thing but a process," a never-ending series of negotiations between cultures using each other to define themselves and their borders.[41]

Acknowledging the fluidity of his newly acquired American identity, though, is precisely what Cahan's protagonist Jake refuses to do. For Jake is unnerved by his hesitation between two worlds, by the possibility in particular that his uncertain status in the New World could reduce him to the status of a foreign spectacle to American eyes, the object of amusement and curiosity. He strenuously resists this possibility, and that resistance takes the form of his insistence upon seeing his wife Gitl through what he thinks of as purely "American" eyes—eyes that would turn upon Gitl and everything she represents the cold stare of the ethnographic gaze, eyes that in turn would award Jake the status of "American" subject.

Even before Gitl's arrival in New York with their son Yosselé, the acclimated Jake is much inclined to think of his wife and son as curiosities of sorts from his past, images safely locked away in his memory and unlikely to disrupt his newly acquired sense of "Americanness." It is as an image in Jake's memory that Gitl makes her first appearance in the narrative, and Jake finds a certain reassurance in the way he can distance himself from that image. Merely working at his sewing machine in the cloak shop seems to carry "him away from the apparition which had the effect of receding, as a wayside object does from the passenger of a flying train, until it lost itself in a misty distance, other visions emerging in its place" (9).

Jake even tends to define his own growing sense of being American by his ability to confine Gitl to the confines of an image to be scrutinized. "From a reality," the narrator says, "she had gradually become transmuted into a fancy" (25). She and his former self have become no more than "fellow characters in a charming tale, which he was neither willing to banish from his memory nor able to reconcile with the actualities of his American present" (26). Indeed, how to make this reconciliation, the narrator adds, and how to bring Gitl and little Yosselé "out of the thickening haze of reminiscence and to take their stand by his side as living parts of his daily life," is a source of considerable anxiety and worry for Jake, and it is not surprising that he avoids thinking about that possibility as much as he can.

Hence it comes as a considerable shock to Jake when Gitl does emerge from those reminiscences and appears with Yosselé in the flesh on Ellis Island. He is openly appalled by the spectacle presented by "his wife's uncouth and un-American appearance" (34). To a startling degree, the short, dark woman with her unwieldy wig resembles "a squaw," and Jake can hardly bring himself to look at her (34). And when Gitl substitutes a kerchief for the wig at Jake's urging, she ends up looking from Jake's perspective "like an Italian woman of Mulberry Street on Sunday" (37).

In a word, Gitl looks *ethnic* to Jake the self-described Yankee, and from that moment he seems to be incapable of seeing her in any other light. Every failing he sees in her—her old-fashioned clothes, her religious observances, her hesitation in learning English—provides him with a tool for widening the distance between them. She is, he tells her over and over again, hopelessly green, and in that pronouncement lies assurance that Gitl the "greenhorn" immigrant, rooted in the habits and customs of Lithuanian Jewry, is everything that Jake himself is not. It is no wonder, then, that Gitl feels herself the object of a withering gaze, scrutinized and judged even by the furnishings of her new home, which "seemed to stare at her haughtily and inspired her with fright." As the narrator notes, "Even the burnished cup of the electric bell knob looked contemptuously and seemed to call her "Greenhorn! greenhorn!" (42).

That Jake does feel compelled to see her only in this light, of course, underscores how vulnerable he himself is to falling under an objectifying gaze. However American he looks at Ellis Island, he falls under the amused scrutiny of the immigration officer, who is struck by "[t]he contrast between Gitl and Jake" and questions Jake closely "to make sure—partly as a matter of official duty and partly for the fun of the thing—that the two were actually man and wife" (35). Later on Jake squirms at the thought of the spectacle he and his wife make to his Americanized friends at the dancing school. Bound to the old-fashioned Gitl, he feels himself abruptly relegated to the realm of the foreign and the backward. "All his achievements seemed wiped out by a sudden stroke of ill fate" (44). Yearning to restore his sense of self as Jake the Yankee, he is increasingly drawn to his old dancing-school partner Mamie, who appears considerably more Americanized than Gitl and who taunts him for being an old-fashioned religious Jew. To her he wants to proclaim that he is "as much of a Yankee and a gallant as ever" (53).

To do so, Jake slowly realizes, means leaving his wife and child and casting his lot with Mamie. This is a decision, though, that also means relinquishing his heritage for a world largely defined by money. For part of Mamie's attraction is Jake's suspicion that she has a large savings account, and when Mamie offers him all of her money to buy his way out of his marriage, the bargain is sealed. Henceforth Jake feels considerably more assured of his Yankee status, but the scene in which he makes his bargain—on a tenement rooftop festooned with drying laundry—hints at what he has lost and what he has betrayed. Waving in the wind, the laundry eerily resembles Jewish burial clothes, and for an instant, the reproachful "figure of his dead father, attired in burial linen, uprose to his mind" (77).

That sense of reproach and loss pursues him to the end of the narrative. Newly divorced and on his way to the mayor's office for his wedding to Mamie, Jake is haunted by the fear that he is "the victim of an ignominious defeat" (89)—as indeed he is. His freedom from the scrutiny of a patronizing and objectifying gaze has been purchased not just with Mamie's money but with his abandonment of the world of his fathers. In a manner of speaking, Mamie's money comes to serve as a substitute for everything that Gitl represents and Jake eventually repudiates—reverence for family and tradition, religious piety, connectedness with the past. Mamie's money makes it possible for Jake to reassure himself that he is indeed Jake the Yankee and not Yekl the greenhorn immigrant. Her money even enables Jake to move closer to the world of the narrator, by implication a thoroughly acclimated, gentile, middle-class world that is fully aware of what money can accomplish. But the Yankee, middle-class world for which Jake has traded his heritage is also disorienting and undefined. On the threshold of his new married life with Mamie and as a newly confirmed Yankee, Jake feels oddly uncertain and fearful of the future.

Almost inevitably, like any good middle-class reader of local color, Jake the Yankee looks wistfully back at his past, at his marriage to the traditionally minded Gitl, for some sense of relief from his present uncertainty: "What if he should now dash into Gitl's apartments and, declaring his authority as husband, father, and lord of the house, fiercely eject the strangers, take Yosselé in his arms, and sternly command Gitl to mind her household duties?" (89). Whether or not that backward glance can be consoling, though, remains to be seen. The conclusion of *Yekl* offers not answers but only Jake's accelerating apprehensiveness.

Cahan's ending, then, slyly brings attention to the motives underlying backward glances, exotic journeys, and nostalgic quests—to the yearning for past certainties amid present irresolution and ambiguity and to what Renato Rosaldo calls "imperialist nostalgia," the compulsion to mourn that which one has conquered and destroyed.[42] The closer Jake approaches his goal of Yankeedom, the more the novella's title—*Yekl*, rather than *Jake*—resonates with nostalgia for the self and world that Jake has lost. Compelled by Howells's sponsorship and his own reading audience to write from the perspective of the ethnographic gaze, Cahan nevertheless succeeds in illuminating its sometimes faltering nature. In particular his novella exposes those anxieties and uncertainties fueling the urgency of the gaze and therefore requiring strict boundaries between ethnic and nonethnic, abnormal and normative, spectacle and spectator. Jake does acquire much-desired Yankee status in the end, but his fierce determination to distance himself from everything that Gitl represents, whatever the costs, hints at the ultimate uncertainty underpinning that status. Those boundaries between spectacle and spectator may, after all, be more mirage than reality, carefully constructed rather than natural and self-evident. And if the ethnographic gaze in *Yekl* wavers the closer Jake comes to Yankee status, so too do the boundaries and lineaments of the native middle-class audience implicitly situated by that gaze. Cahan's reader, in the end, is left in as much uncertainty as is Jake himself.

It is this sort of uncertainty that Charles W. Chesnutt fosters and highlights as well in *The Conjure Woman*, a short story sequence whose quaint black dialect and colorful tales of the antebellum

South were aimed quite explicitly at white middle-class readers who premised their sense of racial superiority on the notion of black inferiority and subordination. In a now-famous journal passage written two decades before the publication of *The Conjure Woman* in 1899, Chesnutt declared, "The object of my writings would be not so much the elevation of the colored people as the elevation of the whites,—for I consider the unjust spirit of caste which is so insidious as to pervade a whole nation. . . ." The problem, as he well realized, though, was that he could not directly confront and attack that "spirit of caste" in an era of burgeoning Negrophobia and racial anxiety. "[T]he garrison will not capitulate: so their position must be mined, and we will find ourselves in their midst before they think it." His part as he saw it was "to accustom the public mind to the idea" of African American equality by simultaneously entertaining his white readers and leading "them on imperceptibly, unconsciously step by step to the desired state of feeling."[43]

Hence *The Conjure Woman* to a great extent offers a short story sequence "about its own complacent reception."[44] Chesnutt was acutely aware that he was writing for white readers well indoctrinated in racist stereotypes of devoted, doglike ex-slaves like Uncle Remus by Old South apologists like Joel Chandler Harris and Thomas Nelson Page, and he defined his own literary mission as disrupting that indoctrination. As he observed in a letter to Booker T. Washington, "The writings of Harris and Page and others of that ilk have furnished my chief incentive to write something upon the other side of the very vital question."[45] Chesnutt himself found both the minstrel-show portrayals of ex-slaves and the self-complacency they fostered in white readers infuriating and thus set himself to the task of complicating the representation of African Americans and unsettling the smug composure of his largely white middle-class audience.

In particular, Chesnutt was all too aware that his readers' self-complacency was bound up with the stereotypic images into which African Americans were cast as quaint, colorful, and distinctly inferior. John, the white northern narrator of *The Conjure Woman*, largely sees the ex-slave Julius McAdoo as nothing so much as a relic of slavery, and that perception colors all his encounters with Julius and his own self-image as a money-conscious, no-nonsense businessman. To John, Julius represents an antiquated sensibility defined partly by race and partly by the institution of slavery. The business

of making money, John confidently assumes, is beyond the comprehension of a black man once defined as chattel. Indeed, Julius, by
John's account, seems to see himself at one with his surroundings,
rather than taking a "proprietary" perspective of land (64), and this
attitude John patronizingly attributes to slavery and, by implication,
race:

He had been accustomed, until long after middle life, to look upon himself
as the property of another. When this relation was no longer possible,
owing to the war, and to his master's death and the dispersion of the family,
he had been unable to break off entirely the mental habits of a lifetime, but
had attached himself to the old plantation, of which he seemed to consider
himself an appurtenance. (64–65)

Similarly, John genially dismisses Julius's tales of conjure as mere
superstition, "revealing," he tells himself, "the Oriental cast of the
negro's imagination" (41). The narrator acknowledges from time to
time, and with a certain irritation, that various ulterior motives
underlie those tales—like protecting a private beehive or making an
elaborate horse-buying deal to buy a new suit of clothes—but for
the most part Julius to him embodies the black slave past—picturesque, superstitious, outmoded in a world now defined by
money.

Julius, in short, provides the narrator with a reverse reflection of
his own thoroughly modern sensibility—one attuned to practicality,
the making of money, and the dismissal of anything smacking of an
antiquated past. John's own sturdy and rather smug sense of self
rests in his confidence that Julius represents everything he himself is
not—blackness and slavery, the past and the South. Hence John
tends to dismiss the stories that Julius tells as sheer nonsense, light
entertainment for a long Sunday afternoon or harmless therapy for
his semi-invalid wife. Such is his reaction, for instance, to the story
Julius tells in "Po' Sandy," the tale of a slave woman named Tenie
who tries to protect her husband Sandy by conjuring him into a tree,
only to lose him to the local sawmill, where he provides lumber for
the slaveowner's new kitchen. To the literal-minded John the story
is merely an "absurdly impossible yarn," yet another reminder of
the distance he sees lying between Julius and himself (61).

To his wife Annie, though, the tale serves as a poignant metaphor
for the dehumanization of slavery. At the end of the story she
exclaims, "What a system it was . . . under which such things were

possible!" (60). As the stories accumulate, Annie reveals herself to be far more attuned than her husband to the masked meanings lying beneath the fantastic surface of the stories Julius tells—to the separation of families, the helplessness, and the sheer misery the tales evoke.[46] To the end John persists in seeing each story as "a very ingenious fairy tale," but Annie increasingly comes to ally herself with Julius's world of conjure by insisting that she believes their deeper truths (159). In "Sis' Becky's Pickaninny," she stoutly maintains, despite John's incredulity, that Julius's story of a slave boy reunited with his mother through conjure "is true to nature, and might have happened half a hundred times, and no doubt did happen, in those horrid days before the war" (159).

John himself remains uncomprehending—both of the stories and of his wife's response, and the contrast his obtuseness presents to Annie's growing sensitivity underscores what Eric J. Sundquist pronounces his "moral and cultural blindness."[47] To a great extent, as Sundquist suggests, he is indeed duped by Julius's storytelling—and not just by the ex-slave's plots to save his beehive or to force through a horse-buying deal.[48] The most impressive feat of Julius's stories is to trick John again and again into revealing—to the reader at least—the full extent of the white Northerner's blindness. John is utterly unable to see beyond the limits of racial stereotypes, unable to acknowledge how dependent his own sense of self is on those stereotypes, unable to read and interpret, as is his wife Annie, beneath the literal, fanciful surface of Julius's stories. He is, in short, unable to see precisely because he sees only with the eyes of the ethnographic gaze.

His blindness ultimately makes him complicit with slavery itself, an institution, as Julius's stories repeatedly show, that reduced human beings to mere objects, not unlike the way, Chesnutt suggests, white stereotypes dehumanized African Americans and the ethnographic gaze reduced all that seemed foreign and Other to the level of mere curiosity. Therein lies Chesnutt's angriest denunciation of the self-complacency that defined white middle-class readers of the late nineteenth century. For the stories Julius tells literally and metaphorically trace again and again the transformation of human beings into mere objects. In "The Goophered Grapevine" the elderly slave Henry becomes yet another crop for his master to harvest when a conjure spell intertwines his vitality with that of a grapevine. And like a crop he is sold every year in an elaborate scam concocted by his owner to earn ever-increasing profits. Similarly, "The Conjurer's Revenge" tells the story of a slave who becomes a beast of burden in earnest when a conjurer's spell turns him into a mule. Other slaves in the stories find themselves traded for horses or sold to Georgia. Still others die of heartbreak or sink into insanity. Julius even takes the trouble in "Mars Jeems's Nightmare" to venture an unflattering comparison between John, who has just fired the old man's nephew, and a slaveowner famous for his cruelty. The fate of Mars Jeems, briefly transformed into a slave himself, Julius hints, could be John's fate as well.

To the end John remains oblivious to the lessons told by Julius's stories. Still convinced of his own superiority, he tells the ex-slave that ". . . your people will never rise in the world until they throw off these childish superstitions and learn to live by the light of reason and common sense" (135). What John finds unsettling, though, is the growing alliance between Julius and his wife Annie, who intuitively understands the deeper meanings of Julius's tales and covertly aids the old man in many of his schemes. In "Po' Sandy" Annie gives Julius the lumber from the old kitchen to build a new church, and in "Mars Jeems's Nightmare" she rehires the old man's nephew against John's wishes. The last story, "Hot-Foot Hannibal," finds Annie and Julius plotting to reunite her sister with her fiancé after a brief quarrel. John even discovers at the end of "Sis' Becky's Pickaninny" that Annie has secretly accepted Julius's gift of a rabbit's foot, a talisman that John has loudly scorned.

There is, in short, a great deal more to these stories than meets John's eye, and the sense of discontinuity created by the breaks between the individual stories only serves to strengthen that impression—as though those brief lapses in narrative hint at the unseen areas of southern rural black life that John's gaze cannot penetrate or fathom. We see only a few fleeting glimpses, for example, of Annie's growing alliance with Julius, but those passages are enough to suggest that the mainstream middle-class world in which John situates himself is not nearly as sturdy and as unified as he would like to think. Annie, for one, just might defect. Nor are the lines between his world and that of Julius as sharply delineated as he is convinced they are. The mere fact that Annie quickly intuits the underlying meaning of Julius's stories and aids him in his schemes suggests that boundaries between white and black, North and South, spectator and spectacle, are not so hard and fast after all. It is also telling, as William Andrews notes, that audience response to *The Conjure Woman* was marked not by unity but by a division into two separate camps—one that pronounced the book a delightful diversion, in the words of one reviewer, "from the serious fiction of the day," and one that stressed the book's tragic realism.[49] To a certain extent, the division between John and Annie anticipates the doubleness of the book's reception.

That doubleness in turn suggests that both the ethnographic gaze and the middle-class sensibility with which it allied itself were riven with certain deep-rooted anxieties and uncertainties, in particular with the fear that boundaries between norm and curiosity, center and margin, mainstream and region, nonethnic and ethnic, might not be so pronounced after all. The very definition of "middle class" was subject to debate and change in the nineteenth century. Something of that class's underlying uncertainty could be detected in the energy with which its members anxiously tried to mark off visible boundaries between those who constituted the norm and those who were consequently defined as marginal and Other.[50] Such boundaries, though, could prove to be elusive, and the ethnographic gaze itself distinctly unreliable and subject to unsettling shifts in perspective. In the rapidly changing world of the nineteenth century, appearances could be deceiving, and nowhere more so than in the realm of otherness and marginality, in those examples of the picturesque and the quaint that both charmed and worried middle-class readers.

If the form and subject matter of local color fiction appeared to set apart the genre as minor and marginal, then, those brief, fragmentary narratives of the quaint and the curious also demonstrated their capacity for unsettling the very notion of center and marginality—and by implication the distinction to be made between minor local color fiction of margins and corners and major narratives of mainstream America. Ultimately both local color fiction and the mainstream novel raised central questions that concerned the nation as a whole—that is, the relation between nation and region, the nature of middle-class identity, and the emergence of ethnicity in relation to nationalism. In local color, surprisingly enough, could be found a medium for exploring those questions from a sharply critical perspective, one that Cahan and Chesnutt—and even Jewett to a certain extent—found particularly effective precisely because the genre's categorizations of spectator and spectacle could be unsettled and rigorously interrogated.

Local color fiction, as *The Country of the Pointed Firs, Yekl,* and *The Conjure Woman* demonstrate, did indeed provide a language for defining middle-class, mainstream America and its Others, but the picturesque and the quaint could also just as quickly turn into devastating critiques of the way local color fiction and the mainstream novel defined region and ethnicity, margin and center. No one illustrated that possibility more than Charles Chesnutt. As an African American writer who somewhat reluctantly identified himself as such to his publishers when *The Conjure Woman* was first issued, the light-skinned Chesnutt knew all too well how ephemeral the boundaries were between middle America's defining oppositions. Born in urban Ohio and raised in rural North Carolina, Chesnutt claimed both white and black ancestry and defined himself in classic middle-class terms—valuing education, self-improvement, property, and rising income. It was, accordingly, a source of neverending irritation to him that whites tended to categorize him with picturesque African Americans like Julius McAdoo rather than with middle-class America. His responsibility as he saw it, even more strongly than either Jewett or Cahan, was to disrupt the steadiness of the ethnographic gaze under which he himself fell and expose nineteenth-century categories of race for the complicated and compromising fictions they were.[51]

In that endeavor he would be joined by writers as disparate as Mark Twain, Frances Ellen Watkins Harper, and James Weldon Johnson. To a certain extent, all three writers used the conventions of local color—in particular, its ethnographic gaze and its preoccupation with the problematic categories of region and ethnicity—to launch their attacks on fictions of race and racism. Having learned the lessons of local color, in particular white America's obsession with otherness, they resolutely set themselves to the task of exposing the fictional nature of racial boundaries and the interdependence of whiteness and blackness. That task, though, would be met with varying degrees of success in a period increasingly preoccupied with erecting barriers between whiteness and blackness.

4

Novels of Race and Racism: Mark Twain, Frances Ellen Watkins Harper, and James Weldon Johnson

Nowhere was the power of the ethnographic gaze to categorize and demarcate invoked more vigorously or passionately in the period's novels than on issues of race—and nowhere was the authority of the gaze more hotly contested. In a period increasingly defined by what Robyn Weigman calls "the reign of the visual," the very act of looking was heavy with the weight of significance. Merely to look could mean assuming the role of consumer ready to purchase commodities on display or designating boundaries between the white middle-class norm and all those who stood in opposition.[1] North Carolina novelist Thomas Dixon, then, felt quite at ease making the astonishing claim in his 1905 Negrophobic novel *The Clansman* that the retina of a dead white woman could retain the unmistakable image of the black rapist who drove her daughter and her to suicide. This is the visual evidence to which Dixon's white characters turn when they seek to uncover the identity of the rapist. On the basis of this evidence—an image lingering in a dead woman's eye—the man is lynched. No passage in the period's literature more effectively illustrates the power attributed to looking—unless it be, perhaps, the scene in James Weldon Johnson's anonymously published 1912 novel *The Autobiography of an Ex-Coloured Man*, in which the protagonist reveals his racial identity to his white sweetheart: "I felt her hand grow cold, and when I looked up, she was gazing at me with a wild, fixed stare as though I was some object she had never seen. Under the strange light in her eyes I felt that I was growing black and thick-featured and crimp-haired."[2] Merely the power of the white glance, these two passages suggest, is enough to designate the configuration and character of blackness.

Determining just where blackness began and ended became one of white America's primary preoccupations in the aftermath of emancipation. With the abolition of slavery, the color line took on heightened importance for a period uneasy with emerging and shifting identities and boundaries. By the early years of the twentieth century, Jim Crow segregation laws were widely in effect in the South, and even more pervasive were popular convictions among white Americans about Anglo-Saxon superiority and the regressive "bestiality" of blacks no longer "restrained" by the institution of slavery. But the more white superiority was touted by white politicians, writers, and even scientists, the more problematic and elusive race and racial differences appeared. Although American and European scientists had energetically searched throughout the nineteenth century for hard-and-fast standards, especially visual criteria defining racial differences, that goal seemed as elusive as ever by the end of the century.[3]

Novelists of the period were as passionately engaged as scientists and politicians in the debate over what race was and what it meant. Many white writers, like Thomas Dixon, continued to insist that blood eventually "tells," that black blood always sooner or later reveals itself to the discerning white gaze, but a growing number of novelists, especially writers who were African American themselves, raised serious questions in their works about the reliability of visual criteria in the determination of racial designations in general. Race itself might just be a matter of who controls and manipulates appearances, and that possibility in particular is explored by the preeminent white novelist of race in the period, Mark Twain, in his 1894 novel *Pudd'nhead Wilson,* and by two of the most distinguished African American writers of the era, Frances Ellen Watkins Harper in her 1892 work *Iola Leroy, or Shadows Uplifted,* and James Weldon Johnson in his 1912 novel *The Autobiography of an Ex-Coloured Man. Pudd'nhead Wilson*—"after *Huckleberry Finn,* Twain's best-known work on race," as Susan Gillman points out—tells the story of a slave who switches the identities of her baby son and her master's son and of the ensuing confusion that results over the next two decades, righted only by the peerless detective work of an outsider named Pudd'nhead Wilson, himself once the butt of social ridicule.[4] Harper's novel *Iola Leroy* recounts the era of Civil War and Reconstruction from the perspective of slaves and freedmen who never reconciled themselves to their servile status and concentrates in particular on the transformation of the eponymous heroine from spoiled white southern lady to black social activist. It was a transformation that Harper, second only to Sojourner Truth among antebellum black women antislavery activists, undoubtedly relished.[5] And if anything, the nameless protagonist of James Weldon Johnson's anonymously published novel *The Autobiography of an Ex-Coloured Man* traces even more startling transformations in the first-person account of a part-white, part-black man who leaves his Connecticut home to pursue a series of adventures as aspiring college student, Florida cigar-maker, gambler, ragtime pianist, valet, and finally white businessman.

In these novels all three writers questioned the authority of the white gaze to detect and define racial differences, and in doing so all three unmasked whiteness as a racial category dependent upon blackness for its very definition. Twain was to draw back nervously from these radical implications, but Harper and Johnson discovered in their interrogation of whiteness and the white gaze possibilities for redefining race in general and black identity and black storytelling in particular. Indeed, their novels served as primers of sorts for dislodging the authority of the white gaze and for finding in its failures and omissions the space necessary for telling oppositional stories about how to create black stories and black identities.

The urgency of the task to which Harper and Johnson in particular set themselves was underscored by the extravagance and extremity of white racism in turn-of-the-century America. Indeed, the 40-year period after the end of Reconstruction in 1877 has often been labeled the "nadir" of African American history.[6] Articles about black crime and violence and accompanying calls to limit the political, social, and economic rights of African Americans had become commonplace in the white press by the early years of the twentieth century, and by and large disfranchisement and legalized segregation in education and public accommodations were quietly accepted as "necessary measures" by whites firmly convinced of the inequality of the races.[7] In the 1890s, lynching, once associated with vigilante punishment of rustlers in the West, became emblematic of the white South's determination to maintain sovereignty over blacks. Historian Joel Williamson estimates that in that decade roughly 138 people were lynched every year in the region and of that number three-fourths were black. "Between 1885 and 1907 there were more persons lynched in the United States," Williamson observes, "than were legally executed, and in the year 1892 twice as many."[8] And never had demeaning stereotypes of black Americans—from the fawning, clowning ex-slave to the "black beast rapist" ready to prey on white womanhood—been more prevalent in the mass media.[9] "Having been placed by a dominant race in circumstances over which we have had no control," Harper herself wrote in the decades after the Civil War, "we have been the butt of ridicule and the mark of oppression."[10]

Never had convictions of white superiority been more loudly pronounced, and never on the face of things had science itself appeared more supportive of those convictions. As early as the 1850s, historian Reginald Horsman reports, ". . . the inherent inequality of races was simply accepted as a scientific fact in America."[11] And if anything, Charles Darwin's theory of evolution hardened that assumption. Evolutionary theory had thoroughly discredited the notion of racial polygenesis—the supposition that races had originated as separate species—propounded by antebellum racial theorists and proslavery apologists like Mobile physician Josiah Clark Nott and English Egyptologist George Robin Gliddon. But Darwin's ideas of evolution still encouraged the century's obsession with measuring and categorizing putative racial differences by arguing that races represented various stages of evolution, "with the white race—or sometimes a subdivision of the white race," historian Thomas F. Gossett observes, "at the top."[12] The scientific paradigm that dominated nineteenth-century racial theory, in short, was, to borrow the terminology of Michael Omi and Howard Winant, "biologistic." Racial differences and racial categories were considered to be biological and inherent.[13] Tampering with those categories was useless and even perilous, according to William Graham Sumner, the preeminent white sociologist of the day. Influenced by the work of Herbert Spencer and Darwin, Sumner argued in *Folkways*, a 1906 publication serving as one of the prime texts of early-twentieth-century sociology, that whites and blacks had lived harmoniously in the South before the Civil War and the abolition of slavery, but in the war's aftermath, he warned, the two races had been unable to establish a new modus vivendi. "The two races," he proclaimed, "are separating more than ever before. It is evidently impossible for anyone to interfere. We are like spectators at a great natural convulsion."[14]

Such sentiments and theories encouraged the late nineteenth century's mania for racial categorization, which had hardened by the early years of the twentieth century into what historian Winthrop Jordan calls the country's "peculiar bifurcation" of race into whiteness and blackness. Originating in southern states, the one-drop rule increasingly became the order of the day, signifying, George Fredrickson notes, "that a person with any known degree of black ancestry was legally considered a Negro and subject to the full disabilities associated with segregation and disfranchisement."[15] In 1920 the U.S. Census bowed to the dictates of the one-drop rule, then widely accepted across the country, by dropping the category of mulattoes altogether from the census rolls and redefining blackness in general as the possession of any black ancestry whatsoever.[16]

Thomas Dixon, then, gave voice to the feelings of all too many white Americans of the time when he declared in his 1902 novel *The Leopard's Spots:* "One drop of blood makes a Negro. It kinks the hair, flattens the nose, thickens the lip, puts out the light of intellect, and lights the fire of brutal passions."[17] But underlying this loudly asserted certainty were profound doubt and anxiety in white America about where racial boundaries began and ended and what whiteness itself constituted. What if one "looked" white but counted blacks among one's ancestors? Just how reliable were visible signs of race after all? Ironically enough, during this era of obsessive racial categorization, passing—the crossing of the color line by Americans who looked white but had some black ancestry—reached its peak. Between 1880 and 1925 anywhere from 10,000 to 25,000 a year managed to cross the color line.[18] Widespread awareness among white Americans that some African Americans could indeed elude visual categorization gave rise to fears of "the specter of invisible blackness," in F. James Davis's telling phrase.[19]

That anxiety in turn was fueled in part by the failure of scientists in Europe and America for more than a century to reach any consensus on the criteria, visible, physical, or otherwise, for determining definitive racial differences or even racial categories. Over the decades theorists had resorted to visible signs as varied as skin pigmentation, cranium size and shape, human hair, and even body lice, but since Linnaeus scientists had differed sharply on the number of human races, which ranged as low as three and as high as 63 in some accounts. Indeed, by the late nineteenth century the evidence indicated strongly that no theory of race was viable. Dr. John Wesley Powell, director of the Bureau of Ethnology at the Smithsonian Institution in the 1880s, even went as far as to declare that "there is no science of ethnology," meaning, that is, that no science of race actually existed.[20] And by the early years of the twentieth century, "biologistic" theories of race had fallen under attack by Progressive reformers like Horace Kallen and by the Chicago school of sociology, led by Robert E. Park, who argued that race was simply a "*social* category," one of many "determinants of ethnic group identity or ethnicity."[21]

At no other time in American history were racial categories and boundaries more loudly and dogmatically proclaimed and at no other time was the very idea of race more weighed down with doubt. It was precisely the contradictory character of race in turn-of-the-century America—the absolute, unyielding vocabulary used to define racial differences and the utterly arbitrary way that vocabulary was wielded—that drew the attention of writers like Mark Twain, Frances Ellen Watkins Harper, and James Weldon Johnson. For each of their novels—Twain's *Pudd'nhead Wilson,* Harper's *Iola Leroy,* and Johnson's *The Autobiography of an Ex-Coloured Man*—took issue with biological definitions of race and suggested instead that race was simply a matter of who has the authority and power to decide what race is. The ultimate authority in matters of race in nineteenth-century America, all three writers suggest, had far less to do with science, measurement, or even visible difference and far more to do with the inequitable distribution of power, measured by access to the traditional tools of law, money, and sheer physical intimidation.

Accordingly, each novel prominently features scenes in which the protagonist, initially taking whiteness for granted, is suddenly confronted with an abruptly assigned black identity. Each protagonist is allocated that new racial identity not on the basis of any perceptible difference but simply on the basis of authority defined by the possession of superior power. Harper's heroine Iola Leroy, for instance, is raised to take for granted her status as the sheltered daughter of white Mississippi planter Eugene Leroy, and so secure and firm is that identity that she vigorously defends slavery as an institution to her classmates in a northern boarding school. But what she does not know is that her mother Marie was once the slave of her father, who freed her in order to marry her. Upon the death of her father, Iola finds her racial identity and her sense of self abruptly reassigned by her father's cousin Alfred Lorraine, who has long disapproved of Leroy's marriage to Marie and who manages to find flaws in Marie's manumission papers in order to remand Marie and her children, including Iola, to slavery. Iola's first inkling that her racial identity is abruptly reassigned comes when she is the target of sexual advances that would have only been made by a white man toward a black woman. In a world ruled by slavery and race, only white women are assumed to be virtuous and chaste. But still uncomprehending, Iola does not learn of her new racial status until her brokenhearted mother tells her and adds that her transformation is dictated by "The law of the strong against the weak."[22] Ahead of Iola lie slavery and humiliation, and not until a runaway slave notifies a Union general of her plight is she released from bondage. But there still remains the issue of how she is to define herself—as white or as black—after the war and the demise of slavery.

Just as abrupt is the crisis that the nameless protagonist of Johnson's *The Autobiography of an Ex-Coloured Man* suffers when he is peremptorily told by his teacher at school to take his place with the black children. Up until that moment, race has never been much of an issue for the boy, who unthinkingly assumes that he is white and accordingly allies himself with white children in racially charged fights at school. But as soon as he is proclaimed black by his teacher, the white boys declare, "Oh, you're a nigger too" (17). The boy's immediate response is to run to a mirror and to examine his image the way whites probably do—as an exotic whose physical beauty is defined by its strange, dark quality: "I was accustomed to hear remarks about my beauty; but now, for the first time, I became conscious of it and recognized it. I noticed the ivory whiteness of my skin, the beauty of my mouth, the size and liquid darkness of my eyes, and how the long, black lashes that fringed and shaded them produced an effect that was strangely fascinating even to me" (17). He ends up sobbing in the lap of his mother, who tells him that she is black and that his father is white but avoids answering his questions about his own racial identity. For the protagonist, that identity has already been assigned by his white teacher, and the moment that he is assigned to blackness remains an extraordinarily painful memory. Looking back, he declares: "Perhaps it had to be done, but I have never forgiven the woman who did it so cruelly. It may be that she never knew that she gave me a sword-thrust that day in school that was years in healing" (19).

A similar upheaval is experienced by the young ne'er-do-well and man about town Tom Driscoll in Twain's novel *Pudd'nhead Wilson,* set in a small antebellum Missouri town called Dawson's Landing. Tom has spent his childhood and youth in the kind of privilege and ease that only a white southern slaveholder can take for granted, casually abusing the slaves who serve him and taking as his due luxury and comfort. But a late-night meeting with a former family slave named Roxana, who raised him from infancy, turns his world upside down when she tells him that he is her son and that she placed him in the privileged—and white—position he now enjoys by switching him in the cradle with the master's son, who now occupies the role of her son and Tom's slave. Tom is utterly thunderstruck by this revelation, which seems to him a "tremendous catastrophe" changing his "moral landscape" forever.[23] Suddenly he is confronted with the arbitrariness of assigned social and racial identities, and that confrontation leads him to speculate in a way he never has before. "Why were niggers *and* whites made?" he asks himself. "What crime did the uncreated first nigger commit that the curse of birth was decreed for him? And why is the awful difference made between white and black? . . . How hard the nigger's fate seems, this morning!—yet until last night such a thought never entered my head" (122).

Of these three novels, interestingly enough, *Pudd'nhead Wilson* initially appears to be the most daring and radical in its speculations about the way that racial differences are constructed. For Tom's racial identity—his place in the world of whites—has been made possible by a black woman, his mother Roxana, who places the infant Tom in the cradle of the master's son to ensure that her own son will never be sold down the river. Roxana herself is "as white as anybody, but the one sixteenth of her which was black outvoted the other fifteen parts and made her a Negro" (32–33). The only thing that identifies her as black is her speech—the dialect of southern black slaves—and in a sense it is to language that she herself resorts when she switches the racial identities of her son and her master's son and proclaims by a change of clothes, cradle, and mere verbal sleight-of-hand that one is white and one is black. The ease with which Roxana undertakes this change suggests just how permeable nineteenth-century racial boundaries are and how susceptible they are to any kind of transgression.

Moreover, the masquerade that Roxana herself pursues—deferring to the child she has proclaimed the master's son—underscores how dependent white superiority is upon black subordination and how easily fictions of superiority and inferiority can harden into perceived realities. Even Roxana is "surprised to see how steadily and surely the awe which had kept her tongue reverent and her manner humble toward her young master was transferring itself to her speech and manner toward the usurper" (48–49). By the time Tom the usurper has grown to manhood, Roxana's masquerade has become reality rather than performance, and Roxana herself, the narrator observes, has been mastered by her own "fiction," deceived by her own deception as "the mock reverence became real reverence, the mock obsequiousness real obsequiousness, the mock homage real homage: the little counterfeit rift of separation between imitation slave and imitation-master widened and widened, and became an abyss, and a very real one" (55, 56). Such is the power, the novel implies, of language and storytelling—for Roxana essentially creates an alternative story for her son Tom, one of whiteness rather than blackness—to create difference and inequality where none previously exists.

Yet the fraud that Roxana perpetuates—and is eventually mastered by—indicates just how susceptible the white gaze is to deception, and that susceptibility is forcefully underscored by all three writers. Briefly paralyzed by Roxana's revelation that he is indeed "black," Tom goes through a short period of guiltily acting and looking "as meek as a nigger," in the words of his puzzled uncle Judge Driscoll (124). But he soon recovers his sense of balance and returns to "his old frivolous and easygoing ways," appearing and performing before the town as a white man (126). In this effort he is counseled by his mother Roxana, who aids and abets his secret robberies in the town and later forces him to reform his behavior to stay in the good graces of his uncle. Tom's "imitation" whiteness, as Eric J. Sundquist terms it, even goes so far as to allow the young man to sell his mother Roxana down the river in order to raise money for gambling debts, and so persuasive is his performance of whiteness that no one is the wiser.[24] As Pudd'nhead Wilson the outsider and resident amateur scientist exclaims when he does indeed discover the "truth" of Tom's identity, "And for twenty-three years no man has ever suspected it!" (277). In the world that Twain creates—and lived in, for that matter—it is apparently all too easy for the white gaze to be misled by the mere appearance of whiteness.

If anything, the white gaze sees what it wants to see, and therein lies its undoing, according to Harper's novel of African Americans

during the Civil War and Reconstruction. For the white suprema-
cists she portrays are far too confident in their ability to discern the
smallest possible gradation between whiteness and blackness, and
even her well-meaning white characters, like Eugene Leroy, Iola's
father, see only as far as their desires lead them. For Harper the
white gaze is defined by its peculiar and willful blindness, and it is
with a certain glee that Harper repeatedly returns to this motif in
her narrative. From the very beginning of the novel, she portrays
white slaveholders as singularly blind to the undercurrent of black
activity that covertly supports the Union cause, and even to "the
legible transcript of Divine retribution which was written upon the
shuddering earth" (14). Time and time again the narrative emphasizes the inability of the slaveholders to see their slaves except in the
most limited of self-serving stereotypes—as willful children and
lower creatures—and that inability renders them peculiarly vulnerable. The young, light-colored slave Robert Johnson, for instance, is
able to keep the rest of the slave community abreast of the war news
precisely because his doting mistress, who taught him to read much
the same way she would teach a pet animal tricks, cannot imagine
Robert putting his skill to the use of giving slaves the hope of emancipation. Even the relatively sympathetic slaveholder Eugene Leroy
is portrayed as being far too confident in his ability to hide the
"secret" of his children's background and to foresee the possible
consequences. In particular, he is unable to see the possible danger
represented by his cousin Alfred Lorraine that his wife Marie anxiously perceives, and telltale indications of approaching civil war
also elude his gaze. As the narrator stresses, ". . . his vision [was] too
blurred to read the sign of the times" (78).

More to the point, though, is the comical self-confidence of the
most racist character in the book, the white Southerner Dr. Latrobe,
who boasts to a gathering of professional men after the war that he
can always detect telltale signs of blackness. "There are niggers," he
proclaims, "who are as white as I am, but the taint of blood is there
and we always exclude it" (229). When asked by the former Union
soldier Dr. Gresham how he can perceive "the taint of blood,"
Latrobe replies: "Oh, there are tricks of blood which always betray
them. My eyes are more practiced than yours. I can always tell
them" (229). And of Robert Johnson, who looks white but declares
himself black, he adds, "I saw it in his eye" (229). One of the men in
the group of listeners, Dr. Frank Latimer, smiles mysteriously in

response, and he later takes a certain amount of satisfaction in revealing to the astonished Latrobe that he is black, in the words of another character, "by blood and choice" (238). As Gresham explains the choice, "His father's mother made overtures to receive him as her grandson and heir, but he has nobly refused to forsake his mother's people and has cast his lot with them" (238). Not only has Latrobe's eye been confounded, then, but the very authority of the white gaze has been challenged by Latimer's refusal to allow his racial designation to be dictated by his appearance and by the gaze of others. To him, race is simply a matter of personal choice.

Johnson's protagonist in *The Autobiography of an Ex-Coloured Man* takes a similar pleasure in outwitting the confining nature of the white gaze. Toward the end of the novel, the protagonist travels throughout the South doing research on black music, and during his travels he is struck by conversations with whites who take him for white and freely discuss race and blacks. Those discussions and other experiences in the region lead the narrator to muse on the limited vision of whites who can see only the literary stereotype of the "happy-go-lucky, laughing, shuffling, banjo-picking being" created by whites themselves (168). "In this respect," the narrator adds, "the Negro is much in the position of a great comedian who gives up the lighter roles to play tragedy. No matter how well he may portray the deeper passions, the public is loath to give him up in his old character; they even conspire to make him a failure in serious work, in order to force him back into comedy" (168). But in the end, when the narrator makes a conscious decision that he "was not going to be a Negro," white blindness works to his advantage (193). Refusing to label himself as either white or black, the narrator is assumed to be white as he rises in the world of New York real estate, and the humor of his situation is not lost on him:

> The anomaly of my social position often appealed strongly to my sense of humour. I frequently smiled inwardly at some remark not altogether complimentary to people of colour; and more than once, I felt like declaiming: 'I am a coloured man. Do I not disprove the theory that one drop of Negro blood renders a man unfit?' Many a night when I returned to my room after an enjoyable evening, I laughed heartily over what struck me as the capital joke I was playing. (197)

To Johnson's protagonist the joke is so amusing because it confirms his suspicion that race is simply a matter of performance following a script of whiteness or blackness and therefore letting the white gaze see what it wants to see. For the man who becomes the ex-colored man and for Twain's character Tom Driscoll as well, "race is theater," in Eric Lott's words, a matter of blacking up for white audiences who already know the lines and roles.[25] And if one wants to cross racial lines, it is necessary only to change the script— to play the white man, in the case of Johnson's protagonist, in times and places where whites expected only to see whites. Noting his own decision to cross the color line, Johnson's protagonist declares: "I finally made up my mind that I would neither disclaim the black race nor claim the white race; but that I would change my name, raise a moustache, and let the world take me for what it would; that it was not necessary for me to go about with a label of inferiority pasted across my forehead" (190). He decides, in short, to act white, to assume that race does not apply to him, and in doing so, of course, he is acting according to the dictates of a culture that has long associated blackness with race and whiteness with the absence of race.

The implications here are startling, for all three novels seem to suggest that the white gaze is so vulnerable to deception precisely because race itself, whether blackness or whiteness, is merely a matter of performance, requiring faithfulness to the scripts determined by white American culture. One could be perceived as white or as black merely by acting out the crucial part—as both Johnson's protagonist and Tom Driscoll do. As soon as Tom learns that he is "black," in fact, he inadvertently begins acting like a "nigger," cringing before whites, giving way before them on the road, and suffering from gestures of implied equality: "The 'nigger' in him went shrinking and skulking here and there and yonder, and fancying it saw suspicion and maybe detection in all faces, tones, and gestures. So strange and uncharacteristic was Tom's conduct that people noticed it, and turned to look after him when he passed on . . ." (124). But when Tom returns to his old behavior of arrogance and assumed superiority, he no longer draws puzzled glances, and he is therefore reassured that if he acts white he'll be perceived as such by the community at large.

What these three novels accomplish, then, is the unveiling of whiteness itself—usually assumed to be the invisible norm, undefined itself by race—as a visible racial category of performance dependent upon the opposition and subordination of blackness for its very definition.[26] Tom Driscoll and Johnson's protagonist are perceived as white because they present themselves as such, assuming in public the privilege of whiteness, its automatic sense of superiority, its confidence that other racial categories are irrelevant to its own status, and its unspoken assumption that whiteness is everything that blackness is not. But implicit in both of these performances and in *Iola Leroy* is the sly suggestion that whiteness in general is a masquerade, an elaborate performance that must be bolstered by subterfuge, deceit, and violence to maintain itself apart from blackness.

That whiteness is simply a matter of performance Twain makes clear not just in Tom's own role-playing but in the novel's probing critique of white southern male honor in general. For the aristocratic families of the small town where the novel is set are thoroughly preoccupied with their family honor—which is to say, with maintaining a flawless appearance before the community. To be honorable, the rules say, one must be perceived accordingly by the community, and the correlation that Twain makes by implication is that to be white is also to be perceived as such by the community. Maintaining that good appearance, though, can require certain strange twists of logic, like the reasoning of Tom's uncle Judge Driscoll that a public insult delivered to Tom can be fully addressed not by a court decision but by a duel. Only through ritualistic violence, the laws of honor dictate, can the Driscoll family honor be restored, and the judge is outraged when Tom himself tries to settle accounts through the courts rather than on the field of honor.[27]

Similarly, Tom's appearance of whiteness requires elaborate deceits and masquerades, like the robberies he pursues to pay back his gambling debts and the disguises of white women and blacks he assumes to throw the authorities off the track. To maintain that appearance he is even willing to sell his mother down the river to ensure that she is safely out of sight, although she has offered herself to be sold temporarily to help him in his financial bind. Finally, he resorts to the desperate act of robbing and killing his uncle to ensure that his masquerade remains intact.

Tom's utter ruthlessness in maintaining his masquerade has drawn a good deal of uneasy commentary from critics who see his characterization as yet another indication of nineteenth-century white America's conviction that blood does indeed tell. Sandra Gunning, for instance, argues that however "scathing" Twain's critique of race in

America may be, his portrayal of Tom and the chaos he enacts offers disturbing "metaphors for malignant blackness."[28] Even more precisely, Michael Rogin has labeled Tom's characterization as indicative of Twain's own susceptibility to the period's extreme racism. Tom Driscoll, he notes, "is not the black child of conservative thought but the black beast of racial radicalism." He is a character who represents white fears that blacks would regress to savagery without the "protective" shelter afforded by the institution of slavery.[29]

But if Tom's characterization does have disturbing implications for Twain's own racial assumptions, his portrayal also has striking parallels to offer with the assertions of black writers like Harper and Johnson that whiteness can be performed and maintained only through elaborate deceits and lies and only through the violent, forced subordination of blackness. Tom's superior status in the little Missouri town where he lives, the narrative of *Pudd'nhead Wilson* tells us again and again, is utterly dependent upon the subordination of Roxana, ostensibly his black nurse but really his mother, and his slave Chambers, who has taken Tom's place in slavery thanks to Roxana's dexterity in manipulating appearances. Roxana is, after all, "mastered" by the fiction she herself has created of Tom's whiteness, and during Tom's childhood the distance between them increases until it becomes an "abyss":

She saw her darling gradually cease from being her son, she saw *that* detail perish utterly; all that was left was master. . . . She saw herself sink from the sublime height of motherhood to the somber depths of unmodified slavery. The abyss of separation between her and her boy was complete. She was merely his chattel now, his convenience, his dog, his cringing and helpless slave, the humble and unresisting victim of his capricious temper and vicious nature. (62–63)

That Tom necessarily requires black subordination for his definition of whiteness is underscored in the episode in which he is rescued from drowning by his "slave" Chambers, who is instantly pronounced by the taunting white boys in the neighborhood " 'Tom Driscoll's niggerpappy,'—to signify that he had had a second birth into this life, and that Chambers was the author of his new being" (61). Tom's response is one of frustrated fury and increased violence against Chambers himself, but the boys' taunt remains as a telling commentary on the politics of subordination required for the definition and maintenance of whiteness.

Similarly, Iola Leroy frankly acknowledges that the privileges she enjoyed as a southern white girl were premised upon the oppression of black slaves who made those privileges possible in the first place by sheer dint of physical labor. Her decision to define herself as black, after she is freed from bondage, serves in a sense as an acknowledgment of that debt. In the interest of honoring it, she first pursues work to make herself financially independent and finally becomes a teacher of ex-slaves in the Reconstruction South. When her white suitor Dr. Gresham expresses dismay at her decision and tells her that she is "unfitted for social life" among blacks, Iola replies frankly, "It was . . . through their unrequited toil that I was educated, while they were compelled to live in ignorance. I am indebted to them for the power I have to serve them. I wish other Southern women felt as I do" (235). Indeed, Iola's decision to embrace blackness is, in the words of one critic, "a clear rejection of the role of the white woman" who requires black subordination to ensure her sense of value and purity.[30] Iola is everything the ideal white southern lady is supposed to be—gently raised, educated to culture, refined, and pure in heart—and her refusal to accept the era's assumption that those traits are automatically white underscores as well her refusal to equate her own value with the subordination of others.

Moreover, she scolds Dr. Gresham for the way his race has taken that sense of privilege, premised on subordination and oppression, for granted. Whites, she tells Gresham, who shamefacedly agrees, have used their position "to victimize feebler races and to minister to a selfish greed of gold and a love of domination" (116). And the most ironic aspect of that drive to dominate, the novel insists again and again, is the refusal of whites to acknowledge their culpability for the rising number of mulattoes in the general population or the inevitable intertwining of whiteness and blackness in the South and the country as a whole. As Gresham himself eventually acknowledges, ". . . the negro, poor and despised as he is, has laid his hands on our Southern civilization and helped mould its character" (217). No progress toward reconciliation between white and black, the novel suggests, can be made until white Americans finally acknowledge their indebtedness to blackness. Such an acknowledgment seems far from forthcoming in the racially charged atmosphere of turn-of-the-century America, and it is significant that the novel ends with a vision of a small but vital black community defining freedom

on its own terms and living utterly apart from whites in the Reconstruction South.[31]

If anything, Johnson is even more insistent in *The Autobiography of
an Ex-Coloured Man* that whiteness must be unveiled as a racial category requiring as the foundation for its definition and construction
the oppression of blacks. What the protagonist discovers in particular in his travels through the South is the utter absorption of the
average white southern man with asserting white sovereignty over
blacks: ". . . most of his mental efforts run through one narrow channel; his life as a man and a citizen, many of his financial activities,
and all of his political activities are impassably limited by the ever
present 'Negro question' " (76). Among his encounters the protagonist records the conversation of a Jewish cigar manufacturer, a professor from Ohio teaching in Alabama, a Union veteran, and a belligerent Texan discussing precisely that "question" in a train
smoking car, and one of the things that strikes the protagonist about
that conversation is the monumental stake white southern men like
the Texan have in the enforced subordination of blacks. The Union
veteran mockingly notes that Anglo-Saxons "ought to remember
that we are standing on a pile of past races, and enjoy our position
with a little less show of arrogance," but it is the protagonist himself
who offers the strongest condemnation of the lengths to which
white supremacy will go to maintain its position (162). For nothing
drives home more fully that determination than the lynching that
the protagonist inadvertently witnesses during his travels in the
South. Watching the mob's fire with horror and later staring obsessively at the spot where only ashes and rubble remain, the protagonist implicitly understands that the spectacle of the lynching is the
logical outcome of the white gaze, and its construction of whiteness
is premised on the subordination of blacks. As the narrator himself
trenchantly observes a few pages earlier, ". . . when the white race
assumes as a hypothesis that it is the main object of creation and
that all things else are merely subsidiary to its well-being, sophism,
subterfuge, perversion of conscience, arrogance, injustice, oppression, cruelty, sacrifice of human blood, all are required to maintain
the position . . ." (167)

Partly as a result of this horrifying lynching, the narrator decides
to cross the color line and thereby forsake his project of collecting
and popularizing black folk music and the larger agenda of intro-
ducing himself to the complexity and richness of blackness. That

this is a decision riven with doubt and anxiety the narrator makes all too plain when he asserts: "All the while I understood that it was not discouragement or fear or search for a larger field of action and opportunity that was driving me out of the Negro race. I knew that it was shame, unbearable shame. Shame at being identified with a people that could with impunity be treated worse than animals" (190). Still, the narrator pursues his plan with diligence and skill, learning to make money in a white world and to climb through its social ranks, but he remains regretful about what might have been and what he has in turn lost. Pondering the struggle of African Americans to assert their political rights, he muses sadly on the distance that lies between those activists and himself: "Beside them I feel small and selfish. I am an ordinarily successful white man who has made a little money. They are men who are making history and a race. I, too, might have taken part in a work so glorious" (211).

The odd thing about this statement, though, is that it emphasizes just how uncertain everything is in the protagonist's world, including the very categories of whiteness and blackness. By adjusting his racial performance to a white script, the protagonist has deftly stepped over the color line, and even in his lament—"I am an ordinarily successful white man"—can be discerned the instability of race and identity. Not only is the protagonist a financially successful white man, but he has also proved himself to be singularly successful in assuming the identity of a white man despite all the racial shibboleths of his era. Indeed, Samira Kawash argues that the novel of "passing," of which *The Autobiography of an Ex-Coloured Man* is so preeminent an example, is decidedly not about "the *representation* of blackness or whiteness," but rather about "the *failure* of blackness or whiteness to provide the grounds for a stable, coherent identity."[32] The ease with which the protagonist takes up the mantle of whiteness and the success he achieves in wearing it suggest how vulnerable the era's most hard-and-fast categories of identity are to disruption and revision.

It was just this suggestion that racial boundaries could indeed be blurred and confused that southern white reviewers found so objectionable. Instantly proclaiming the book a "lie" and, more revealingly, an "insult to Southern womanhood," the *Nashville Tennessean*, for instance, denied that there could be any such thing as "an ex-colored man" and added, for good measure, "once a negro, always a negro."[33] Johnson's book had, in short, struck a nerve in the white South among those for whom white supremacy was a prime consideration, and no doubt Johnson himself intended that effect by having the book published anonymously and thereby blurring the volume's generic boundaries. Was it a work of fiction or a genuine autobiography? That was the question immediately raised by the author's anonymity. Johnson had actually based the book's first-person narrator on a friend from his youth in Jacksonville, Florida, an attorney named J. Douglass Wetmore, who had successfully passed the color line and was by 1908 living as a white man in New York City—just like the book's narrator. But that was not a fact that Johnson ever acknowledged in print. He preferred, rather, the very confusion and anger that the book incited. As he told one friend, "When the author is known, and known to be one who could not be the main character of the story, the book will fall flat."[34] But as a book with an author who remained anonymous, the story of the ex-colored man fairly vibrates with uncertainty and instability, hesitating between the genres of fiction and autobiography as surely as it hesitates between whiteness and blackness. Therein lies the novel's multiple rendering of the very idea of passing, suggesting not just "shifting identities" but "shifting perceptions [of] what the world takes the narrative, or the protagonist, to be."[35]

The world the narrator of *The Autobiography of an Ex-Coloured Man* creates, then, is ultimately one of radical instability, where everything—race, identity, social position, even perception itself—is marked by radical doubt highlighting the ephemeral nature of artificial categories like race. Representations of uncertainty in the novel underscore the era's profound doubt and anxiety about its most cherished social boundaries and categorizations, and in this respect, Johnson's book has a good deal in common with both *Iola Leroy* and *Pudd'nhead Wilson*. All three novels raise questions so far-ranging and fundamental that they eventually touch on issues of epistemology—that is to say, how one perceives the accepted difference between whiteness and blackness, where one category ends and the other begins, and how reliable any individual perceptions of those differences are. Beneath the surface of late-nineteenth- and early-twentieth-century American life, with its penchant for rigidly defined categories of race and class, just might exist the fluidity of multiple possibilities, multiple perceptions, and ultimately multiple identities, and the specter of those looming multiplicities hovers ominously over each narrative.

Of the three writers, Frances Harper, an abolitionist lecturer and Reconstruction activist, was probably the most explicit in articulating just what those possibilities of fluidity and uncertainty were. She was, after all, wryly aware that she herself—as a woman, an African American, and a writer and public speaker—confounded a good many stereotypes and social expectations in her multiple roles as poet, journalist, lecturer, and reformer. Two decades before writing *Iola Leroy*, she had commented ruefully on the contradictory and confused responses her very presence at lecture podiums in Georgia had attracted. Writing to a friend in 1870, she observed: "I don't know but that you would laugh if you were to hear some of the remarks which my lectures call forth: 'She is a man,' again 'She is not colored, she is painted.' Both white and colored come out to hear me, and I have very fine meetings. . . ."[36] In *Iola Leroy*, her literary portrait of that period, she captures something of that confusion and flux by emphasizing again and again in her narrative how all the rules of race and identity have changed radically with war and emancipation. One of her older black characters, Aunt Linda, observes with glee that the house she and her husband have lived in since the end of the war once belonged to her husband's old master, who is now in "de pore-house" (155). And of her relationship with her former mistress, she adds, ". . . things is turned 'roun' might quare. Ole Mistus war up den, an' I war down; now, she's down, and I'se up" (159). As she herself says, "My! But ain't dem tables turned" (155). In this postwar world everything related to race, including the configuration of social space, seems subject to radical change, and even casual greetings between whites and blacks seem to require "learning a new language" (151). But however unsettling this flux is to the whites in the novel, it signifies to former slaves the freedom to assume new identities at will, and the energy with which they do so signifies their delight in that new freedom. Aunt Linda's husband John, for one, takes pleasure in having not one but two names, one for his pension as a Union veteran and another one assumed after emancipation. As he says himself, "Got 'nuff ob my ole Marster in slave times, widout wearin' his name in freedom" (167).

Mark Twain's character Tom Driscoll is, of course, nowhere nearly as admirable as the former slaves Harper portrays in *Iola Leroy*, but like Harper's characters Tom revels in the freedom he discovers as he crosses boundaries of race and even gender throughout most of *Pudd'nhead Wilson*. Paired with Roxana, who initiates his masquerade and collaborates in maintaining it, Tom cavorts across the narrative like an anarchic imp, crossing racial lines at will, acting white with the townspeople but black with Roxana, needling Pudd'nhead Wilson for his hobbies of fingerprinting and palm-reading, robbing white households, and instigating incidents of confusion from duels to court trials. Tom even raises the daring possibility that crossing gender lines is all too feasible when he assumes disguises as a young girl and as an old woman to cover his tracks after his robberies. Together he and Roxana suggest that just beneath the tidy surface of Dawson's Landing lie multiple possibilities for self-definition. It is little wonder, then, that Tom puzzles the Italian twins when he meets them, inspiring one twin to find him amiable and leaving the other suspicious. And it is little wonder that up until the end of the novel, Tom and Roxana together thwart the best efforts of the town in general and Pudd'nhead Wilson in particular to solve the mystery of the mounting confusion into which the community is thrown. Tom is, after all, running amok in a community with little gift for looking beyond the superficial or for understanding the sort of wit and irony that characterizes the remarks of Pudd'nhead Wilson, who has long been the object of ridicule in the town simply on the basis of being incomprehensible to his fellow townspeople.

But if the townspeople of Dawson's Landing—and the whites in *Iola Leroy* and *The Autobiography of an Ex-Coloured Man*, for that matter—remain singularly blind to the uncertainty and fluidity of late-nineteenth-century American life, African Americans are portrayed by Harper and Johnson in particular as being gifted with a special kind of vision alerting them to alternative—and liberating—possibilities. After being told that he is "black," Johnson's protagonist emphasizes that his world has been utterly transformed because he now "looked out through other eyes" (21). He is, he asserts, forced to see everything "from the view-point of a *coloured* man," and that perspective frees him from the limitations of a strictly white vision. In words strikingly similar to those by W. E. B. Du Bois on the "twoness" of black identity, the protagonist suggests that African Americans remain "a mystery to the whites," that it "is a difficult thing for a white man to learn what a coloured man really thinks; because, generally, with the latter an additional and different light must be brought to bear on what he thinks. . . ." This quality, the protagonist adds,

gives to every coloured man, in proportion to his intellectuality, a sort of dual personality; there is one phase of him which is disclosed only in the freemasonry of his own race. I have often watched with interest and sometimes with amazement even ignorant coloured men under cover of broad grins and minstrel antics maintain this dualism in the presence of white men. (21–22)

To see and act doubly, he emphasizes, makes it possible for him to move "from one world into another," and while that ability suggests on one level the restrictions of race as they are defined in turn-of-the-century America, it also implies a certain freedom, the ability to see, as it were, otherwise, beyond the sweep of the white gaze (20).

This possibility of seeing otherwise also intrigues Harper, who emphasizes that those characters, like Iola and her brother Harry, who are revealed to be "black," learn to "see things in a new light," as Harry himself observes (124). In particular, *Iola Leroy* emphasizes again and again, they learn to see far beyond the range of the white gaze, and that new way of seeing enables them to invent new definitions and stories of blackness in opposition to white definitions and narratives. To see "in a new light," in fact, takes on crucial importance in both *Iola Leroy* and *The Autobiography of an Ex-Coloured Man*, for seeing anew enables Harper's ex-slaves and Johnson's protagonist to learn how to define blackness and race, not according to the criteria of white society but according to their own standards and needs, and above all how to tell stories that are black. Both novels serve self-consciously as primers on how to tell black stories, and the key to that task lies in seeing beyond the white gaze and learning ways to reinterpret white narratives of blackness.

Accordingly, *Iola Leroy* features one slave after another who recounts visions of approaching freedom and of retribution for cruel slaveholders, and those visions, the narrative emphasizes, enable them to receive white narratives skeptically and offer instead their own narratives in opposition. Their masters tell them of Confederate victories and of the atrocities that Union troops will commit, but aided by their visions and by their ability to see otherwise, slaves like Aunt Linda learn to tell alternative narratives of what has happened and what will happen. Aunt Linda has been deprived of the ability to read the newspapers, but her mistress's face, she notes, "is newspaper nuff for me. I look at her ebery mornin' wen she comes inter dis kitchen. If her face is long an' she walks kine o' droopy den I thinks things is gwine wrong for dem" (9–10). Similarly, her friend Jake, she declares, plays the happy-go-lucky slave while he collects letters for his masters. "But Jake's listen' all de time wid his eyes and

his mouf wide open," Aunt Linda observes, "an' ketchin' ebery-
thing he kin, an' a heap ob news he gits dat way" (11). In a like vein,
a vision that comes to another slave, Uncle Daniel, of his dead master suffering the torments of hell, helps the old man redefine his
relationship with his young master as one of obligation and honor,
not of mere servitude.

This ability to see beyond the range of the white gaze and to
detect possibilities for multiplicity and fluidity enables the slaves in
Iola Leroy to create an underground world undetectable by whites,
one defined by their fervent anticipation of liberation, their angry
denunciation of cruelties committed by slaveholders, and even a
secret code to pass on news of the war. In such beginnings, Harper
implies, can be found the tools for constructing black identities and
black stories. For the inhabitants of her novel, choice becomes a crucial element of defining black identity, and her scenes of war and
Reconstruction emphasize the multiplicity of choices that her characters weigh and ponder—joining the Union forces, deciding to stay
behind to look after unprotected white women, choosing new
names, and reconstructing families. Choice can even mean, in the
case of Iola and her brother Harry, the decision to define oneself not
as white but as black, despite the opportunities to do otherwise.

To define black identity, above all, means to tell black stories, and
Iola Leroy is nothing if not a novel, in John Ernest's words, "about
writing (authoring) the self—and, beyond that, about writing the
race."[37] Hence in scenes of family reconciliation that modern readers frequently find unrealistic and incredible, Harper portrays
African Americans telling their stories before public gatherings and
discovering not just long-lost relatives but new identities in the act
of reciting their tales. At one such church meeting in the South, "a
dear old mother" rises and tells the story of the time when she lost
her children in slave sales; in response, the former slave and Union
veteran Robert Johnson tells his own story of losing the mother who
used to see him only at night and of his search for her since the
war's end. Telling these stories brings about Robert's reconciliation
at last with the "dear old mother" who is in truth his own long-lost
mother, and in that moment of storytelling and reunion both Robert
and his mother create new identities for themselves—as son and as
mother. Not surprisingly, his mother declares, "I feel's like a new
woman!" (183). And so she is, for the telling of their individual stories has released them not just from the confines of slavery and the

havoc it wreaked on black family life and identity, but from the narrow bounds of white narratives about blacks. Those scenes of reconciliation and storytelling are necessary from Harper's perspective because they represent staged scenarios of what it means for an African American to define blackness and to tell a black story. To tell one's own story, Harper emphasizes, is the first real step toward freedom—from the white gaze, from white narratives, and from white definitions of race.

That these are stories often told by mulattoes—in *Iola Leroy* and in *The Autobiography of an Ex-Coloured Man*—is equally significant. For the figure of the mulatto in these two novels, and in Twain's novel as well, serves as a living contradiction of white narratives about race and "telling" signs of color. African American writers like Harper and Johnson have frequently been condemned for giving mulatto characters center stage because their prominence has often been interpreted as a sop to white audiences, and certainly a good case can be made for this particular criticism when applied to abolitionist narratives of the tragic mulatto. But if Iola Leroy and Johnson's protagonist look white, they both make decisions to choose blackness (although the latter later moves on to choose whiteness as well), and in making that choice they serve as living embodiments of all those contradictions and ambiguities undermining racial categorizations in turn-of-the-century America. As Nancy Bentley succinctly notes, "The Mulatto figure was a scandal—not only a sexual but an intellectual scandal, confounding as it did the racial categories that were as fundamental to social life in the North as in the South."[38] Harper's and Johnson's protagonists, after all, have held both white and black positions in society, and as such they serve as potent reminders of the limitations of the white gaze.

Perhaps even more to the point, their choice and exploration of blackness in these two novels provide outlines for future black stories. Once Iola embraces blackness as her identity, she commingles with soldiers, doctors, runaway slaves, urban northern blacks, professionals, and southern black folk, and the range and richness of experience she finds in those black communities indicate directions for future black stories to take. At one point Iola herself is urged to tell her story, and in response she says that when she does indeed write a book, she will take as her hero Dr. Frank Latimer, yet another figure who eschews whiteness for blackness and who eventually marries Iola. As far as these two characters are concerned, to be black is to choose blackness, to define blackness according to one's own needs and beliefs and within the confines of black narrative.

Similarly, Johnson's protagonist leaves his Connecticut home after his mother's death and travels South to learn something of his mother's heritage. There he undertakes what Kenneth Warren calls "a picaresque journey through blackness," meeting black students, preachers, railroad men, factory workers, gamblers, and musicians.[39] Having earlier "formulated a theory of what it was to be coloured," Johnson's protagonist discovers "the practice" particularly in Florida, where he learns firsthand of "the tremendous struggle which is going on between the races in the South," the complicated intertwining of whiteness and blackness, and the intricacy of class stratification among African Americans themselves (74, 75). He learns, in short, the diversity of raw material for black stories, and at the end of the novel, when he contemplates the cost of his decision to cross over into whiteness, he sadly ponders the music he could have written and by implication the new black narratives he could have created. Sometimes, he says in the conclusion, he opens "a little box in which I still keep my fast yellowing manuscripts, the only tangible remains of a vanished dream, a dead ambition, a sacrificed talent." Then, he adds, he "cannot repress the thought that, after all, I have chosen the lesser part, that I have sold my birthright for a mess of pottage" (211). The price he pays for whiteness, in short, is the multiplicity of black stories he might have created but never will.

Mark Twain would have undoubtedly sympathized with this sense of loss and, more generally, with the imperative explored by Johnson and Harper of breaking away from the white gaze and creating black stories. One of his intended goals in writing *Pudd'nhead Wilson*, after all, as can be easily discerned from the narrator's asides and from the aphorisms of *Pudd'nhead Wilson's Calendar* heading each chapter, was to offer a blistering denunciation both of the slave South and of the mounting tide of racism in the 1890s. And indeed, as Sandra Gunning observes, "the novel's play on skin color and its farcical indictments of the nostalgia for life before the Civil War suggest not only Twain's questioning of a white notion of social control, but also his critique about racial essence."[40] But the radical implications of the novel—its sly portrayal of whiteness as racial masquerade, its probing of racial and gender boundaries, and its evocation of a world in which nothing, not even individual identity or the act of perception itself, is assured of any certainty—proved to be too much for Twain, who ultimately backs away from those implications in the novel's climax, the trial for the murder of Judge Driscoll, after which everyone, including Tom and Roxana, is restored to an original "rightful" identity and racial category.

Due to Pudd'nhead Wilson's superior detective work, and not incidentally, his hobby of fingerprinting everyone in Dawson's Landing for the last two decades, Tom is dramatically revealed not just as the murderer whose fingerprints can be found on the murder weapon but also as a "sham" white man whose "proper" identity is that of a black and a slave. Wilson's revelation immediately puts an end to the chaos that has troubled Dawson's Landing, that is, the robberies and social dissension that Tom has generated and above all his antic masquerades across race and gender boundaries. Tom is promptly sold down the river to pay for the debts of the Driscoll estate, and Roxana is thoroughly broken and subdued by the unmasking of the charade that she instigated so long ago. As the narrator notes, ". . . the spirit in her eye was quenched, her martial bearing departed with it, and the voice of her laughter ceased in the land" (301). The "real heir," in turn, is reinstated in his "rightful" place as a white man, but his long years as a slave and as a black man make that position thoroughly uncomfortable for him—as it is made uncomfortable for his creator, who abruptly declares, ". . . we cannot follow his curious fate further—that it would be a long story" (302).

Such a story, of course, would undoubtedly pursue the possibility that race is simply a matter of circumstance and performance, since Chambers the "rightful heir" and white man suffers under the burden of his new white identity after years of living as a black man. He may be white by immediate family lineage, but he continues to feel black—a contradiction that Twain himself is unwilling to pursue in an ending that resorts to the conventions of the detective story to set all the confusion of the narrative aright and to assert, rather unexpectedly, that identity is a sure thing after all.[41] As commentators like Susan Gillman and Eric Lott have suggested, Twain was probably as attracted to the notion of "certainty as held out by the law and by the science of heredity" as he was critical of the era's racism and imperialism.[42] And indeed, it is nothing if not telling that in the trial of the accused murderer of Judge Driscoll, the defending lawyer, Pudd'nhead Wilson, seeks out the real murderer by resorting to the era's criteria for racial categorization—visual evidence, this time in the form of fingerprints. Also telling, as Gillman points out, is the way that Wilson's superior intellect is finally revealed to the town at large "through superior visual observation."[43] Wilson alone in the town is capable of unmasking Tom Driscoll because as an amateur practitioner of fingerprinting he is far more attuned to the visual than the rest of his fellow white townspeople. He alone, it appears, is capable of reading the "tell-tale" signs of race, and that ability suggests that Twain, almost in spite of himself, did believe on some level, like Thomas Dixon, that blood in the end does "tell," that "one drop" of black blood "kinks the hair," that race is after all a matter of biology. The novel that begins so promisingly as a critique of the era's white gaze ends, tragically, with its confirmation.

But what lingers on in the imagination after a reading of *Pudd'n-head Wilson* is the anarchic spirit of confusion and uncertainty that Tom and Roxana foster throughout most of the narrative. However much Twain might have retreated from the radical implications of the uncertainty Tom and Roxana embody, he nonetheless goes far enough in his critique of race and racism to point, like Harper and Johnson, to a world of flux and multiplicity where storytelling itself emerges as a crucial element of defining one's identity. In the act of storytelling one could actually shift one's position, remove oneself from the glare of social scrutiny and categorization, and bring about a realignment of social space in general. That discovery in particular would be explored by women writers, white and black, seeking for themselves a space in the community of artists and for their fictional characters a redefinition of narratives of and by women. For Edith Wharton and Pauline Hopkins in particular, acquiring the gift of narrative would become crucial in determining whether or not their central women characters would survive their struggle with the consequences of falling under public scrutiny.

5

New Women and New Stories: Edith Wharton and Pauline Hopkins

As the political and economic status of African American men and women deteriorated in turn-of-the-century America, the symbolic stock of white women, as historian Paula Giddings has observed, rose considerably.[1] Since the antebellum period, civic virtues like justice and liberty had been personified as women in public rites and ceremonies, and by the late nineteenth century white women were charged with the responsibility for perpetuating the standing and "superiority" of the white race.[2] And as the "crown of creation," the very cornerstone of white society, white women were expected, Bram Dijkstra suggests, to maintain that lofty position by remaining within a specifically feminine sphere, by "being passive, malleable, and focused on motherhood." They were also expected, not incidentally, to be the polar opposites of black women, stereotyped since slavery as sexually insatiable and aggressive. The traits of white women, argued sociologists like William Graham Sumner, had emerged over the long course of evolution, and as the species slowly "progressed" toward perfection, the more distinct and separate became the defining characteristics of masculinity and femininity. The more advanced the race, the more aggressive and domineering the male and the more pliable and submissive the female.[3] In literature and painting, ideal white femininity was celebrated as civilization's cornerstone and highest ornament—much to the exasperation of feminist writers like Charlotte Perkins Gilman, who noted caustically that only in the human species does the female "carry the burden of ornament."[4]

The possibility that white women could be other than ornaments and cultural symbols of civic and domestic virtue, that black women could be something more than mere foils for white women, engaged the narrative energy of a growing number of women writers, white and black, respectively, in the closing years of the nineteenth cen-

tury and the opening years of the twentieth, among them Frances
E. W. Harper, black educator Anna Julia Cooper, white writers like
Ellen Glasgow and Kate Chopin, and women of color like Sui Sin
Far, the pseudonym for Chinese American writer Edith Maud
Eaton, and Hum-ishu-ma, a Native American writer whose only
novel did not appear in print until 1927.[5] And while white women
novelists were seldom as likely as black women writers to acknowledge how closely intertwined the cultural definitions of white and
black womanhood were, writers of both races sought to expand the
range of narratives for women. They sought as well to establish
themselves as genuine artists in the largely masculine world of high
art, rather than assuming the less lofty role of writers who wrote for
a living, as their literary foremothers had largely done in the 1850s
and 1860s. And by setting their sights on that larger ambition, they
also found themselves, as Barbara Hochman argues, "redefining
their position as women within turn-of-the-century America."[6]

Two novelists in particular, Edith Wharton, the most prominent
white woman novelist of the period, and Pauline E. Hopkins, one of
a growing number of activist African American women writers, produced important novels exploring just that possibility of expanding
stories for women. In Wharton's best-selling 1905 novel *The House of
Mirth* and Pauline Hopkins's 1900 novel *Contending Forces,* both
writers focus on the confining and dehumanizing nature of single
stories imposed on women and the dangers of being confined to a
small social space circumscribed by male vision and desire and traditionally male narratives. And perhaps even more to the point,
both writers—Wharton implicitly and Hopkins explicitly—insisted
in those works upon the necessity of writing oneself out of dangerous and suffocating spaces through the act of storytelling. If women
are to escape the fate of being told by stories not their own, these
two novels assert, they must take on the task of creating their own
stories and, by implication, their own selves.

The House of Mirth, accordingly, tells the story of a society beauty
named Lily Bart who diligently pursues marriage as the logical conclusion of her life's training, only to discover herself thwarted by
her own fastidiousness and by mounting gossip that eventually
destroys her. Originally titled "A Moment's Ornament," *The House of
Mirth* was the first of a long line of novels by Wharton to explore the
plight of a young woman confronted with marriage as the only
available denouement of her life's narrative.[7] The novel propelled

Wharton to the front ranks of American novelists and helped crys-
tallize her sense of self as a writer. Serialized in *Scribner's Magazine*
from January to November of 1905, *The House of Mirth* quickly
proved itself a popular success, selling 140,000 copies by the end of
1905 and topping Upton Sinclair's *The Jungle* on the best-seller list.[8]
In many respects, it was an intensely personal story for Wharton,
whose childhood nickname was Lily and who felt herself trapped in
an unfulfilling marriage, but it was also a novel sharply critical of
common cultural assumptions about the "proper" and "improper"
roles to be played by American women and of the limited options
available to women.[9]

Pauline Hopkins's novel *Contending Forces*, first serialized in *The
Colored American Magazine* in 1900 and then published separately as
a novel that same year, was, if anything, even more critical of the
limitations facing women in general, but in notable contrast to
Wharton's novel, Hopkins's story ends with the main character's
successful marriage and sturdy claim to "respectability." *Contending
Forces* traces the painful efforts of a young black woman named Sappho Clark, caught in historical forces set in motion long before her
birth, to extricate herself from white stereotypes proclaiming her
sexual prey and to redefine herself as happy wife and mother.[10] As
Claudia Tate aptly declares, "The text transforms Sappho from a
passive and impure heroine—the sexually experienced object of
perverse male desire—into an active female-hero, the subject of her
own desire."[11] Hopkins herself was less successful. In the 1890s she
worked as a stenographer for Republican politicians and the Massachusetts Bureau of Statistics and then for four years helped edit *The
Colored American Magazine.* She returned to stenographic work after
Booker T. Washington, whom she had sharply criticized in print,
bought the magazine and in all likelihood fired her.[12] Unlike Wharton, whose fame and critical appreciation seemed to mount with
each passing year until she became something of a grande dame of
American letters, Hopkins died obscure and long-forgotten, still
making her living as a stenographer.[13]

Both Hopkins and Wharton undertook their respective fictional
interrogations of conventional black and white womanhood at a
time when American public life was becoming increasingly diverse
and complicated and cultural expectations about gender roles and
boundaries—about the way that men and women were supposed to
define themselves—conversely appeared more stark and opposi-

tional than ever before. Drawing sharply defined boundaries between masculinity and femininity, in fact, seemed to serve as a way of imposing manageable order on an increasingly chaotic and diverse social sphere.[14] So too were the finely tuned distinctions made between "virtuous" and "fallen" women, and in particular between white and black women. If the ideal white woman did appear to be so lofty on her pedestal, it was because she stood on the stereotype of her defining opposite—the woman who had fallen from virtue, and in particular the black woman, who in the words of one critic served as "the cultural repository of all the white bourgeois lady's denied sexuality."[15]

Indeed, to tell the age-old story of womanly virtue rewarded by marriage, bequeathed to nineteenth-century American and English culture by Samuel Richardson's popular eighteenth-century novel *Pamela*, was to premise the tale of ideal femininity on its opposite— the woman who succumbs to temptation and thereby falls by the wayside.[16] In late-nineteenth-century and early-twentieth-century America, where ethnic, class, and racial categories were acquiring ever-growing importance, to tell a tale of ideal femininity was by implication to evoke the untold narrative of its opposite—the black woman who had served as sexual prey since antebellum times, the working woman excluded from characterizations of fragility and ornamentation, the public woman denied male solicitude and protection. These were the figures who lingered in the shadows and the margins of the Richardsonian narrative, which did its best to impose orderliness on representations of femininity by drawing sharp distinctions between "successful" and "unsuccessful" womanhood.

Yet this was a time when the increasing diversity of American life, produced by urbanization, immigration, class differentiation, and the growing restlessness of white and black women and black men, was giving rise to a multiplicity of often competing and contradictory narratives. The cacophony created by those stories implicitly and often explicitly interrogated hard-and-fast social categories of race, class, and gender and the narratives accompanying those categories. African American writers like Pauline Hopkins were acutely aware of the necessity of using the novel to generate their own stories about African Americans and to refute racist narratives of black "inferiority" popularized by novelists like Thomas Dixon. *"No one will do this for us,"* Hopkins declared in the preface to her 1900 novel *Contending Forces; "we must ourselves develop the men and women who will faithfully portray the inmost thoughts and feelings of the Negro with all the fire and romance which lie dormant in our history,* and, as yet, unrecognized by writers of the Anglo-Saxon race."[17] In *Contending Forces,* Hopkins explicitly refutes stories of rape by black men to justify lynching in the South by presenting a character who asserts that such tales can nearly always be countered by opposing black versions: "If every case of Negro lynching could be investigated, we should discover fearful discrepancies between the story of the mob and the real truth" (299). The answer, the character concludes, is to use "the methods of the South"—that is, to "create sentiment for the race *against* its detractors" (300). In other words, the cultural narrative of white women endangered by black rapists, created by the white South to justify the practice of lynching, could be effectively countered only by an opposing narrative generated by African Americans themselves.

Charlotte Perkins Gilman, for her part, observed in the early years of the twentieth century that "the art of fiction is being re-born in these days" because of the proliferating creative activity of white women writers. Narrative plots had until recently, she noted, been limited to two main forms—adventure stories implicitly masculine in form and content and love stories written for and about women. But women writers of the early twentieth century, she added, were rapidly multiplying those possibilities. Already they were expanding their narrative purview beyond love stories into at least five general categories of narratives: (1) stories of women who give up their careers for marriage; (2) stories of middle-aged women who find themselves radically dissatisfied with their lot; (3) stories of women's relationships with one another; (4) stories of mothers and children; and (5) stories of "full-grown" women who face "the demands of love with the high standards of conscious motherhood."[18]

The sense of multiplying narrative possibilities available to women pondered by writers as wide-ranging as Gilman and Hopkins suggested just how much public space was expanding for women in the years after the Civil War. Before the war, especially in the period between 1825 and 1840, as historians, among them notably Mary Ryan, have argued, the public sphere appeared relatively unproblematic and uncomplicated in its primarily masculine character, with concessions to the presence of women only "at the border" of the public realm as symbols of civic virtues. Public ceremonies, Ryan suggests, like parades and patriotic celebrations in antebellum cities, "gave public expression to a blunt and familiar gender asymmetry: in public it would seem, men were vigorous social actors, women a docile audience."[19] To be a public woman, in fact, was to invite the characterization of a Jezebel, the wife of Ahab in the Book of Kings in the Old Testament, who exerted an unsavory influence upon her husband and who came to figure as the stereotypical fallen, impure woman whose very presence was perceived as threatening to the public order.[20]

The Civil War, however, had greatly expanded the possibilities for public contributions made by women. Both Harriet Beecher Stowe, the author of the best-selling and highly controversial *Uncle Tom's Cabin*, and Julia Ward Howe, author of "The Battle Hymn of the Republic," came to figure as public inspirations for the Union cause, and on both sides, Union and Confederate, women took central roles as custodians of public culture—as poets, journalists, and novelists in particular.[21] The best-selling novel of the Confederacy *Macaria*, by Augusta J. Evans, took as its primary narrative concern the public contributions to be made to the Confederate cause by two intellectually and artistically aspiring single women who eventually eschew their individual ambitions for the Confederacy.[22]

And if the war bestowed upon women a new role as cultural custodian, the postbellum period saw the rise of yet another public role for women—that of shopper. In the expanding and increasingly complicated marketplace of the postbellum years, marked by the birth and rise of department stores, women generally had the responsibility for shopping for their families, and in that capacity they took on the increasingly important role of consumer, thereby expanding the boundaries of women's sphere.[23] The department store, in fact, as historian Glenna Matthews observes, "was coming into its own as *the* grand public space for women."[24]

Precisely because of the expanding marketplace, the widening range of employment for women in offices and shops, and new forms of transportation, like public streetcars, women had never appeared to have so much freedom in the public realm. Those women, born between 1850 and 1900, who took increasing advantage of that freedom to redefine themselves came to be known as New Women.[25] This was a term largely limited to white women, but it nonetheless demonstrated its appeal to African American women moving into the public sphere as well. New Women were regarded as the daughters of True Women, the mid-nineteenth-century ideal of white femininity defined by piety, submissiveness, and domesticity. Appearing in growing numbers in the 1880s and 1890s, New Women invaded colleges and universities, offices and businesses, and often resisted marriage itself. By 1888, 35,000 women were enrolled as students in 563 colleges and universities, and women in the workplace constituted 17 percent of all workers.[26] Over the next two decades women made their presence felt outside the home. Between 1870 and 1900 the number of women working outside the home increased by three times—in offices, factories, and shops.[27] The invention of the typewriter in 1867 led to the emergence of a new kind of office worker—the stenographer or "typewriter girl"— 200,000 strong in offices across the country by 1900.[28] So striking was this growing presence of women in universities and the workplace, in women's clubs and in reform movements ranging from suffrage to temperance, that the New Woman—and her disinclination to succumb automatically to marriage and domesticity— attracted considerable public comment. One 1890s magazine ventured to offer a half-humorous, half-anxious poetic definition:

> She flouts Love's caresses
> Reforming ladies dresses
> And scorns the Man-Monster's tirade;
> She seems scarcely human
> This mannish New Woman
> This Queen of the Blushless Brigade.[29]

African American women tended to be a little more resistant to some of the iconoclastic aspects of New Womanhood—resisting love and marriage, for example—since slavery had historically barred black women from legally defined marriage and racism had long defined black women in stereotypes directly opposite to that of True Womanhood—that is, as sexually voracious, aggressive, and physically hardy.[30] But women of color were nonetheless moving into the public sphere nearly as rapidly as white women. By the opening years of the twentieth century, 4,000 black women had graduated from normal schools and universities, and growing numbers were actively pursuing professions ranging from law to medicine to teaching. Increasingly, black women pursued the possibilities of organizing themselves for public action in university sororities like Alpha Kappa Alpha and Delta Sigma Theta and in women's clubs. The latter in particular were established in part to refute the myth of black women's sexual availability and voracity. Paula Giddings notes that in the wake of African American journalist Ida B. Wells's 1890s antilynching crusade, aimed at debunking white stereotypes of black sexuality and white women's vulnerability, black women's clubs sprang up first in Manhattan, Brooklyn, and Boston, and then all over the country.[31] What was needed, many of these new clubwomen asserted, was a concerted effort to emphasize the great untold story of race and sexuality in late-nineteenth-century America—"the sexual vulnerability of black women."[32] One of those women, Fannie Barrier Williams, a graduate of the New England Conservatory of Music, frankly articulated that agenda at the World Columbian Exposition of 1893. Black women's "own mothers can't protect them," Williams told an Exposition audience, "and white women will not." Years later Williams wrote: "It is a significant and shameful fact that I am constantly in receipt of letters from the still unprotected women in the South, begging me to find employment for their daughters . . . to save them from going into the homes of the South as servants as there is nothing to save them from dishonor and degradation."[33]

The challenges that New Women, black and white, posed to the gender status quo aroused considerable public debate and unleashed sizeable anxieties about an increasingly fluid public sphere. Public spaces in nineteenth-century cities appeared increasingly unsettling because of the ever-present possibility of meeting a wide range of strangers not readily susceptible to reassuring social categorizations, including women, white and black, who appeared to transgress traditional gender boundaries and who disrupted time-honored assumptions about women who were public and thereby linked with sexual impropriety.[34] Even speaking out in public as an author who was also a woman could be an ambiguous and dangerous endeavor. For women writers who were perhaps too open and frank there still lay the possibility of being vulnerable to the kind of characterizations linking sexuality and public prominence made by Stendhal in 1819: "The publication of a book is fraught with difficulties for anyone but a harlot. . . ."[35] Several generations later, public commentaries and common assumptions, responding to an increasingly heterogeneous public sphere, warned of sexual danger awaiting women who made themselves too public; women could place themselves in danger by venturing too far into that sphere, just as they could also, as "women of the streets," themselves embody that sexual danger. "Warning of sexual danger and admonitions to maintain scrupulous gender differences," Mary Ryan suggests, "might express and assuage the anxiety portended by such diversity." Defining precise boundaries between masculinity and femininity and between "dangerous" and "endangered" women, as Ryan puts it, was one way of creating "symbolic order out of social multiplicity."[36] Hence public debates about New Women resounded with lamentations about the new "mannishness" of women. Fears were expressed about the effect of higher education upon the capacity of women to reproduce and to absorb "beyond" their biological abilities, and anxieties about New Women as an emerging "intermediate sex" contributed to the newly articulated sexual category of Lesbianism created by equally new experts in sexology.[37]

Partly in response to these efforts to retain women within traditionally defined spaces and narratives focusing on love and marriage, a good many novels of the period by women writers took as their focus the problem of how to tell a woman's story that breached the boundaries of those spaces and narratives. Indeed, what concerned a wide range of women writers in turn-of-the-century America was the confining nature of those traditional spaces and narrative plots. These were writers, like Kate Chopin, Ellen Glasgow, Alice Dunbar-Nelson, Frances Harper, and the apprentice Willa Cather, who had inherited two centuries of "heroine's texts," in Nancy Miller's phrase, novels that feature female protagonists vulnerable to sexually predatory behavior, whose only real option for survival and success appears to be marriage and, by implication, integration into society. To triumph was to follow the plot defining Samuel Richardson's famous heroine Pamela, whose stalwart virtue is eventually rewarded by marriage to her pursuer. To fail was to be Ophelia, left with no alternative to marriage and the happy ending but death.[38]

What happens, both Edith Wharton and Pauline Hopkins ask in *The House of Mirth* and *Contending Forces*, respectively, when female protagonists with artistic sensibilities and even aspirations are trapped within such narrow narrative confines, especially when those stories are not of their own making? For the protagonists of both novels—Wharton's Lily Bart and Hopkins's Sappho Clark—are indeed figures with strong artistic inclinations who find those inclinations repressed and frustrated as they themselves are reduced to beautiful objects of art and scrutiny. Lily, as her sometimes friend and strikingly reluctant suitor Lawrence Selden tells her, is very much an artist who makes the most of the smallest opportunity, even a chance meeting with him, to display herself in the best possible light as marriage material. Everything she does, from strolling along a woodland path to caressing the fine leather bindings of old books, reveals what the narrative calls "the instinctive feeling for effect which never forsook her."[39] Yet for all her artistic sensibilities, Lily never seriously considers pursuing the possibility of art as a vocation. Part of the problem lies in the world that defines her, for everything in Lily's environment conspires to channel "her sense of beauty and her craving for the eternal finish of life" into mere appreciation of material comfort and possession, of the expensive clothes she has been taught to wear to present herself on the marriage market and the luxurious surroundings her mother has tutored her to see as both the price and the reward of her beauty (26). But Lily's plight is also defined by a sense of self imposed upon her by stories not of her own making, stories that decree woman's fate as ornamental and aimed solely toward the goal of marriage. Similarly, Hopkins's protagonist Sappho Clark reveals her artistic inclinations in her very name, as well as in her proclivity for creating beauty in her modest boardinghouse room and even in her occupation as a typist.[40] But she too finds herself barred from undertaking the act of artistic creation itself by a complex of forces beyond her control—by stereotypes that pronounce her as sexually available, by men willing to victimize her, and by historical forces so powerful that they threaten to make her reenact the patterns of past generations and keep her silent forever.

Sappho tries desperately throughout *Contending Forces* to seek a way out of those narrative confines. Having been raped and impregnated by her white uncle at an early age, thereby reenacting the age-old story of the black woman as sexual victim, Sappho tries to redefine herself and her story, first by assuming the name Sappho Clark and making a new life for herself in Boston, and then by resisting the efforts of an unscrupulous lawyer named John Pollock Langley who seeks to reinsert her in the role of black woman as sexual prey by making her his mistress. Lily Bart, in contrast, can never quite manage to set her sights beyond the confines of the heroine's text, beyond the limits of the marriage plot. She may complain early on to Selden about "what a miserable thing it is to be a woman," but she is incapable of imagining a narrative outcome for herself apart from marriage (7). When Selden asks her if marriage isn't her vocation, she replies quite simply, "I suppose so. What else is there?" (9). The alternative represented by her friend—and Selden's cousin—Gerty Farish, a woman who lives alone on her own income and devotes herself to philanthropy and cultural activities—does not exist for Lily because the spinsterish Gerty is not "marriageable," not a figure in the marriage plot (7).

It is a plot with which Lily herself feels vaguely dissatisfied, even though she tirelessly cultivates opportunities and friendships that may bring her closer to the prescribed culmination of marriage. But being of a fastidious nature, Lily can never quite bring herself to inspire a marriage proposal from the extremely wealthy but boring and unimaginative Percy Gryce or to consider accepting the proposal presented her by the social-climbing Simon Rosedale, a Jewish financier regarded contemptuously by her social set, or even the tentative approaches to marriage presented by the unhappily married George Dorset. "Sometimes," her friend Carry Fisher muses, "I think it's just flightiness—and sometimes I think it's because, at heart, she despises the things she's trying for. And it's the difficulty of deciding that makes her such an interesting study" (197).

It is also a plot that underscores how closely intertwined Lily's very sense of self is with the reflection she sees in other people's eyes—in Selden's amused, detached admiration, in the appreciation that people show for her striking beauty, in the stir that she creates whenever she ventures out in public. It just may be that one of Lily's failings is a too-easy pliability, a willingness to be what others want her to be, and significantly enough, she prides herself in her "power to look and to be so exactly what the occasion required" (93). A striking number of scenes, in fact, portray Lily peering into the mirror, striving to see what others see—the beauty that sets her apart from other women, the lines that are beginning to touch her face at the age of twenty-nine, and even the ugly rumors that begin to follow her when she only half-knowingly engages herself in an elaborate and ultimately compromising financial relationship with Gus Trenor, the wealthy husband of her socialite friend Judy Trenor. To a great extent, Lily does not exist to herself without the reflection she sees in others' eyes. Her beauty and ultimately her very sense of self are radically dependent upon the regard of others. Selden discerns something of this truth when he unexpectedly stumbles upon a solitary and distracted Lily during a country-house visit and thinks to himself, *"That is how she looks when she is alone!"* (71). In this respect, it is significant that the story of Lily's unsuccessful pursuit of the marriage plot begins and ends with Selden's measured, voyeuristic survey of her, pondering her beauty, weighing her motives, and ultimately reducing her to the object of his gaze and his own reluctant, half-hearted sense of desire. Ultimately, Lily is incarcerated by Selden's measuring, judgmental gaze—the gaze, after all, of "a negative hero," as Wharton herself termed Selden—and by the images and reflections that other people have of her.[41]

Caught in the gaze of others, Lily has no room or inclination for looking within, for being introspective, for defining herself on her own terms. Indeed, as a woman who seeks her sense of self in the eyes of others, she finds introspection singularly frightening, an endeavor full of doubts, shadows, and dangers, and she does everything in her power to avoid the soul-searing experience of looking within. Hence when Lily has a terrifying late-night interview with Gus Trenor, who implicitly, half-consciously demands sexual payment for the financial aid he has given her, Lily retreats to the arms of her friend Gerty rather than face her inner demons on her own. "Can you imagine looking at your glass some morning and seeing a disfigurement—some hideous change that has come to you while you slept?" she asks Gerty. "Well, I seem to myself like that—I can't bear to see myself in my own thoughts—I hate ugliness, you know—I've always turned from it . . ." (173).

In particular, one of the doubts and shadows revealed to her in those brief, always resisted moments of introspection is the vague realization that her cherished position as society beauty and *jeune fille à marier* is made possible by the sweeping aside and marginalization of other women's stories—of Gerty, an independent, plain young woman who apparently has no chance at a fashionable marriage; of Nettie Struther, the office girl suffering from the consequences of a sexual adventure and finding redemption of sorts in a modest flat with a baby and hardworking husband; and above all, of Mrs. Haffen, the charwoman who literally blocks Lily's way on two occasions and who extorts money from Lily for compromising letters to Selden written, not by Lily, as Mrs. Haffen supposes, but by a powerful and unscrupulous socialite named Bertha Dorset. Lily herself has always noted with satisfaction how favorably her beauty compares with that of other women in society and how her own possibilities for happiness *appear* to outweigh those of Gerty. To contrast herself with others "seemed only," the narrative tells us, "to throw her own exceptionalness into becoming relief" (93). Selden in turn comes to a similar conclusion at the outset of the novel when he ponders "a confused sense that she must have cost a great deal to make, that a great many dull and ugly people must, in some mysterious way, have been sacrificed to produce her" (5). But to ponder the possibility of other stories on which hers is premised also suggests the instability of the marriage plot in which she is cast—a sense, in particular, of her own insecurity and of competing stories lying just beneath the surface. In Mrs. Haffen's clumsy, brutal attempt at extortion, in her exposure of some of the uglier secrets underlying the glittering society world and the wealth for which Lily yearns, the charwoman reveals "the other side" of Lily's world, "the volcanic nether side of the surface over which conjecture and innuendo glide so lightly" (109).

This is a possibility that Wharton, very much a part of the upper-crust world that she so vigorously criticized and satirized, raises almost in spite of herself. Hardly an egalitarian and very much marked by the snobbery and anti-Semitism of her class, as her portrait of the financier Simon Rosedale reveals, Wharton nonetheless ponders, if only briefly and uneasily, the alternative stories lying beneath the surface of Lily's story as ornament. That fleeting contemplation uncovers a world on the brink of the atomism and fragmentation of traditional narratives and pieties that define modernist novels of the twentieth century. Lily herself glimpses something of that atomism and fragmentation toward the end of the novel, when she briefly conjures up a vision of men and women resembling "atoms whirling away from each other in some wild centrifugal dance" (337).

That there are alternative, submerged narratives of women to be considered and excavated, that Lily's story of a lovely white woman incarcerated in the marriage plot is not the only story of women to be told, is Pauline Hopkins's primary concern in *Contending Forces*. In a sense, Hopkins brings to the surface what Wharton uneasily ponders and quickly discards. For what interests Hopkins is the intertwining of women's stories that are supposedly defined by their radical difference from each other—the story of the white woman valued for her untouchable, pristine beauty, embodied by

Grace Montfort, the Englishwoman married to Bermuda planter Charles Montfort, and the stories of black women, like her maid Lucy, like Sappho Clark living generations later, and like Grace herself, suddenly labeled a black woman—all of whom make that pristine, precious quality possible by the simple fact of contrast. To stand on the pedestal, Hopkins's narrative suggests, is to stand on the bodies of black women whose devaluation determines the precious value of white women.[42]

Hopkins makes the intertwining of women's stories startlingly clear in the novel's strange, almost hallucinatory introduction, titled "A Retrospect of the Past," which initially appears strangely disconnected from and independent of the novel's main narrative—that of Sappho Clark, the Smith family, with whom she boards, and the African American community in Boston in which they all live. The novel opens with a scene in 1790s Bermuda, where a planter named Charles Montfort announces his decision to leave his paradisiacal island home for North Carolina in order to sidestep the inevitable prospect of emancipation under British rule. An immensely wealthy owner of some 700 slaves, Montfort resists the prospect of submitting his will and his fortune to plans for gradual emancipation and decides to move his family and his slaves to eastern North Carolina, where ". . . he would gradually free his slaves without impoverishing himself . . ." (24). Hence the arrival of the Montforts and their establishment in the little North Carolina town of Newbern causes something of a stir. Arousing particular interest is the appearance of Montfort's wife, Grace, "a dream of beauty even among beautiful women," attended by her loyal maid and foster-sister Lucy (40). Her beauty and very inaccessibility attract the eye of an unscrupulous local planter named Anson Pollock, whose passion for her mounts after she angrily and virtuously spurns his advances. In retaliation Pollock vows to ruin her husband, confiscate his fortune, and possess Grace, and his most potent weapon turns out to be stories that his henchmen spread about the community alluding to the possibility that Grace is part black and that her husband plans eventually to emancipate his slaves.

Whether or not Grace is indeed part black and part white remains to be seen. That possibility is obliquely referred to by the narrator, who nonetheless maintains a noncommittal tone on the topic. The authority for the stories about Grace Montfort rests ultimately on the mere suspicion that one white man has about "too much cream color in the face and too little blud under the skin for a genooine white 'ooman" (41). But what is notable about these stories is the rapidity with which they change her status in the neighborhood and eventually topple her from the pedestal of white womanhood. On the strength of gossip and sheer envy, Grace is transformed from pristine and distant white lady to sexually vulnerable black woman. Spurred on by the gossip, a local mob attacks the Montfort house and kills Montfort, thereby leaving Grace open to a vengeful whipping by a white man in a passage, as Hazel Carby observes, evoking nothing so much as a graphic rape scene.[43] Grace dies shortly thereafter, leaving her two young sons, Charles and Jesse, to the tender mercies of Anson Pollock, who relegates them to slavery as the sons of a black mother. Only the thin membrane of narrative, it would appear, separates Grace the ornamental, pristine white lady from Grace the black rape victim, and her sons from the condition of human chattel. The value of one apparently cannot be separated from the degradation of the other, and as if to underscore the intertwining of the two stories that come to define Grace, Anson takes her foster-sister Lucy as his mistress after Grace's death.

The narrative pattern established in the seemingly unrelated story of Grace Montfort—the remote and chaste white woman instantly transformed into black female prey through the power of stories—is repeated by Sappho Clark, a young African American woman who supports herself as a stenographer and takes up lodging in the Smith house several generations later in Boston. Precisely because she appears so white, so beautiful, and so distant, she exerts a peculiar fascination for the aspiring young black lawyer and politician John Pollock Langley, who is engaged to the daughter of the Smith household, Dora. When Langley discovers the truth of Sappho's background—that she has through sheer force of will transformed herself from the rape victim of white men stranded in a New Orleans brothel to a virtuous and remote young lady of independent means—he resolves to "bend her to his will" by confronting her with her past and forcing her to resume her old narrative position as a *fille de joie* (274). Unrelated to Grace Montfort in any way, Sappho finds herself reenacting the old story of black women's sexual vulnerability, of Grace's victimization and of her own, for that matter, merely on the basis of being a black woman vulnerable to narrative plots—and plotting—seemingly beyond her control. And as if to underscore the repetitive nature of narrative plots in which black women are incarcerated, the narrative later reveals that Langley is himself the part-white offspring of the Pollock family that produced Anson Pollock, the white man responsible for destroying the Montfort family. Both Sappho and Langley, the novel implies, are playing roles that were scripted for them long ago by narratives and historical forces seemingly far beyond their individual control and subjecting them to endless repetitions of the past.

Hopkins shares with Wharton, then, a conviction that traditional narratives for women—marriage plots for white women and plots of victimization for black women—create suffocating spaces for women that are nothing if not dehumanizing and confining. Nowhere is this conviction displayed more openly—and in more strikingly similar terms—than in two scenes of exposure and public scrutiny placing Sappho Clark and Lily Bart on display—the first, very public telling of Sappho's story of sexual victimization, and Lily Bart's exhibition of herself as Mrs. Lloyd, as painted by Sir Joshua Reynolds, in the famous *tableau vivant* scene staged for a society event. In *Contending Forces*, Sappho finds her story and, in a manner of speaking, herself on exhibit in the speech given by a black man named Luke Sawyer at a public meeting responding to yet another lynching of a black man in the South. To emphasize the connection to be made between "lynching and concubinage"—as Hopkins terms the twin phenomenon in the novel's preface—Sawyer tells the gathering first of the lynching of his father, a businessman too successful for his white neighbors in Louisiana, and then of the sexual victimization suffered by the young daughter of a friend at the hands of her white uncle. She was eventually found, Sawyer declares, in a New Orleans brothel, pregnant and half-mad, and when her father threatened to go to the legal authorities for satisfaction, he was set upon and lynched by a white mob incited by the white uncle.

Sawyer's indignation is heartfelt, but it is significant that Sappho's story, the possibilities of which have intrigued all of those around her, is told for the first time not by Sappho herself but by another, a well-meaning man who casts her in the role of rape victim. Genuinely outraged by the fate of the young girl once called Mabelle Beaubean, Sawyer takes up the task of telling her story himself. In doing so, he reinforces the narrative bonds that Sappho, who has come to Boston with a new identity and a new life, has worked so hard to elude. Sappho's response to the telling of her

story in public is to faint—what other response could there be?—
and John Langley's response is to ensure that she remains in the
exposed and vulnerable space she now occupies by "crush[ing] her
with the weight of his surmises" and forcing her to resume her role
as sexual prey in the age-old plot incarcerating black women (318).
In a word, Langley tells her that he knows her secret and threatens
to expose her unless she gives herself to him. For Sappho, then, to
stand before a crowd while her story of victimization is told by
another is to experience that victimization again, to be vulnerable to
endless reenactments of brutalization.

Lily Bart, in contrast, yearns to put herself on display as much as
Sappho shrinks from it. Acutely aware that her marriage prospects
crucially depend on being seen in the right places and by the right
people, Lily deliberately places herself in the public eye to calculating effect, exhibiting herself on the upper-class marriage market.
The culmination of that effort, she feels, will be to take her place in
the ultimate spectacle—being "the principal part" in a wedding, the
bride, instead of being "a casual spectator" (91). Hence Lily is very
much "in her element" when she is asked to participate in a series of
tableaux vivants at a social event orchestrated by a couple aspiring to
status in the inner circle of society (138). Choosing just the right
painting to impersonate—Sir Joshua Reynolds's portrait of Mrs.
Lloyd on the eve of her marriage—gives her the opportunity to
express "her vivid plastic sense, hitherto nurtured on no higher
food than dress-making and upholstery," in the arrangement of
color, light, and texture, in the creation of something very like art
itself (138). But most gratifying of all to Lily is "the exhilaration of
displaying her own beauty under a new aspect; of showing that her
loveliness was no mere fixed quality, but an element shaping all
emotions to fresh forms of grace" (138).

But however much the *tableau vivant* appears to provide Lily with
the opportunity to give free rein to her artistic sensibilities and even
the possibilities of self-expression, the scene ultimately underscores
her own imprisonment in traditional narratives confining women.
For the portrait Lily has chosen to portray depicts Mrs. Richard
Lloyd—then the young Joanna Leigh—in the act of carving her
future husband's name on a tree.[44] The scene does display Lily's
beauty to great effect, and the response of the watching crowd is
indeed deeply gratifying to a woman who constantly seeks her
sense of self in the eyes of others. But portraying a woman carving

her future husband's name in a tree nonetheless reinscribes Lily in the marriage plot, emphasizing the narrowness of narratives available to her and ultimately confining her to a single story not of her own making. It is, admittedly, a scene that displays Lily's deepest ambition—to be married—and the method by which she seeks to fulfill that ambition—by being on display. But it is also a *tableau* that emphasizes how little of the scene is of Lily's own making. The portrait is the creation of another artist, and the scene it depicts is of an age-old narrative for women—an approaching marriage as the final culmination of a woman's story. Ultimately, the scene in which Lily is allowed to give the fullest and freest expression of her artistic inclinations is also the one in which her imprisonment in traditional narratives—in particular, the marriage plot—is underscored with chilling finality.

Curiously enough, the *tableau vivant* also renders Lily a little too public for her own good. Lily herself is well aware that at the age of twenty-nine she has been "too long before the public" as a marriageable girl and that she is beginning to attract a little too much gossip (91). In the *tableau vivant* Lily displays her beauty to full effect, and while the spectators voice their appreciation, they also begin to give voice to the suspicion that Lily is somehow blurring the lines between propriety and impropriety. Her cousin Ned Van Alstyne, for one, pronounces her "a deuced bold thing," and even Gus Trenor begins to mutter about "damned bad taste" (142, 146). Those early expressions of doubt and disapproval foreshadow the gossip that accelerates around Lily as the narrative proceeds, and significantly, Lily's declining fortunes are obliquely but implicitly linked with yet another painting proclaiming her fate of narrative imprisonment—that of Beatrice Cenci. Fixed on the lid of a bronze box in her aunt's sitting room, where Lily is reproached for being "disgraced," the picture portrays the legendary Italian girl who was raped by her father and who killed him in retaliation, thus inspiring a host of nineteenth-century writers ranging from Percy Shelley to Nathaniel Hawthorne (182). For Lily, though, the image of Beatrice Cenci—in a sense the quintessential fallen woman—is a painful reminder of the fate awaiting any marriageable girl who is talked about too much, who is, to use the word of her gossipy and vindictive cousin Grace Stepney, too "conspicuous" (130).

Having failed to reach the culmination of the marriage plot in a wedding of her own, Lily slips inevitably into the underlying narrative on which the marriage plot rests—that of the fallen woman. One action after another is interpreted by those who view her as yet another indication of her fall into impropriety and scandal. She becomes in a sense something of a "public" woman, a figure in other people's stories about her. It is that gossip that frightens away Percy Gryce as a potential suitor, that eventually turns Lawrence Selden away from her when he unexpectedly spots her in a compromising night encounter with Gus Trenor, that results in Lily's disinheritance by her aunt, who is horrified by rumors of Lily's gambling and dalliances with married men. Ultimately, gossip about Lily estranges her from her entire family and nearly everyone else except Gerty Farish. Lily herself, penniless and driven to life in a shabby boardinghouse, is reduced to aimlessly roaming the streets of New York City day after day in a manner disconcertingly close to that of a woman of the streets.

By her own lights Lily does her best to resist the confining bonds of the "other" woman's story—that of the fallen woman—but she finds herself slipping repeatedly into those narrative confines in scenarios not of her own making. An invitation to travel on the yacht owned by George and Bertha Dorset appears on the face of things to offer her an escape from the gossip linking her name with Gus Trenor's—and from the debt that she finally learns she owes him—but once aboard the yacht in the Mediterranean, she learns "the part allotted her," that of distraction for George Dorset as Bertha pursues a romantic relationship of her own (311). Lily ends up playing the part too well, for although she resists any real romantic entanglement with Dorset, she nonetheless is turned off the yacht in a very public manner in a maneuver by Bertha to camouflage her own indiscretions. For those few who know the real facts of the story, Lily appears to be very much the injured party, but gossip labels her the other woman in a ménage à trois and results in Lily's virtual ostracism by society and her own family. Similarly, Lily accepts a position as secretary and companion to an ambiguous wealthy divorcée whose friends plot her marriage to an impressionable young man of impeccable family, and though Lily extricates herself from what she herself sees as an increasingly compromising situation, gossip about her nonetheless mounts and wreaks further damage on her reputation.

It is no wonder, then, that Lily feels herself hemmed in on all sides by stories not of her own making. When Gus Trenor brutally refers to gossip that implicitly questions her character and reputation, Lily suddenly realizes how vulnerable she is: ". . . this was the way men talked of her. She felt suddenly weak and defenceless; there was a throb of self-pity in her throat" (153). As far as she is concerned, "The words—the words were worse than the touch!"—worse than any physical advance made to her by the likes of Trenor (155). It is no wonder, considering the devastating effect of those words and others, that Lily feels herself doomed by the gossip that places her firmly and unmistakably in the narrative confines of the fallen woman. As she herself tells her friend Gerty, ". . . the truth about any girl is that once she's talked about she's done for . . ." (236). And indeed, Lily appears "done for" as early as the episode of being turned off the Dorsets' yacht. For when Selden unexpectedly meets up with her and her party, he is struck by the newly "impenetrable surface" of Lily's beauty, suggesting "a process of crystallization which had fused her whole being into one hard brilliant substance" (199). It is as though Lily has been turned into stone, not by Medusa but by the stories about her, rendering her so much the object of other people's stories that no sense of an individual self, an individual voice, remains.

For Lily—and for Sappho Clark in *Contending Forces*—the only way out of this narrative entrapment is to appropriate the power of storytelling itself. Lily is in fact urged by her friend Gerty to tell her story, to counter the gossip that Bertha Dorset and her friends have circulated to their own advantage. Lily's response, though, is to say merely: "My story?—I don't believe I know it myself," and she adds, "Why, the beginning was in my cradle, I suppose—in the way I was brought up and the things I was taught to care for" (236). From Wharton's perspective, this inability on Lily's part to tell her own story is probably her greatest tragedy, for Wharton herself, like Pauline Hopkins and so many other women writers of the period, deeply believed that she had defined who and what she was through her writing, despite the various obstacles presented by her family and by the world in which she lived. And as a writer who was also an African American woman, Hopkins made it quite clear to her readers that African Americans in general and African American women in particular must write themselves out of the scripts devised by whites. Revealing both her personal and her political agenda, Hopkins observed quite simply that her motive in writing *Contending Forces* was "to do all that I can in a humble way to raise the stigma of degradation from my race."[45]

As different as Wharton's and Hopkins's backgrounds were, both writers associated the act of writing and storytelling with their own personal struggles to define themselves in opposition to external social forces largely beyond their control, from family and class expectations to dehumanizing racial stereotypes. As numerous commentators have observed, Wharton herself was by no means a self-conscious feminist or even a friend to fellow women writers, whose works she dismissively categorizes in her autobiography as "rose-and-lavender pages."[46] But Wharton was acutely aware of all the pressures, familial and social, that conspired to place her in a narrowly defined identity as a woman born in the nineteenth century. She notes rather ambiguously in her autobiography that her earliest memory was of her delight as a toddler in a new bonnet and the opportunity to adorn herself, and later biographers would point out that when Wharton's first engagement was broken, well before her marriage to Teddy Wharton, popular sentiment in her social circle blamed her for over-large and inappropriate literary ambitions.[47] Precisely because she did indeed understand all too well the forces that militated against her literary ambitions, Wharton quite explicitly traced her sense of self-defined identity and consciousness to her writing and to the publication of her first collection of short stories, *The Greater Inclination,* issued in 1899. Until then, she observed, she had "no real personality of [her] own." Writing, she felt, made her, determined the outlines of her soul.[48] It was, finally, her "secret garden"—and the very term revealed just how much of a refuge from the outside world and its various pressures writing represented for her.[49]

Hopkins in turn tended to see writing as an arena of struggle, both personal and collective. Significantly, in a biographical sketch in the *Colored American Magazine,* probably written by Hopkins herself, her life is defined in distinctly combative terms: "Pauline Hopkins has struggled to the position which she now holds in the same fashion that *all* Northern colored women have to struggle—through hardships, disappointments, and with very little encouragement. What she has accomplished has been done by a grim determination to 'stick at it,' even though failure might await her at the end."[50] Hopkins saw the shape of her own life, in other words, as emblematic of the history of African Americans struggling to define and to advance themselves. Nowhere was that struggle more evident than in the realm of history, whether it be individual or national, as the writer makes clear in the very title of her first novel, *Contending Forces*.[51] These are the forces, Luke Sawyer argues in his pivotal speech, culminating in the telling of Sappho Clark's story, that are bent on destroying African Americans—"conservatism, lack of brotherly affiliation, lack of energy for the right and the power of the almighty dollar which deadens men's hearts to the sufferings of their brothers, and makes them feel that if only *they* rise to the top of the ladder may God help the hindmost man" (256).

Posing herself and her novel against those forces, Hopkins explicitly portrays the act of storytelling in her novel as a liberatory act, as the central means to write history anew and to write oneself into being as well—and not just for Sappho Clark, whose own story is first told by another, but for the entire Smith family as well. Sappho is initially described as a woman with an untold story that desperately needs telling if she is ever to take genuine charge of her life. Surrounded by storytellers from the beginning, in a vibrant and even clamorous community, Sappho is singularly silent about her early life, even though her new friend Dora Smith shrewdly observes that if ever a face told a story it was Sappho's. Profoundly guilt-stricken about the acts of victimization and brutalization that have seared her life, Sappho remains silent even in the midst of other storytellers, like Dora, who tells her of her engagement to John Pollock Langley, like her fellow boarders, Mrs. Davis and Mrs. White, who tell tales both of their slave past and of their lively present, like the wealthy widow Mrs. Willis, who makes her living speaking on the woman question, and like Dr. Abraham Peters, the church janitor, who claims he possesses the gift of words to "hoodoo" white men.

Not until Luke tells her story—and thereby inadvertently exposes her to the possibility of reenacting its narrative through Langley's advances—does Sappho recognize the necessity of speaking up herself and claiming control of both her story and her very sense of self. And tell her story she does—first to her aunt, the fortuneteller Madame Frances, who has been caring for the boy who is really Sappho's unacknowledged son, then to the mother superior at the New Orleans convent where Sappho eventually takes refuge, and finally, with Will Smith, the son of the Smith family, to the wealthy Louisiana man of color who has given her employment. The frequency with which Sappho does tell her story in the latter part of the novel—after remaining silent for so long—suggests just how

crucial that act is in liberating her from the repetitive force of the
past, from age-old narratives that define African American women
as sexual prey and from exploitation by unscrupulous men ranging
from her white uncle to John Pollock Langley himself. And significantly, the multiple tellings of Sappho's story free her from the bur-
dens of her past, from the guilt she feels for having once been sexually exploited, and from the constraints she has felt standing
between herself and marriage to Will Smith. Ultimately, then, telling
her story herself enables Sappho to remake her very sense of self—
from rape victim to a new kind of African American woman who is
free to embrace love, marriage, and respectability on terms defined
by her and not by "contending forces."

As if to underscore the power of storytelling to liberate, yet
another character, Mrs. Smith, Will's mother, tells her family's story
in an effort to reclaim that strange, hallucinatory prologue to the
novel that floats uneasily over the narrative of the Bostonian Smiths.
Relating the story of the Montforts, which she says she never speaks
of "for fear of ridicule," Mrs. Smith tells the sad tale "in almost the
exact words of the story we have given as the first part of this narrative" (374). Once told, the story finally becomes a part of the Smith
narrative, rather than the strange, autonomous tale looming over
their lives like a narrative doppelgänger, threatening to take over
the events and shape of their own lives and force them into never-
ending reenactments of the past. The story is told again by Will
Smith to the Louisiana man of color who is Sappho's employer, and
then finally to the United States Supreme Court. This last retelling of
the Montfort-Smith narrative wins Mrs. Smith a settlement for dam-
ages suffered by her family and long-lost relatives in England, the
descendants of one of the Montfort sons. Telling the story repeatedly allows the Smiths not only to unite their present with their past
but also to redefine themselves as a family and to put behind them
their own age-old narrative roles as victims.

This is a feat of self-definition that Lily Bart in *The House of Mirth*
never succeeds in making, precisely because Lily can never quite
manage to acquire the ability to tell her own story on her own terms.
Conditioned by a family upbringing in which money is all-important
because there is never enough, taught to see her beauty as her prime
asset on the marriage market, and tutored to shun all other narrative
possibilities except the triumphant climax of a financially successful
marriage, Lily can never quite conceive of a sense of self apart from

the reflection she sees in others' eyes or of a story for herself apart from the marriage plot. Everything in her life, it would seem, has conspired to make her see herself as a beautiful object of art rather than a creator of art in her own right. Tellingly, Lawrence Selden has a sudden vision of her narrative imprisonment at the very beginning of the novel: "She was so evidently the victim of the civilization which had produced her, that the links of her bracelet seemed like manacles chaining her to her fate" (7).

Even once Lily has been banished into social limbo, condemned to wander on the far outskirts of society, she does everything she can to reinstate herself into the traditional marriage plot rather than assume the task of storytelling herself. She clings to what old associations she can to maintain a precarious foothold on the margins of society, to keep herself as visible as she can to her old world, and resorts to telling Simon Rosedale, whom she can never quite bring herself to like, that she is now willing to marry him. But as Rosedale frankly informs her, her value as marriage material, as an object of art and beauty, has plummeted. The stories that have circulated about her have for all intents and purposes removed her from the marriage plot and placed her in the ambiguous region of tales of compromised and fallen women. Banished from the traditional plot of marriage, Lily discovers, as she later tells Selden, that her beauty and her deft skill at putting that beauty to its best advantage are singularly "useless" without that framing narrative (324). "What can one do when one finds that one only fits into one hole," she asks him. "One must get back to it or be thrown out into the rubbish heap . . ." (325).

Lily does, though, catch glimpses of other possibilities, other narrative plots for women, like the twilight demimonde world of the divorcée for whom she briefly works as a secretary and companion. There she has "the odd sense of being behind the social tapestry, on the side where the threads were knotted and the loose ends hung" (290). Similarly, Lily sees in the lively gossip in the millinery shop, where she unsuccessfully tries to learn the millinery trade, a strangely "fragmentary and distorted image of the world she had lived in"—bits and pieces of stories about the society women who were once her friends (301). And in a like vein, she discovers in the modest flat of Nettie Struther, the working girl she once thoughtlessly helped, an alternative ending to the narrative of the fallen woman. Nettie has found a husband who trusts her and a comfortable, if financially fragile existence, after feeling herself condemned for an unfortunate romantic relationship. These are fleeting glimpses that suggest possibilities for retelling stories of the world in which Lily once lived, of retelling and reshaping Lily's own story, of resisting the conclusion that no alternative to the marriage plot exists except the age-old story of the fallen woman. These are also glimpses that point the way to a modernist perspective of narrative in general, one that views hard-and-fast unitary narratives with suspicion, subjects them to fragmentation, and couples them with competing stories.

But these are narrative possibilities that prove too unsettling, too disorienting for Lily, who longs for the single, straightforward narrative from which she has been banished, "for that other luxurious world, whose machinery is so carefully concealed that one scene flows into another without perceptible agency" (317). She longs as well for her former, privileged position as the cherished object of art, ornamentation, and admiration, and ultimately, for the passivity implicit in the triumph she experienced in the *tableau vivant*. Rather than pursue the arduous task of telling her own story, of fitting together the fragments she sees as an exile from her former world, Lily yearns for that perfect moment when she received the accolades of the watching crowd and saw in their eyes the self-reflection she sought. That yearning eventually presents itself in its strongest form in Lily's intense longing for dreamless, comforting sleep, which more often than not eludes her in her constant worries about her final fate. In sleep that she can bring about finally only through a sleeping potion, she finds the perfect passivity for which she longs,"the gradual cessation of the inner throb, the soft approach of passiveness," and "the dim abysses of unconsciousness." Only in sleep can she happen upon "the sense of complete subjugation" and the unqualified happiness that eludes her in her waking moments (340).

Ironically, Lily is finally able to return to that perfect moment of passivity and admiration in the end when she dies from an overdose of the sleeping potion, and in this respect *The House of Mirth* functions as nothing so much as a novel of admonition on the dangers awaiting any woman who succumbs to age-old narratives of marriage and ornamentation and resists the opportunity to tell her own story and thus bring her own sense of self into being.[52] Only on her deathbed is Lily able to draw to her that reluctant and doubting suitor Lawrence Selden, and there at her side, pondering her beauty one last time, Selden provides Lily with a reenactment of her tri-umph in the *tableau vivant*. For a brief moment she is once again the object of admiration, the woman "fashioned to adorn and delight," but to fill that function, to acquiesce to that traditional narrative of womanhood, is to forfeit the opportunity to tell her own story (316). Significantly, Selden acknowledges to himself as he gazes at Lily that he will never know the real truth about her, the real story that lies buried under the gossip mounting with each year. He will never, he tells himself, be able even to piece the story together—implicitly because Lily herself could never tell the story, could never bring her-self to pursue narrative possibilities outside the traditional story of womanhood in which she was incarcerated.

The House of Mirth becomes in the end a cautionary tale about the dangers of clinging to one's precarious post on the pedestal, of shut-tling aside other stories of other women. If Lily Bart is, like Sappho Clark in *Contending Forces,* a prisoner of traditional narratives of womanhood, largely a victim of external circumstances beyond her control, she is also a figure who complies with her fate by failing to seize the opportunity to tell her story herself. She can neither bring herself to tell the real story of what happened on the Dorset yacht to counter gossip, nor make calculating use of the letters she buys from Mrs. Haffen, however ambiguous that latter course might be. Unlike Sappho, Lily never relinquishes the space she occupies as the object of intense scrutiny and admiration, and that failure turns out to be her undoing.

Telling women's stories, though, rather than being told by them, can realign the space women occupy and the social space of others as well—that is the lesson counseled by both these novels, by exam-ple in *Contending Forces* and by counterexample in *The House of Mirth*. Sappho Clark manages to break free of the space that con-fines her—that uncomfortable spotlight of voyeuristic scrutiny—by telling her own story again and again and thus reshaping the world around her, the expectations that define her, the way people per-ceive her, and the way that they perceive and define themselves. Her marriage to Will Smith suggests something of the momentous nature of those changes. In marrying Will, Sappho resists the fate usually awaiting fallen women—death—and redefines the notion of womanly virtue in turn-of-the-century America as something not just reserved for white women. That redefinition in turn changes Will, who does not, as she initially anticipates, scorn her for her dark past, but rather expands his own notions of womanhood and manhood to accommodate stories as complicated and as ambiguous as Sappho's. Lily Bart, in contrast, never manages to wrench herself free of the space defined by the *tableau vivant* or to change or expand its perimeters. In death she returns to it, once more scrutinized by Lawrence Selden and still silent, still unable to tell her own story, still told by the stories of others. What effect she might have had on Selden if she had told her story, redefined her space and his, remained to be seen, but those possibilities—and those consequences—would be explored in disconcerting detail by naturalist male writers like Theodore Dreiser and Frank Norris. Their work, in particular Dreiser's *Sister Carrie* and Norris's *McTeague,* would make all too clear and all too disconcerting and unsettling just what happened when stories and social spaces of women and men were reshaped and redefined, subject to one rapid change after another.

6

Naturalism and Novels of Besieged White Masculinity: Theodore Dreiser and Frank Norris

White male novelists in turn-of-the-century America knew all too well that the growing presence of women in the public sphere and the literary realm—and the proliferation of their stories—would directly affect the artistic efforts of male writers, the social spaces they occupied, and even their very identities as men. The success of the New Woman in breaching the boundaries of the public sphere, historian Gail Bederman points out, "undermined the assumption that education, professional status, and political power required a male body." White men could no longer assume exclusive access to certain professions and public activities, and accordingly, they could no longer take for granted traditional notions of manhood associated with that exclusive access.[1] New Women, in short, meant trouble for Old Men, and just what that trouble entailed was suggested in part by an emblematic story circulated—and largely fabricated—by Theodore Dreiser about the difficulties he faced in getting his pathbreaking novel *Sister Carrie* published. According to the story told over and over again by Dreiser, the wife of Dreiser's publisher, Neltje Doubleday, had read the book in manuscript, denounced it as immoral, and insisted that her husband Frank refuse to publish it. As a recent biography of Dreiser observes, the story presented Mrs. Doubleday as "a veritable Titaness, a stand-in for all the snobbish, meddling, do-gooding clubwomen who sought to tame the new realism."[2] The book was eventually published in 1900, despite the controversy it generated at Doubleday, and for years Dreiser was lionized in certain critical circles as the novelist of professional integrity and sexual frankness who was brave enough to stand up against the forces of prudery—and not incidentally the growing power of women in the public sphere.

Sister Carrie was indeed a pioneering novel of sexual frankness, but it was also one of many novels produced in the 1890s and 1900s that responded with anxiety and uncertainty to rapidly changing gender roles and to the increasingly problematic status of traditional white masculine authority amid a chorus of competing voices. In novels by Dreiser, Frank Norris, Hamlin Garland, Jack London, Stephen Crane, and Richard Harding Davis, a new, loosely defined movement of naturalism emerged, one that was peculiarly male in the writers it attracted and in the concerns it addressed. Both in primary themes and in formalistic preoccupations, naturalist novels brought attention to the period's fragmentation of inherited stories and notions of authority, and in particular to the difficulties of white masculine self-definition in a rapidly changing world. With startling frequency, naturalist novels took as their central and defining image a suffering male body succumbing to decay and disintegration. Nowhere was that image probed more energetically or poignantly than in *Sister Carrie* itself and in *McTeague* (1899), by one of Dreiser's earliest and most energetic supporters, Frank Norris.[3] In the hands of Dreiser and Norris, this image provided the means for questioning traditional American assumptions about the agency of the implicitly male individual self, about wide-ranging social, economic, and historical forces apparently arrayed against the self, and about the kind of narratives that could be produced about the plight of the besieged self. Ultimately, novels like *Sister Carrie* and *McTeague* revealed deep white male unease about the rapid changes transforming American life, particularly about the emerging chorus of voices transforming and pluralizing the public sphere, where traditionally defined masculine voices and spaces no longer fully ruled the day. In turn that unease voiced in naturalist novels, almost in spite of itself, pointed the way toward literary modernism—toward a new thematic and formalistic concern with the fragmentation of the self, toward the deterioration and growing suspicion of inherited narratives and narrative in general, and even toward the gender battles that recent critics see as central to literary modernism in the twentieth century.[4]

Naturalism's anticipation of many modernist concerns, even to the extent of blurring conventional boundaries between naturalism and modernism, suggests some of the difficulties in defining naturalism. Coherent definitions of naturalism seem elusive precisely because novels associated with this loose and sprawling movement, embracing writers as different as Stephen Crane and Frank Norris, are more often than not shaped by tensions and oppositions, most notably between overwhelming socioeconomic forces, embodied by confining environments, and individual free will.[5] Nevertheless, the usual view, as Donald Pizer notes, is that naturalism is simply a form of "social realism laced with the idea of determinism"—that is, a philosophical perspective emphasizing that the individual and even the individual's intentions, desires, acts, and will are shaped by material, physical forces far beyond his or her control.[6] Indeed, George Becker resorts to three words to sum up his own definition of naturalism: "pessimistic materialistic determinism."[7]

As a matter of fact, literary naturalism arose at roughly the same time that the social sciences, marked by the dominating presence of Charles Darwin and Darwinian evolutionary ideas, emerged between 1880 and 1920. Writers of the period—like Dreiser and Norris in particular—paid tribute to the new prestige of science by modeling their methods, their language, and even their roles as writers upon science, emphasizing documentation, objective point of view, the unadorned presentation of facts, the acknowledgment of the shaping forces of environment and heredity, and the everyday and the mundane.[8] Above all, the novels these writers produced acknowledged the new currency of evolutionary science as it had emerged with the publication of Darwin's *The Origin of Species* in 1859 and *The Descent of Man* in 1871. Darwin had argued in those key texts that in the "struggle for existence," as he termed the competition for food and survival, those individuals within a species who possessed the traits most beneficial in that struggle would be the most likely to survive and to pass on their superior features. Determining the evolutionary history of any one species, then, were two key processes "discovered" by Darwin, random variations and "natural selection"—his particular term for the inevitable outcome of the "struggle for existence."[9]

The picture of the universe emerging from Darwin's theories was very different from the one delineated by nineteenth-century Christianity. The very idea of divine "design" appeared to be "unnecessary," as Cynthia Eagle Russett points out. "Natural phenomena," Russett explains, "could be explained solely in naturalistic terms with no need to appeal to the supernatural or religious."[10] Instead of a paternalistic deity overseeing all, immense, impersonal forces of evolution and natural selection seemed to be at work in a universe defined not by divine order but by simple indifference. Human beings in turn no longer appeared to hold a place halfway between the animal world and the angels. From a Darwinian perspective they were merely animals themselves. Even long-held American notions of individualism seemed problematic, since evolutionary theory placed no special importance on the individual. In Darwin's scheme, individuals succumbed to the forces of natural selection so that the species itself might survive. What mattered in the end was the preservation of the species, not the sanctity of the individual.[11]

Writers influenced by these developments understandably turned to a new and profoundly deterministic perspective to trace the impact of huge, impersonal forces of environment and heredity upon the individual, and in that move they were aided by the popularity of Émile Zola's novels in 1890s America. Motivated by a strong anticlericalism, Zola frankly argued for the death of "the metaphysical man" and proclaimed that ". . . our whole territory is transformed by the advent of the physiological man." This new man, he added, thought and felt "according to the fixed laws of nature" and as such raised serious questions about the extent of the physiological man's free will and agency.[12] In a world of things and impersonal evolutionary forces, there seemed to be little room for the exertion of the individual free will. Indeed, the strongly deterministic picture drawn by Zola and his disciples, like Frank Norris, who enthusiastically proclaimed himself "the boy Zola," offered hardly any room at all for an autonomous self. Far from existing as independent and free-willed, the self in the determinist picture drawn by literary naturalists tended to merge into its surroundings.[13]

If these ideas about determinism seemed to be accepted with bewildering ease in the 1890s by writers and the public alike, it is at least partly because of the unsettling speed with which the country was transforming itself in the latter half of the nineteenth century from a loosely defined coalition of regions, small towns, and agrarian communities into a corporate, bureaucratized society all too recognizable to late-twentieth-century eyes. In these years some 11 million people moved from farms to the cities even as the country's population as a whole was swelled by the arrival of some 20 million immigrants, most of whom also settled in the cities. The total labor force expanded by a full 50 percent, but the total number of self-employed individuals increased by only 10 percent. By World War I, in fact, almost 40 percent of the workforce could be found in factories.[14] And as the country grew, it appeared to be all the more susceptible to inscrutable forces beyond individual control, like the cycles of prosperity, depression, and unemployment that gripped the national economy from 1873 to 1896, and disruptive events like the great railroad strike of 1877 and the Pullman strike of 1894.[15] It is no wonder, then, that many Americans at the turn of the century felt profound unease about their times and voiced their fears about living, in June Howard's words, "in a perilous time, a period of change and uncertainty, of dislocations and disorders."[16] So rapid were the social and economic changes transforming the face of American life and culture that the individual suddenly seemed puny and powerless, dwarfed by the immensity of forces arrayed in opposition. Indeed, Americans' very faith in the American Dream, in the possibility of the individual's self-fulfillment through hard work and sheer stamina, appeared to be severely shaken by the 1890s.[17]

These were developments that would bear directly on how American white men in particular would define themselves and how masculinity in turn would be portrayed in novels by naturalist writers. In the past decade, critics have pointed out how thoroughly "masculine" naturalist fiction as a rule is—in terms of the writers it attracted and the narratives that were produced—and if anything, this is a point that needs to be emphasized even more heavily than it has been by students of the period.[18] For naturalist novels about white men under siege were written at a time when gender identities, and in particular Darwinian notions of sexual selection, were being weighed carefully by figures as wide-ranging as sociologist William Graham Sumner and feminist Charlotte Perkins Gilman. Indeed, Bert Bender argues that Darwin's ideas about sexual selection were even more popular and pervasive, especially in turn-of-the-century fiction, than were his theories on natural selection. Basically, the theory of sexual selection consisted of two main principles: male competition, what Bender calls "the violent and passionate struggle among males for possession of the female," and female choice, leaving to the female the decision to choose the worthiest and most outstanding competitor for her favors.[19]

Emerging from Darwin's scenario of sexual selection were two far-ranging implications for literature. First, from the perspective of many of Darwin's followers and interpreters, sexual selection defined sexual love and relations between men and women in terms of struggle. As Darwin himself noted, "The season of love is that of battle."[20] This view of sexual love and man/woman relations would have a profoundly dark impact upon fictional representations of sexuality and romance in turn-of-the-century novels, as Bender argues throughout his study of sexual love in the period's fiction marked by Darwinism.[21] Certainly in naturalist novels of the period, in Stephen Crane's *Maggie: A Girl of the Streets* (1893) and in Harold Frederic's *The Damnation of Theron Ware* (1896), for instance, sexual love increasingly was portrayed in terms of conflict and animosity. Second, Darwin had argued in *The Descent of Man* for a sharply defined differentiation between men and women—between men, on the one hand, defined by their compulsion to create and to act, and women, on the other, defined by their need to re-create themselves and to resist action with passivity.[22] Such a scenario tended to confirm the dominant Victorian ideology of separate spheres for men and women, one public and competitive, the other domestic and nourishing.[23]

In the hands of Darwin's popularizers, like William Graham Sumner, Darwinian theories of masculinity and femininity were utilized to argue for and to celebrate even more pronounced distinctions between men and women. Evolutionists proclaimed that sexual divergence was quite simply, as Lisa Tickner argues, "part of the evolutionary process: the higher the order of civilization, the more refined and distinct the attributes of masculinity and femininity." Indeed, representatives for the new "science" of eugenics, calling for the improvement of the "race" through scientific and social manipulation, maintained that the nation's putative decline—worrying many *fin de siècle* commentators, who claimed to see that decline in the era's social, political, and economic turmoil, general indirection, and intellectual "flabbiness"—could be reversed "by 'manly' men and 'womanly' women regenerating the population."[24] It was, in short, in the nature of things, in the nature of evolution, for men and women to be as different as possible, for men to be aggressive and domineering and for women to be submissive and pliable, and the more pronounced those gender characteristics became in the evolutionary process, the more "advanced" human beings and their societies became.[25]

Ironically, Darwinian theories preaching the glories of sexual differentiation came at a time when social and economic developments increasingly appeared to contradict the very idea of an exaggerated and aggressive masculinity. Before the Civil War, the United States had been predominantly agrarian, and more than 50 percent of its adult male population had been self-employed—a status that reinforced antebellum free labor ideology, which dictated that to be a real man was to be economically self-sufficient, whether as a small farmer or as an independent mechanic. But by the turn of the century, it had become something of a rarity to be self-employed. Most white men worked for someone else and under conditions that had become increasingly regimented, with the advent of new techniques of labor efficiency developed by Frederick Winslow Taylor, and with the emergence of the assembly line requiring precisely timed teamwork. The pace and rhythm of work increasingly was determined not by the individual but by efficiency methods stressing speed, regularity, and quotas of output. Horatio Alger ideals, celebrating the individual who climbs to success on his own, persisted in popular novels and legend, but the reality, as Alan Trachtenberg points out, was much more akin to the elaborate teamwork required by Thomas Edison's research laboratory.[26]

As social and economic conditions narrowed the possibilities for establishing an autonomous, self-made manhood, so too did the plurality of masculine roles available to white men during the earlier part of the century decline. Most conspicuous among antebellum male roles was probably the white middle-class ideal of manliness, as defined by conscience, self-discipline, hard work, and self-mastery, traits encouraged by the period's evangelical orientation.[27] Historian Clyde Griffen argues persuasively, though, that white middle-class notions of manliness faced competing styles of masculinity. There was, for example, the cult of elite honor associated with white upper-class men of the South, defined in part by the subordination of white women and slaves. There was also the grittier and rougher sense of honor claimed by southern backcountry frontiersmen—the world that Mark Twain captures in *Adventures of Huckleberry Finn*—who sought to prove their manhood to themselves and to their fellows in appallingly brutal eye-gouging, nose-pulling fights.[28] Also offering competing styles of manliness were northern urban working-class groups, like Irish immigrants who were still very much concerned with honor and preindustrial habits of work, evangelically oriented working-class groups stressing self-discipline and restraint, northern white male abolitionists who espoused freely expressed fraternal love, and certain professions

like the law, which cultivated a certain style of male competitive-
ness. But by the closing years of the nineteenth century, Griffen
adds, this plurality of masculine roles had slowly eroded and the
"rougher forms of masculinity associated with preindustrial occupations lost ground as their former settings disappeared." Male
independence appeared increasingly elusive as more and more men
found it necessary to subordinate themselves to the dictates of others in the workplace. New habits of leisure and consumption in turn
contributed to more homogeneous lifestyles.[29]

The result of these combined pressures was the emergence of "a
unifying national norm" of masculinity cultivated in part by mass-
circulation magazines, a norm, moreover, that appeared highly suit-
able for a bureaucratized age. This more standardized notion of
masculinity emphasized the importance of being a team worker
who nonetheless maintained a certain toughness and virility. The
new, turn-of-the-century ideal still emphasized the importance of
work in defining male identity, but being a white man in the new
corporate age also meant devotion to family as the most important
aspect of an individual's life outside of work. Marriage itself
increasingly came to be seen as companionate rather than patriarchal, and marriage manuals frankly informed male readers of their
responsibility in helping their wives achieve sexual fulfillment.[30]
Above all, the most vaunted ideal of antebellum white masculinity—independence—became ambiguously charged. As historian
Anthony Rotundo succinctly notes, "In the new order, every businessman had to submit. The successful one was the man who submitted to the fewest others."[31]

Implicit as well in the emergence of this new norm of masculinity
was the disturbing sense that narratives available for achieving
manhood were narrowing. Throughout the nineteenth century,
manhood in general had been perceived in something of a narrative
sense, as a plot to be followed culminating in the final acquisition of
manhood, more often than not defined by independence and by the
proving of oneself before one's fellows.[32] But how, novels in turn-of-
the-century America increasingly came to ask, were men to follow
through the plot of manhood and achieve autonomy in an age
marked more and more by bureaucracy and impersonal forces
largely beyond individual control? And what space could men find
in the public sphere if they found themselves increasingly in competition with women—women, moreover, who seemed to serve as

symbols of social disorder precisely because they were busy at the task of redefining the boundaries between femininity and masculinity and the very ideal of femininity itself?[33]

Most disturbing of all was the growing sense that the masculine social spaces and the narratives that remained to male writers in particular were fraught with increasingly complicated and ambiguous possibilities. For it was in the closing years of the nineteenth century that the concept of male homosexuality began to emerge in medical scholarship and in the new field of sexology presided over by figures like Richard von Krafft-Ebing and Havelock Ellis. As developed by physicians and sexologists in the late nineteenth century, the persona of the male homosexual was defined as an "abnormal" male identity, one that had succumbed to effeminacy.[34] From this perspective the male homosexual was an "invert," someone who had "inverted" his gender and acquired "feminine" traits and mannerisms, becoming for all intents and purposes what was known at the time as a "third sex," defined by both male and female elements. Indeed, as historian George Chauncey argues, the figure of the "fairy" emerged in the late nineteenth and early twentieth centuries "as the dominant pejorative category in opposition to which male sexual 'normality' was defined."[35] The stereotype of the fairy, in short, was seized upon in medical discourse and in the popular imagination as a cautionary figure, a warning of what "failed" masculinity could lead to if one did not abide by the "norm."

It was that possibility, unacknowledged but unmistakably present in cultural definitions of "normal" masculinity, that Eve Kosofsky Sedgwick aptly calls "male homosexual panic." As Sedgwick observes, to be a man in the nineteenth century "required certain intense male bonds that were not readily distinguishable from the most reprobated bonds," those of homosexuality, and the possibility that "homosocial" bonds between men could merge all too readily into the realm of homosexuality was the source of considerable homophobia and anxiety, that is, "male homosexual panic."[36] If one takes into consideration how anxiety-fraught and ambiguous cultural notions of heterosexual masculinity were in the waning years of the nineteenth century, it perhaps comes as no surprise that the image of the suffering male body, embodying "a struggle of masculine identity with emotions or physical stigmata stereotyped as feminine," increasingly became emblematic as the object of sentimental pity in the popular imagination. Sedgwick herself argues that the suffering male body supplanted that of the suffering woman as the most representative figure in sentimental novels and stories attempting to elicit the sympathy of readers.[37]

The spectacle of a man suffering, of a tormented male body, generated considerable interest in the period's popular imagination. It was at the turn of the century, after all, that widespread fears were voiced that American culture had become "overcivilized" and implicitly feminized with the new emphasis on leisure and creature comforts readily available for purchase, and partly in response to those fears, Teddy Roosevelt himself made his famous call for "the strenuous life"—for a new manliness based on athletic prowess, aggressiveness, and imperialism—to "restore" the nation's health.[38] The fear of womanly men emerged in the period as an issue of public concern, and nowhere more so than among writers like Frank Norris who were haunted, in the words of Michael Davitt Bell, by "the specter of 'effeminate' irrelevance" by virtue of being novelists and driven to produce a new self-consciously "virile" fiction as a form of rebuttal.[39] *Their* fiction, they repeatedly insisted, was not concerned with issues of literary style or with appeals to genteel female readers but with representations of real life—and by association real masculinity. As Norris himself declared, taking it upon himself to speak for his fellow naturalist writers, "We don't want literature, we want life."[40]

From the perspective of both Norris and Dreiser, "life" and the spectacle of men suffering, men trying to define a sense of masculinity in an increasingly confusing age, required novels with a frank new emphasis upon sexual relationships. Those relationships followed a certain trajectory in a fluid and complicated public sphere and had a distinct impact on the way that men in particular defined themselves as men. Both writers begin their narratives of sexual relationships as romantic triangles linking two men and a woman, and their representations of sex and sexuality resemble nothing so much as the traffic in women that Gayle Rubin describes in her famous essay, which was based on Claude Lévi-Strauss's equally famous definition of society and sociality as founded on the exchange of women between men.[41] According to the paradigm explored by Rubin, society defines men as actors and women as goods and signs to be exchanged between men, who derive their primacy in society from their ability to participate in this form of traffic.

Something very like that traffic characterizes the erotic triangle that Dreiser sets up in *Sister Carrie*, which links his heroine Carrie Meeber with the salesman Charlie Drouet and his friend George Hurstwood, the manager of a famous and elite Chicago saloon, and that Frank Norris portrays in *McTeague*, binding his central character, the crude and powerful dentist McTeague, to his best friend Marcus Shouler through their mutual desire for Marcus's cousin Trina Sieppe. In *Sister Carrie*, 18-year-old Carrie Meeber arrives in Chicago fresh from small-town Wisconsin only to discover that the city offers not endless delights and discoveries to new arrivals but routine and hard work in tedious factory jobs. Fired from her job and fearful of the hardships awaiting her in the urban marketplace, Carrie drifts into a liaison with Drouet, whose wallet seems to offer the shelter she seeks. But that relationship soon becomes complicated by the arrival of Drouet's friend Hurstwood, whom Drouet seeks to impress with Carrie's youth and beauty. Drouet finds his desire for Carrie intensified by Hurstwood's frank admiration for Carrie and even feels "closer to [Hurstwood] than ever before" precisely because of that admiration.[42] Hurstwood's measuring eye, marked by his growing appreciation of Carrie, in turn coolly begins "to 'size up' Drouet from the standpoints of wit and fascination" (108). Drouet, in fact, starts to serve Hurstwood as something like a gratifying reverse image of faults and weaknesses highlighting Hurstwood's own strong points and sense of self: "There was no disputing that whatever he might think of him as a good fellow, he felt a certain amount of contempt for him as a lover. He could hoodwink him all right" (108). Eventually, Hurstwood succeeds in winning Carrie's affection and luring her into running away with him, albeit initially under false pretenses. He does so in part, the narrator tells us, "because he thought her fate mingled with his was better than if it was united with Drouet's" (122). Carrie, in short, serves as the medium through which each man sizes up the other and adjusts his own sense of self. She becomes, in an odd sense, the means by which both Drouet and Hurstwood define themselves as men and as competitors for her favor.

A similar erotic triangle, linking two men whose desire for a woman is heightened in part by their awareness of the other's desire, shapes the early stages of the narrative in Norris's *McTeague*. At Marcus's insistence his cousin Trina, with whom he has been "spending" time, visits McTeague in his capacity as a dentist, and when McTeague reveals his infatuation with Trina to Marcus, the former suddenly sees his "time" with Trina in a more serious light than he has—as though to underscore the rivalry that has been revealed between the two men. In a grand gesture to save and solidify their friendship, Marcus formally gives up Trina for McTeague, and as a result, both men feel a closer bond than ever:

> It was a great moment; even McTeague felt the drama of it. What a fine thing was this friendship between men! The dentist treats his friend for an ulcerated tooth and refuses payment; the friend reciprocates by giving up his girl. This was nobility. Their mutual affection and esteem suddenly increased enormously. It was Damon and Pythias; it was David and Jonathan; nothing could ever estrange them. Now it was for life or death.[43]

That moment of intense affection, though, does not last long, for when Marcus learns that Trina has won a $5,000 lottery, his envy flowers into a general sense of frustrated anger and desire for his "missed" chances with Trina. McTeague's triumphant marriage to Trina throws Marcus's very sense of self into disarray, and eventually McTeague's best friend becomes the dentist's worst enemy. Once again, then, a woman serves to mediate two men's sense of themselves and their bonds with one another.

The curious thing about these two novels, both written at a time when anxiety about gender boundaries in general and masculinity in particular was openly voiced and pondered, is that they both raise the question of what happens when the woman in the triangular relationship eventually refuses to serve as a passive medium through which men can define themselves and each other. In particular, what happens, both novels ask, to the men who find themselves dispossessed of the power to traffic in women? The answer in both novels is stark and direct: their manhood withers away and disappears altogether, and the social space they occupy shrinks slowly but steadily until it very nearly vanishes as well. In a word, the men in these two novels suffer irreversible decline, and therein lies, according to a good many critics in recent years, the main distinguishing feature of naturalist novels: the plot of decline, which traces the inevitable defeat of the individual, nearly always portrayed as male, at the hands of forces far beyond his control.[44]

Initially, of course, George Hurstwood in *Sister Carrie* feels a considerable sense of triumph in his success at wresting Carrie away from his rival Drouet, but that triumph is muted to a striking degree by the fact that his triumph necessitates the loss of his family, his job, and his position in Chicago—in short, his very sense of self. For Hurstwood's flight with Carrie first to Montreal and then to New York City to start a new life under a new name is precipitated by his half-conscious, half-inadvertent theft of his employers' money, an act that is finally decided for him by circumstances beyond his control when his employers' safe closes while he is holding and contemplating their money. And though Hurstwood delights for a while in his hard-won intimacy with Carrie, he gradually realizes what he has lost in leaving his world of Chicago behind. In New York City, Hurstwood is quite simply "nothing," a man who has no standing in a setting already crowded with "celebrities" (305). In that unfamiliar setting, Hurstwood no longer has the glamour of the Chicago saloon to frame his sense of self, and in particular he no longer enjoys the appreciative glances and camaraderie of the saloon's habitués, which told him, in a sense, who and what he was. It is for that lost sense of self—the confident George Hurstwood presiding over Hannah and Hogg's saloon and lionized by equal and superior worthies—that Hurstwood increasingly mourns as his new life in New York City and the modest bar into which he buys a partnership prove disappointing and diminished in comparison. Perhaps even more to the point, the money he has lost in giving up his position and his family robs him of the expansive sense of self that he has always presented to Carrie: "This was not the easy Hurstwood of Chicago—not the liberal, opulent Hurstwood she had known. The change was too obvious to escape detection" (311).

Carrie herself proves to be disconcertingly unpredictable. No longer the apex of the erotic triangle between Drouet and Hurstwood, she begins to show an unsettling inclination not to serve as a passive medium for Hurstwood's self-regard or as acquiescent goods to be exchanged between men. Nor is she willing, for that matter, to remain in the role and narrative designated for her as a "fallen" woman. Indeed, she extricates herself from that role and narrative with surprising ease, not succumbing to decline and death as dictated by traditional plots of fallen women but determinedly remaking herself and her future narrative plots. Increasingly distressed by Hurstwood's diminishing financial resources, especially after his share in the modest saloon is lost, Carrie turns again to her interest in the stage, first aroused in Chicago, where her experience of acting in a fund-raising theatrical event brought her surprising success.

On the stage, after all, Carrie is able to turn her impressionable and pliable qualities to good use, becoming any self required by the parts she plays, and therein lies the most striking difference between the narrative possibilities awaiting Carrie and the shrinking narrative space awaiting Hurstwood, who becomes increasingly paralyzed by his diminishing fund of money. Hurstwood, in fact, finds it more and more difficult to envision alternative selves and stories that depart from the self and narrative he left behind in Chicago. Indeed, the more Carrie energetically pursues future possibilities awaiting her on the stage, making the rounds of offices and theaters, moving from chorus line to small part to larger part to growing public acclaim, the more Hurstwood retreats into the past, pondering past glories and hearty male camaraderie at Hannah and Hogg's, even to the extent of reliving old conversations. And the farther afield Carrie explores those possibilities, away from Hurstwood, the more incapacitated and helpless Hurstwood himself appears, unable to get another job, unable to think of himself as anything but the ex-manager, the man who lost his chances and opportunities in Chicago. Watching Carrie leave to look for work, he feels, the narrator tells us, "some faint stirrings of shame, which were the expression of a manhood rapidly becoming atrophied" (381). As Carrie rises in the theatrical world, Hurstwood increasingly retreats to newspapers in his rocking chair, and shortly after she leaves him to throw in her lot entirely with the theater, Hurstwood is well on the way to becoming a Bowery bum, driven from one cheap lodging to another. By the time, in fact, that Carrie's image, larger than life, looks down on Broadway from a billboard, Hurstwood has been reduced to a "type"—waiting in line with other bums for charity (491). Not without reason, then, have a number of critics pointed out that Carrie's rise is premised on Hurstwood's decline.[45] Carrie's world expands and Hurstwood's shrinks in part because Carrie simply removes herself from Hurstwood's narrative, shows herself unwilling to serve any longer as goods to be exchanged between men.

Carrie's very impressionability, her ability to become in a sense anything that people want her to become, emerges as her greatest asset in a marketplace where increasingly people have to market themselves according to the demands of rapidly changing economic conditions. As a good many critics have already pointed out, Carrie seems to be able to exchange one identity with its accompanying narrative for another with impressive speed—from Carrie Meeber the raw country girl to Mrs. Drouet, the pseudo-wife of Charles Drouet, to Carrie Madenda, the aspiring amateur actress in Chicago, to Carrie Wheeler, the wife of a modest saloon owner in New York City, to Carrie Madenda once again, the Broadway actress who makes her fortune moving from one part to the next.[46] She succeeds in the competitive New York theatrical world precisely because she can change her sense of self according to the demands of the marketplace, and as each self changes, so in a sense does the narrative plot she follows. No wonder, then, that she becomes, in the word pronounced by the admiring men in her audiences, "capital," both a "delicious little morsel" to be pondered by the male gaze and a highly profitable commodity (447).

Hurstwood, in contrast, has emerged as mere debris, an unprofitable product in the marketplace for whom there are no takers. As Carrie's image on the billboard looms over Broadway, Hurstwood's image shrinks and even disintegrates, reduced to one of the many anonymous bits and pieces of broken men on a charity line waiting for a bed for the night:

There was a wooden leg in the line. Hats were all drooping, a collection that would ill become a second-hand Hester Street basement collection. Trousers were all warped and frayed at the bottom and coats worn and faded. In the glare of the store lights, some of the faces looked dry and chalky. Others were red with blotches and puffed in the cheeks and under the eyes; one or two were rawboned and reminded one of railroad hands. (467)

Significantly, Dreiser himself once remarked that the origin of Hurstwood's character lay in just that assortment of down-and-out figures. In his own hard-pressed financial days, Dreiser noted, while he was in City Hall Park surrounded by men hard on their luck, "the idea of *Hurstwood* was born."[47] Hurstwood's own fate, from Dreiser's perspective, unearthed the untold stories of those men. Deprived first of his position and his wealth and then of Carrie herself, Hurstwood has nowhere to go but down, and his decline becomes precipitous once Carrie extricates herself from his narrative.

It is a pattern of decline oddly echoed by the disintegrating relationship, in Norris's novel *McTeague,* of McTeague and his wife Trina, who, like Carrie, turns to other possibilities, and by implication other narratives, when McTeague suddenly loses his ability to serve as financial provider. Probably at the instigation of the eternally bitter and antagonistic Marcus Shouler, McTeague is suddenly informed by the city authorities, after his twelve years of practice as a dentist and three relatively peaceful years of marriage, that his lack of professional credentials requires that he cease his practice immediately. McTeague himself is unable to make sense of the notification, sent to him by authorities he has never seen and evoking professional standards of which he is only dimly aware. He initially declares that he is not about to quit his profession simply because of a piece of paper sent to him by an impersonal and remote city hall. "They—they can't make small of me," he tells his wife Trina (450). But of course "they" can—serving as reminders that McTeague lives in a world where government and bureaucracies are beyond both his ken and his control and as such can directly challenge his sense of autonomy and, not incidentally, his very sense of manhood. Trina, for one, quickly and intuitively senses McTeague's loss of status and autonomy, and like Carrie she takes action by appropriating the role of family provider to the detriment of McTeague's own vaguely defined sense of manhood. "Are you my boss, I'd like to know?" he angrily demands when she insists on moving to smaller and cheaper quarters. "Who's the boss, you or I?" And in reply she triumphantly asks, "Who's got the *money*, I'd like to know?" (454). In that exchange alone can be detected the major shift in power from McTeague to Trina, and in spite of his anger and resentment, not to mention his growing taste for brutalizing Trina, McTeague finds himself unable to recapture the initiative, and by implication his rightful place of male dominance in the marriage. And rather tellingly, his decline in the novel was read as a loss of masculinity by at least two contemporary reviewers, who described the plot as following "the decay of McTeague's prosperity, and accompanying it the decay of his own manhood."[48]

Too "slow-witted" to learn a new trade, McTeague becomes increasingly helpless and even paralyzed, much like the besieged and increasingly unmanned Hurstwood, and finds himself forced slowly to "[abandon] his profession" (450). Trina, in contrast, becomes decidedly more energetic, stepping out of the role of goods to be trafficked in and taking the initiative in controlling their financial circumstances. Intent on sheer survival, she is no longer content to function as helpmate and devoted wife.[49] Selling their household goods at Trina's behest, the McTeagues move first to smaller and cheaper lodgings and then once again, to a horrible hovel that would have been unimaginable from their formerly comfortable perspective. And as McTeague proves himself unable to find another stable job, Trina becomes maniacally obsessed with saving as much money as she can. However miserly she may be, she becomes the moving force in their straitened situation, but unlike the expanding future Carrie finds in *Sister Carrie*, Trina's narrative possibilities narrow considerably. The narrator tells us that her emotions shrink to "her passion for her money and her perverted love for her husband when he was brutal" (479). Nevertheless, her passion for money draws her more and more away from McTeague's sphere until finally, abandoned by her husband, the once meticulous and pretty Trina emerges in a new avatar and in a sense a new story altogether, no longer the prize to be competed for by McTeague and Marcus but a dingy and prematurely aged scrubwoman, "a solitary, abandoned woman lost in the lowest eddies of the great city's tide" (509).

McTeague himself, in turn, suffers a decline as precipitous as Hurstwood's, and to an unsettling degree the narrator attributes that decline from the very beginning to his relationship with Trina. Initially suspicious "of all things feminine" and content in his unthinking routine of weekly work and Sunday leisure, McTeague is thoroughly shaken by the entrance of Trina into his life: "With her the feminine element suddenly entered his little world. It was not only her that he saw and felt, it was the woman, the whole sex, an entire new humanity, strange and alluring, that he seemed to have discovered" (279, 281). His whole life, the narrator tells us, has to be rethought and remade accordingly. Above all, his newly aroused sexual desire for Trina awakens "the animal in the man," alerting McTeague in a sense (and us as readers) to the presence of "the brute" within for the first time (283, 285). Indeed, more than one critic has pronounced Trina the fatal woman whose sexuality eventually means the end of McTeague, for it is at least partly because of their increasingly brutal and violent relationship that McTeague experiences his rapid deterioration. Trina's sexuality is embodied first in her wonderful black hair, long figuring in Western literary tradition the potency of female sexuality, and then in the gold that she obsessively collects and that increasingly draws McTeague's own driven desire.[50]

Unmanned by the loss of his profession, by his wife's struggle for power with him, and even by her sexuality, McTeague eventually falls victim to his brutish family legacy of drunkenness and violence. Once abstemious in his drinking and wary of whiskey, McTeague becomes vicious and calculating, propelled as much by his growing hatred of Trina as he is by the desire for liquor. That he finally kills Trina in the end, the narrative suggests, should come as no surprise, for there is something fatal both in his destructive and debilitating relationship with Trina and in his very heredity. Early on, the narrator delivers a warning of McTeague's dangerous vulnerability to forces far beyond his control: "Below the fine fabric of all that was good in him ran the foul stream of hereditary evil, like a sewer. The vices and sins of his father and his father's father, to the third and fourth and five hundredth generation, tainted him. The evil of an entire race flowed in his veins. Why should it be? He did not desire it. Was he to blame?" (285).

The irreversible decline suffered both by McTeague and by George Hurstwood suggests not just two portraits of a self battered and ultimately defeated by forces far beyond its control—by a cold and calculating marketplace that penalizes those who cannot adapt and bend themselves to its demands and by the weight of a family legacy—but two strikingly similar lamentations on the plight of besieged masculinity. In both *Sister Carrie* and *McTeague,* we discover depictions of a diminished, shrunken masculinity that is eventually destroyed by competing narratives of womanhood and a newly assertive female sexuality, and by an increasingly complicated and heterogeneous public sphere of multiple voices and stories. In the brave new world of turn-of-the-century America, both novels assert, even the very space allocated to manhood seems in danger of disappearing altogether.

Above all, both novels focus on the plight of the suffering male body and its deterioration. Hurstwood's physical decline, in fact, begins nearly as soon as he leaves his impressive position and money behind in Chicago. Deprived first of his opulent surroundings in Chicago and then of his much more modest saloon, he no longer has, the narrator says, "the same impressive personality which he had when he first came to New York" (344). From time to time, with the little savings still left to him, he occasionally indulges in masquerades of his old life, eating in restaurants, buying cigars, getting shaves, and sitting in fine hotel lobbies. But those times disappear when his money does, and Hurstwood proves himself singularly unable to play any masculine role except that of moneyed gentleman. Even a brief stint as a strikebreaker for a tram company proves beyond him, and after a day of cold and physical danger, he retreats gratefully to newspaper accounts of the strike in his rocking chair. And as his financial situation deteriorates, so too does his physical appearance, succumbing more and more to age, weakness, and shabbiness. By the time Hurstwood has suffered abandonment by Carrie and illness from exposure and bad food, he bears little resemblance indeed to "the once hale, lusty manager." The narrator notes: "All his corpulency had fled. His face was thin and pale, his hands white, his body flabby. Clothes and all, he weighed but one hundred and thirty-five pounds" (463).

If Hurstwood's body bears the mark of his decline, social and financial, so too does the very space that he occupies, shrinking first from the expansive and glamourous environs of Hannah and Hogg's to the more modest saloon in New York to the small, cheap rooms to which he and Carrie move, to the rocking chair at home and the armchairs in hotel lobbies that he occupies for brief forays into newspapers and nostalgic thoughts of the past, and finally to the soup kitchens and breadlines and the tiny, suffocating flophouse room in the Bowery where he finally decides to turn on the gas. As his options narrow, so too do the very settings that he occupies, and those spaces in turn become increasingly ambiguous and fluid as the man who once took supreme confidence in his place in life among hail-fellows-well-met takes up a residency of sorts in the Bowery. For the Bowery in turn-of-the-century New York was known not just for its poverty and its down-and-out denizens but also for its role as the city's center of "commercialized vice" and, more to the point, as the center of increasingly visible homosexual culture. So visible was that culture, in fact, that it had become fashionable as a form of slumming in certain quarters to visit well-known homosexual resorts. At resorts like Armory Hall in the Bowery, flamboyantly dressed homosexuals already known in the late nineteenth century as "fairies" had become central attractions, luring middle-class crowds eager for titillation and for glimpses of what was fast becoming "the dominant public image," historian George Chauncey says, of "male sexual abnormality."[51] To set George Hurstwood so prominently in this world, then, is to underscore by association his own aberrant manhood, to allegorize, in a sense, his own male homosexual panic, where nothing—not his financial status, not his sense of manhood, not his sexuality—seems to be much of a sure thing. Now confined to the Bowery, Hurstwood moves in a world where the homosociality by which he once defined himself—the rare good camaraderie that he enjoyed so much in his Chicago days—suddenly reveals possibilities of blurring into reprobated homosexuality.[52]

Those possibilities are never explicitly articulated in *Sister Carrie*, but they nonetheless haunt the narrative by virtue of Dreiser's vivid evocation of the Bowery and the whole underside of white middle-class culture that it represented in this period, including newly emerging notions of male homosexuality defined by effeminacy and male "abnormality." For Dreiser himself knew intimately what it was like to be "on the Bowery" from his own down-and-out newspaper days during the Depression of 1893. The experience of his own father's economic failure, moreover, exemplified by his plunge from mill manager to laborer within two short years in the 1870s, made the novelist acutely aware how fragile both middle-class status and masculinity itself could be in an unpredictable and often havoc-inducing economy. His father's failure, Dreiser's latest biographer notes, "banished" the entire family from middle-class status and rendered his sisters, one of whom served as the model for Carrie herself, especially vulnerable to sexually compromising situations. Hence Dreiser himself reveals an extraordinary sense of empathy and even identification with Hurstwood in his days of precipitous decline. Hurstwood's plight was in a sense his own, replicating his own experience of coming to New York, fresh from triumphs as a star reporter in St. Louis, only to be confronted by one failure after another.[53] In a period when failure could be equated with failed masculinity—and by implication and association with homosexuality—Hurstwood's plight of being "on the Bowery" resonated with a host of disturbing associations both for Dreiser personally and for his representation of masculinity under siege. To be unmanned by competing female narratives—like Carrie's rise to stardom—by economic misfortune, by shame, and by self-condemnation was to raise other, less readily speakable specters.

Norris's sense of identification with McTeague, in contrast, was slight if anything, in particular since the distance between narrator and character and between reader and character increases markedly as McTeague descends into a brutish realm far beyond the range of experience implicitly associated with the half-pitying, half-condemnatory narrator.[54] Nevertheless, like Dreiser, Norris makes it unmistakably clear that McTeague's sense of status, self, and manhood are never really quite sure things in the fluid world of Polk Street in San Francisco, where the dentist lives. For Polk Street, situated just a block from the "high life" of the avenue and bustling with a bewildering mixture of people and occupations, is representative of a new urban world very much in the process of becoming, and in that world nothing is secure. Everything—from one's sense of what is respectable and what is not, to social position and the way it is defined—is subject to rapid and disorienting change:

> The shop girls, the plumbers' apprentices, the small tradespeople, and their like, whose social position was not clearly defined, could never be sure how far they could go and yet preserve their 'respectability.' When they wished to be 'proper,' they invariably overdid the thing. It was not as if they belonged to the 'tough' element, who had no appearance to keep up. . . . There were certain limits which its dwellers could not overstep; but unfortunately for them, these limits were poorly defined. They could never be sure of themselves. At an unguarded moment they might be taken for 'toughs,' so they generally erred in the other direction, and were absurdly formal. No people have a keener eye for the amenities than those whose social position is not assured. (328)

In a curious sort of way, the junk shop of the strange and gold-obsessed Zerkow, into whose hovel the McTeagues eventually move, exemplifies the fluidity and dangers of Polk Street and, by implication, the rapidly expanding and increasingly complicated public sphere in turn-of-the-century America: "Everything was there, every trade was represented, every class of society; things of iron and cloth and wood; all the detritus that a great city sloughs off in its daily life. Zerkow's junk shop was the last abiding-place, the almshouse, of such articles as had outlived their usefulness" (293). In Zerkow's shop there is no perceptible sense of order and no signs to indicate how to negotiate one's way through this conglomeration of debris, just as there appear to be few guides available for making one's way through an increasingly bewildering public realm. The refuse available in the junk shop also hints at the dangers lurking in this strange new public world, where people and occupations can be taken up and then discarded just as easily as things and where individual identities can be lost all too quickly amid the press of different and competing groups and ethnicities and amid a clamor of dissonant voices.

That this expanding and complicated public realm is frightening and even threatening to certain notions of identity, particularly those of white men, is repeatedly voiced by Marcus Shouler, McTeague's early boon companion and later enemy, who complains periodically of the threats presented by Chinese immigrants to good, honest

"American" laborers. This is a world, after all, where white men like Marcus Shouler and McTeague jostle for room with an unfamiliar variety of other identities, represented by characters like Zerkow, Old Grannis the Englishman, Maria Macapa, the Mexican woman who insists on telling stories of family gold, and Trina's Swiss-German immigrant family. And in such a world, the narrative implies, it may be as easy for Marcus and McTeague to lose their professional identities—as animal hospital assistant and as dentist—as it once was for them to acquire those identities in the first place.

In this respect, it is significant that McTeague comes to some dim understanding of his increasingly problematic status in this fluid public space through his rivalry with the ambiguous and hostile figure of "a young fellow just graduated from the college, a poser, a rider of bicycles, a man about town, who wore astonishing waistcoats and bet money on greyhound coursing" (281). This is a rival who evokes professional standards—a college degree and the confidence of systematically acquired scientific knowledge—of which McTeague himself has only the vaguest inkling. Perhaps even more to the point, especially when one takes into consideration Norris's own loudly expressed disdain for "sissies" and "stuffed shirts" in his fiction as a whole, the rival dentist, repeatedly referred to as "the Other Dentist, . . . the poser, the wearer of waistcoats, who bet money on greyhound races," evokes something akin to male homosexual panic in McTeague (457).[55] Rather tellingly, McTeague develops a genuine hatred, laced with envy, for his rival and notes with growing scorn the Other Dentist's "salmon-pink neckties and his astonishing waistcoats" (298). This is a figure that underscores McTeague's increasing sense of disorientation in the strange urban world in which he is cast adrift—disorientation that frequently prompts him to ask, "What did it all mean, anyway?" and to declare, more menacingly, "You can't make small of me!" (364, 330). The Other Dentist embodies McTeague's fears and anxieties: the fear that his manhood and his identity are not what he thinks they are, that hale and hearty male comradeship may reveal itself as something other than what it appears to be, that failing in work and in marriage may cast one into a vaguely defined and comprehensive category of "abnormal" manhood, and that abiding by the new rules and standards of a strange new public sphere—conversely—may impose upon a man a status very like that of a "fairy." Ultimately, McTeague finds it necessary to sell his most prized possession—the huge gold tooth he once used as a sign outside his "dental parlors"—to the Other Dentist, and he does so in a scene that underscores the differences in their physical appearance: on the one hand, the Other Dentist's "velvet smoking jacket" and supercilious air, and on the other, McTeague's increasingly shabby and dirty clothing and air of abstracted neglect (498). That act of surrender, of course, suggests just how fluid and permeable McTeague's own sense of identity and manhood have become despite his pronounced scorn for the Other Dentist.

Finally deserting Trina, McTeague, like Hurstwood, becomes a street bum, and like Hurstwood again, his descent into that underworld is vividly evoked by the shrinking spaces he occupies as the McTeagues quickly plummet down to the levels inhabited by the likes of Zerkow the junkman and Maria Macapa, the brutalized wife Zerkow eventually murders. That murder in turn foreshadows McTeague's murder of Trina for the sake of her gold, and as the ultimate outlet for his now uncontrollable fear and anger at being confined in one increasingly narrow space after another. Fleeing the legal authorities, McTeague takes refuge first in the mines where he worked as a boy and then in the backcountry badlands of California. His flight is as much from the ever-narrowing spaces in which he finds himself—from the last hovel he shares with Trina to the streets of the city to the mine where he temporarily works—as it is from the unknown pursuer whom he instinctively senses and who drives him from one remote spot to the next.

The more McTeague runs, the more he flees into widening spaces—into the mountains and eventually into Death Valley—and those spaces are so expansive that he appears in contrast increasingly small and even more vulnerable. Something of that fate, of being diminished and finally overwhelmed by the great vistas of the American West, is evoked in the short, hallucinatory encounter McTeague has during a water stop on a freight train that he has hopped in his ceaseless movement south. Encountering an Indian begging silently for money, McTeague watches as the now-moving train leaves the Indian shrinking in the distance, "still standing motionless between the rails, a forlorn and solitary point of red, lost in the immensity of the surrounding white blur of the desert" (538). That final diminishment by expanding space becomes McTeague's fate as well. Finally run to ground in Death Valley by none other than Marcus Shouler, who has learned of Trina's death and who has decided to take revenge by tracking McTeague down, McTeague finds himself in a hand-to-hand struggle with Marcus, who suc-ceeds in handcuffing his quarry only to be killed by the revolver over which the men fight. Our last glimpse of McTeague, then, is of the ex-dentist handcuffed to the body of a dead man, stranded with-out water and certain to die amid "the measureless leagues of Death Valley" (572).

No other image—that of McTeague locked to a dead man's body, dwarfed by the vast expanses of Death Valley—could illustrate so well the plight of the suffering male body in an increasingly ambiguous and danger-fraught setting, one in which men could no longer be assured of sole ownership or of readily accessible narra-tives leading inevitably to manhood. In the wide-open expanses of the fabled American West, where men were once urged to go and prove themselves, McTeague finds himself bound to the weight of a dead man's body—a man once his rival for Trina's love and the bit-ter competitor who helped shatter the dentist's once-comfortable life. It is also a burden that alludes, not insignificantly, to the demands of traditional masculinity that drive McTeague to this des-olate place, and in particular to the sense of entitlement that has been frustrated at every turn in the suddenly complex and fluid world of urban San Francisco. And it is a burden, not incidentally, that is also a compelling reminder of the increasingly ambiguous nature of turn-of-the-century American masculinity as it becomes more and more defined by its vulnerability in a rapidly changing world of competing narratives, by the curiously symbiotic inter-twining of "normal" and "abnormal" manhood, and even by the violence and rage aroused by that very ambiguity.

Ultimately, we see McTeague, as we see the dying Hurstwood in his flophouse room, across a great distance, as though through a telescope, revealing to us men reduced to small fragments of their former selves and thoroughly diminished by forces beyond their control. And as fragments, bits and pieces of the men they once were, McTeague and Hurstwood very nearly merge into the settings that overwhelm them in the end—McTeague into the landscape of the seemingly endless Death Valley and Hurstwood into the dark spaces and debris of the Bowery. Each man becomes, in a sense, just another physical phenomenon in an expanse of meticulously observed details defining their settings as a whole. As critic Lee Mitchell says of naturalist characters in general, they become virtu-ally "indistinguishable from [their] surroundings."[56]

If the final effect in both novels is one of disorientation, it is because the narrative structures themselves of *McTeague* and *Sister Carrie* take on something of the deterioration that befalls both George Hurstwood and McTeague. We move between episodes that are connected only by the motif of decline and by disintegration.[57] The very narratives that Hurstwood and McTeague inhabit tend to fall apart as the characters themselves succumb to fragmentation, and what remains in the end—at the conclusion of both *Sister Carrie* and *McTeague*—are shards and fragments, small details like the tint of the desert, the contours of the mountains, the narrowness of Hurstwood's flophouse room, and the darkness of Bowery streets, that Dreiser and Norris so carefully describe and ponder. Locked to a dead man, dying in a flophouse, McTeague and Hurstwood are just two more details in meticulously observed settings, granted no special status, no special privilege, no single feature that sets them apart from their background.

Narratives failing to hold together and succumbing to fragmentation, characters themselves reduced to bits and shards in a mosaic of multiple, disconnected details, selves robbed of agency and free will, besieged by forces far beyond individual control, plagued by doubts and uncertainties—these are the qualities that would also mark to a striking degree Stephen Crane's *The Red Badge of Courage* and Gertrude Stein's *Three Lives*. Vivid and unsparing in their details and descriptions, these two texts are designated naturalist works just as often as they are pronounced to be texts that elude ready labels like naturalism. Indeed, one could argue that both *The Red Badge of Courage* and *Three Lives* question the very notion of the novel as a continuous narrative, assuming the coherence of a story and theme and even of an individual self. If they both suggest something of the materialistic determinism usually associated with naturalist novels, of individuals dwarfed and buffeted by the forces of environment and heredity, they also radically question assumptions about the ability of narrative to "reflect" life, and even the very validity and solidity of narrative itself. In this respect, both works point as much toward modernism as they hearken "back" to naturalism and suggest, ultimately, the curious bonds of affinity binding naturalist novels to avant-garde, experimental modernist novels emerging by the second decade of the twentieth century.

7

Toward Modernism: Stephen Crane and Gertrude Stein

However singularly masculine literary naturalism appears to be, it is nonetheless a label often affixed to the early work of Gertrude Stein, specifically to an anomalous and experimental text, seemingly part novel and part short story collection, titled *Three Lives* and published in 1909. "Naturalism" is also a term that has been readily applied to the novels and short fiction of the restless and iconoclastic Stephen Crane, who delighted in exploring the parodic possibilities of a wide range of genres, from the war novel to the western to the tale of the fallen woman. In many respects Crane's most famous work, the 1895 novel *The Red Badge of Courage*, and *Three Lives* do indeed seem to exemplify some of the central concerns usually associated with naturalism, in particular the evocation of large, deterministic forces underscoring the fragility and suffering of puny individuals. Crane's *The Red Badge of Courage*, after all, concentrates on the plight of a frightened young soldier trying to make sense of his own fears and of the confusion of battle. Stein's triptych of three women's lives in the same city brings attention to figures who exist on the margins of society and are eventually defeated by forces far beyond their control—by the overwork and exploitation suffered by two immigrant servant women and by overly zealous moral condemnations of an African American woman judged too free in her exploration of sexuality.

From the time of their publication, though, both *The Red Badge of Courage* and *Three Lives* generated considerable confusion among readers and reviewers, and therein can be detected their transitional nature as texts "betwixt and between" naturalism and modernism.[1] Hearkening back to naturalistic antecedents, both works evoked strongly deterministic themes of individuals buffeted by bewildering forces and circumstances largely beyond their comprehension or control, but both works also puzzled and sometimes outraged their contemporary readers by drawing attention to the very style of their writing—to certain unexpected or torturous turns of phrase, to persistent forms of repetition, and to paragraphs and sentences that seemed somehow radically incompatible with each other. Equally unsettling was the resistance *The Red Badge of Courage* and *Three Lives* seemed to show to arranging themselves into narratives with discernible plots and unified, understandable characters. Crane's and Stein's books offered the abundance of carefully observed detail considered so necessary by turn-of-the-century novelists, but those details somehow failed to submit themselves to larger patterns of orderly narratives. Even the characters themselves seemed to disintegrate into fragmentary moments of consciousness, changing from one moment to the next. And in the midst of these narrative shards and fragments, no guidance was to be had from a unifying narrative voice or perspective. In *The Red Badge of Courage* and *Three Lives*, the narrator's voice tended to mingle with that of the characters, and the result was a singular absence of narrative authority and unitary perspective.

In a word, *The Red Badge of Courage* and *Three Lives* take as both their narrative form and their central thematic concern the growing multiplicity and fluidity of turn-of-the-century American life—that is, the pluralization of the public sphere by loudly competing voices. As such both texts anticipate the modernist narrative techniques of montage, juxtaposition, multilayering, and fragmentation wielded by twentieth-century writers like Sherwood Anderson, Ernest Hemingway, and William Faulkner. These are narrative techniques that bring attention to what many commentators call the most pressing issue in modernism: the problem of representation, that is, how to designate the relationship between a narrative on the pages of a book and the world "out there" that the narrative purports to represent. Nineteenth-century literary realism, as novels like Rebecca Harding Davis's *Waiting for the Verdict* and William Dean Howells's *The Rise of Silas Lapham* revealed, had always been tinged with a certain doubt about that relationship and in particular the accessibility of the world of reality to representation in novels, but in protomodernist works like *The Red Badge of Courage* and *Three Lives*, doubt is highlighted and uncertainty in interpretation is underscored.[2] Indeed, Crane and Stein in their books repeatedly bring attention to the difficulties of interpretation, understanding, and knowing in an increasingly complicated arena of multiple and competing voices and of vividly evoked details of setting and character seemingly resistant to assimilation into any sort of unitary narrative pattern. And at the same time that Crane and Stein emphasize the centrality of doubt in the fictional worlds they create, they also allude to a lingering yearning for certainty and authority capable of resolving doubts and apparently unanswerable questions. These were concerns that directly linked Crane and Stein with modernist writers to follow, and perhaps even more to the point, their odd and disorienting narratives were hailed as precursors by modernist writers in the 1920s, writers as different as William Carlos Williams, Sherwood Anderson, Carl Van Vechten, Eugene O'Neill, and Edmund Wilson.[3]

But if modernist writers to come would praise Crane and Stein for their experimentalism and their exploration of radical doubt, contemporary readers and reviewers judging *The Red Badge of Courage* and *Three Lives* by late-nineteenth-century standards of fiction were often hard pressed to describe or even define these two books. To be sure, *The Red Badge of Courage* was widely hailed for its "realistic" treatment of the Civil War. Its vivid, moment-by-moment evocation of the battlefield even prompted one veteran to declare, quite wrongly, that he remembered fighting at Antietam with Crane, who was actually born six years after Robert E. Lee's surrender at Appomattox.[4] But the language and narrative form of Crane's novel also attracted commentary ranging from bewilderment to outright condemnation. In one now-famous review of *The Red Badge of Courage,* General Alexander C. McClurg, a Civil War veteran, denounced the book as "a mere riot of words" and castigated the 23-year-old Stephen Crane for writing "a vicious satire upon American soldiers and American armies."[5] The much more sympathetic Harold Frederic, whose own novels, like *The Damnation of Theron Ware* (1896), frequently eluded easy labeling, observed that *The Red Badge of Courage* was a novel that defied classification and hinted that Crane's narrative could not even be properly described as a book.[6] Reviewers of Stein's *Three Lives* in turn were stumped by the book's very form—three narrative histories with no ostensible connection among them other than setting—although a number recognized that fiction-making itself seemed to be a central concern. One perceptive review written for the *Kansas City Star* in 1909 noted the "originality of its narrative form" and added: "As these human lives are groping in bewilderment so does the storytelling itself."[7] Stein herself was impatient with questions inquiring whether or not *Three Lives* was actually a novel. To such queries she replied, "I hate labels. It's just a book, a book about different characters, three different people I knew long ago."[8]

Readers also found the very style of each book to be obtrusive, disconcerting, and unsettling. Crane, a recent biographer noted, wanted to "shock and surprise," and often he succeeded all too well.[9] One contemporary critic complained of *The Red Badge of Courage* that "the short, sharp sentences hurled without sequence give one the feeling of being pelted from different angles by hail—hail that is hot."[10] After reading *Three Lives* in manuscript in 1906, the critic and writer Hutchins Hapgood complimented Stein on the power of her three portraits and noted that she had managed to produce a stirring effect "without any of the ordinary devices of plot, piquancy, conversation, variety, drama." And precisely for that reason, he added, her "stories" were "not easy reading." Urging her to revise, Hapgood declared that the stories of Stein's three women "often irritate me by the innumerable and often as it seems to me unnecessary repetitions; by your painstaking but often clumsy phraseology, by what seems sometimes almost an affectation of style."[11] Two decades later the British artist Wyndham Lewis was decidedly more brutal in his assessment of *Three Lives*. "Gertrude Stein's prose-song," he wrote, "is a cold, black suet-pudding. We can represent it as a cold suet-roll of fabulously-reptilian length. Cut it at any point, it is the same thing: the same heavy, sticky, opaque mass all through, and all along."[12]

These complaints about Stein's and Crane's styles are revealing because they indicate a very real frustration with the lack of narrative direction and coherence provided by *Three Lives* and *The Red Badge of Courage*. Reading both books meant being at sea for readers more familiar with plots of rising action, culmination, and resolution; and for both Stein and Crane, who self-consciously saw themselves as challenging tradition in general and rebelling against what one might call the paternal authority of narrative in particular, that sense of disorientation was precisely the point. A self-styled rebel at an early age, Crane had originally conceived of *The Red Badge of Courage* as a quick way to make money during the Depression of 1893, when he and other aspiring writers in New York City were suffering strained financial circumstances. "I deliberately started in to do a potboiler," he later recalled, "something that would take the boarding-school element—you know the kind. Well, I got interested in the thing in spite of myself, and I couldn't, couldn't! I *had* to do it my own way."[13] His way apparently meant to take direct aim at the traditional tales of battle glory that his young protagonist Henry Fleming takes with him into his first battle, tales that he associates with the greatness of the past, "vague and bloody conflicts that had thrilled him with their sweep and fire."[14] These are narratives that inspire his enlistment in the 304th New York Regiment despite his mother's worried, practical opposition, and for Henry personally they point the way to his achievement of manhood through the trial of battle: "The youth had been taught that a man became another thing in a battle. He saw his salvation in such a change" (104). But they are also tales that ill equip Henry first for the monotony of camp life, the very opposite of the "Greeklike struggles" he envisions, and then for the confusion and panic of actual battle, so frightening to him that he joins half his regiment in a headlong flight away from the line of attack (86). Indeed, the very aimlessness of battle—the smoke, the shouting, the barrages, the cries of fear and anger—seems to have nothing at all to do with narratives of manhood tested and won. It is the nature of this contrast—between the narratives of war Henry inherited, his abstract notions of glory and manly prowess, and the chaos of actual combat—that interests Crane the most, that is, how rigid abstractions play out against the confusion of experience. *The Red Badge of Courage* as a whole is shaped by the opposition between the tidy, straightforward narratives of battle that Henry has inherited and the disorienting, episodic multiplicity of combat itself.

Accordingly, the actual battle serving as the backdrop for Henry Fleming's experiences, Chancellorsville, fought on May 1 and 2 in 1863, provides a highly appropriate setting for the "dark ironies of war," as Lee Clark Mitchell notes, that Crane set out to explore. For Chancellorsville proved itself to be one of the bloodier and more "senseless" battles of the entire war, a battle where the lines between the two armies were never clearly defined, where no discernible objective was won by either side, and where 27,000 men lost their lives. After two days of heavy losses, both the Confederate and the Union armies were left in their original positions, and to compound the irony, Confederate general Stonewall Jackson was accidentally shot by one of his own men.[15] No setting could have been more appropriate for Crane's purpose of evoking a world of confusion, made up of atomistic elements that never achieve any sort of coherent whole. Chancellorsville was quite simply a battle that resisted any sort of coherent explanation, and that was its primary attraction for Crane.[16]

Gertrude Stein, in contrast, was not so much interested in inherited narratives at radical odds with the world of actual experience as she was in their suffocating and destructive nature. Writing *Three Lives* at a time when she was "steeped in naturalist novels," as her most recent biographer Linda Wagner-Martin observes, Stein tended to see inherited narratives, especially those outlining a rigidly defined and limited array of fates for women, in distinctly naturalistic terms, as large, impersonal, overwhelming forces posed against a fragile and ultimately helpless individual.[17] Accordingly, the portraits offered in *Three Lives*—"The Good Anna," "Melanctha," and "The Gentle Lena"—present three women from the lower walks of life who are eventually crushed by narratives that specify traditional roles and expectations for women—selfless service for others, disgrace and punishment for fallen women, and submission to authority.

In "The Good Anna" we watch the title character, a hardworking German-born servant woman, literally work herself to death in the service of others, whether they be employers whom she especially cherishes, friends who require help, or simply poor neighbors in need of financial aid. In "Melanctha" the central character by that name, a restless, complicated, and independent African American woman, pursues one sexual relationship after another and in consequence faces condemnation by everyone from her authoritarian father to friends on whose support she relies. And in "The Gentle Lena" we follow the life of a simple and submissive immigrant woman as it is plotted out first by her aunt, who brings her to America, finds her a job as a servant, and then marries her off, and then by her husband, her husband's family, and her own children. She dies abruptly in childbirth, submissive to the end to the dictates of those around her who decide what direction her life should take.

In a sense, these are characters who inhabit not their own stories but the margins and corners of other people's stories, those of the employers who hire them as servants or the people with whom they briefly become emotionally involved. Stein's characters quite simply live out stories that are not of their own making. Nowhere is their subordination to the storytelling of others more strikingly drawn than in "The Gentle Lena," in which Lena's aunt Mrs. Haydon surveys the effects of her wholesale rearrangement of Lena's life—bringing Lena to America and finding her first a job and then a husband—with nothing so much as the satisfaction of an omniscient narrator.[18]

And if it is dangerous to live in the corners of other people's stories, as Lena's fate suggests, it is just as precarious to rely too heavily on traditional narrative roles and expectations, as Anna appears to do in "The Good Anna." We are told by the narrator that "Anna had always a firm old world sense of what was the right way for a girl to do"—specifically, to stay in her place as a servant, to submit to authority, to receive obeisance from those servants under her, and to dress accordingly.[19] The world that Anna lives in, though, seems to be particularly resistant to Anna's fine sense of order and hierarchy, and as the narrative proceeds, it becomes increasingly clear that Anna's firm sense of how people should act—in a sense, the narratives she has inherited and through which she sees the world—can be misleading at best and dangerously burdensome at worst. Anna's community appears to be populated by those who come and go at will, drift in and out of her life without rhyme or reason, act and speak out of no predictable pattern whatsoever. The more those around her defy her expectations, the more stymied and frustrated Anna herself becomes. The narrator shortly observes: "The good Anna could not understand the careless and bad ways of all the world and always she grew bitter with it all. No, not one of them had any sense of what was the right way for them to do" (117).

In this respect, the setting of Bridgepoint, a thinly disguised portrait of Baltimore, where Gertrude Stein lived for several years as a medical student at Johns Hopkins University, offers a highly appropriate backdrop against which she explores the impact of traditional narratives on the lives of the women of *Three Lives*. For the city of Bridgepoint is as fluid and as disorienting in its way as the battlefield is in *The Red Badge of Courage*. It is a setting filled with recently arrived immigrants, with black men and women struggling for a marginal existence, with others, white and black, who aspire to improve their status and push their way up into the middle class. It is also an oddly public world, especially in "Melanctha," in which the title character is portrayed restlessly exploring the world of the railroads and the docks to satisfy her hunger for "wisdom" of the body and the mind and energetically moving amid commercial travelers and office workers to learn something of the volatile nature of sexual relationships. In "Melanctha" in particular, there scarcely seems to exist any interior domestic space at all, for nearly everything appears to take place under the glare of the public eye. Even the long and torturous arguments between Melanctha and her conventional, middle-class lover Dr. Jeff Campbell indicate that they are both highly conscious of the gossip their actions and movements inspire. Similarly, in "The Good Anna" and "The Gentle Lena," concentrating on the lives of domestic servants, home space is portrayed as endlessly permeable to an outside world of markets, shops, money-making schemes, mysterious charlatans drifting in and out of sight, job applicants seeking to go into domestic service, neighbors and friends begging for financial help, and even stray dogs wandering in from the cold.

Here in these confusing, complicated, and highly layered settings—in Stein's Bridgepoint and on Crane's battlefield—multiple voices from all corners and all walks of life never seem to cease and if anything heighten the confusion of these crowded and labyrinthine public arenas. Negotiating one's way through those voices and confusion, trying to establish some sort of order upon surrounding chaos, becomes a crucial task for Crane's soldier and for Stein's women. Hence the very process of interpreting those voices, discovering a path through the confusion, and establishing some ephemeral sense of order, however artificial, emerges as a central concern in both *The Red Badge of Courage* and *Three Lives,* and in each text the mere activity of interpretation—of reading the signs that are there and trying to understand them accordingly—turns out to be difficult indeed amid all those voices resonating through the public arena.

From the beginning of *The Red Badge of Courage,* in fact, Henry feels compelled by the plethora of voices he hears and the multiplicity of disconnected details around him to impose some sort of sense and order on his perceptions and experiences.[20] The very first chapter opens with the army awakening and stirring "at the noise of rumors" (81), and our initial glimpse of Henry finds him eagerly listening to those rumors and to the comments of soldiers speculating on whether or not the regiment is indeed going to move into battle. Everything he hears and sees appears to be charged with significance, and accordingly he tries to read meaning in everything he comes across—in chance encounters, in passing comments, in the foliage he passes, and in the very contours of the landscape: "The skirmishers in advance fascinated him. Their shots into thickets and at distant and prominent trees spoke to him of tragedies—hidden, mysterious, solemn" (101).

Having been taught by past narratives to assume an inherent order in nature and to read flora and fauna as though they offered a reassuring scripture, he peers for signs and omens in the movements of squirrels and in the canopy of trees overhead. Indeed, early on in the novel, after he has fled the battlefield in the general panic engulfing his regiment, Henry becomes briefly persuaded that nature itself will give him final "assurance" and "the religion of peace" (125). Plunging into the woods, he desperately seeks solace and the means to understand his own panic-stricken behavior. But the only answer that awaits him is the one he earlier received on the way to the battlefield with his regiment—that is, the dead eyes of a corpse in which he fruitlessly seeks "the answer to the Question" (102). There in the woods where he takes refuge, in a chapellike enclosure formed by the dense trees, Henry stumbles upon yet another corpse, this one covered with red ants—in itself a pointed and ironic commentary on the youth's attempt to read reassuring meaning in nature.

Nevertheless, Henry and his comrades persist in their efforts to impose some sort of order on the chaos around them, to find a way of interpreting and unifying the radically disconnected details and impressions that bombard them. Early on, when Henry's brigade marches into action for the first time, the men ponder the unfamiliar scene that awaits them by passing along one rumor and story after another, and they do so in an effort to make the unfamiliar familiar, to domesticate the unknown. Stories and rumors, along with the figurative use of language, are repeatedly resorted to in a collective effort to interpret, understand, and order. The company lieutenant, for one, periodically indulges in rounds of curses to render the anxiety and anticipation of battle less frightening and inscrutable, and Henry himself grasps for one simile after another to try to make sense of his own feelings and the multiplicity of impressions greeting him on every side. Confronted with his first real experience in combat, Henry thinks of the regiment first as "a firework that, once ignited, proceeds superior to circumstances until its blazing vitality fades" (112). He then compares it to "a mysterious fraternity born of the smoke and danger of death" (113). He himself feels "like a carpenter who has made many boxes, making still another box, only there was furious haste in his movements" (113). A moment later he compares his feelings to "a pestered animal, a well-meaning cow worried by dogs" (113). Firing his rifle frantically, he then likens his plight to a "babe being smothered" (113). Still later, during the second attack, he "became like the man who lost his legs at the approach" of a terrifying dragon, his image for the still unseen enemy (119). Finally, Henry breaks and runs "like a proverbial chicken" (119). He is driven, the narrator tells us, by a multitude of anticipated fears: "On his face was all the horror of those things which he imagined" (119).

The most disorienting aspect of Henry's frantic effort to make sense of the chaos is the haste with which he rapidly shifts from one set of interpretations to another, one potential story after another, to render the confusion of the battlefield readable. Having learned that his regiment is not routed after all, as he fears during his headlong flight, Henry first tells himself that he "proceeded according to very correct and commendable rules." Summing up, the narrator notes: "His actions had been sagacious things. They had been full of strategy. They were the work of a master's legs" (124). Then he begins to feel "a great anger against his comrades" who held the position despite the horror of the attack (124). Self-pity rapidly follows: "He was ill used. He was trodden beneath the feet of an iron injustice. He had proceeded with wisdom and from the most righteous motives under heaven's blue only to be frustrated by hateful circumstances" (124–25). Later yet Henry fiercely castigates himself as the lone coward amid a crowd of heroes bearing red badges of honor: "He could never be like them. He could have wept in his longing" (143). But after a passing moment he envisions the possibility of exchanging places with one of the men he envies and achieving great heights of glory in battle: "For a few moments he was sublime" (143). Later still he anticipates the scorn and derision of his fellow soldiers and sees himself as the butt of jokes, "a slang phrase" in other men's stories about him (147).

Henry, in short, goes through so many interpretations of his experiences that he himself ends up appearing as fragmented as the battle confusion he tries to read and understand. His frantic efforts to rationalize his actions, ironically enough, reduce him to the very disorder that he has been trying to resolve into some sort of meaningful, discernible pattern. From moment to moment, his perceptions of self undergo distinct and sometimes drastic transformations—from self-righteousness to fear to shame to yearning to heroic posturing—and no discernible sequence appears to link those transformations in any understandable order or logic. He becomes, in a sense, part of the chaotic battlefield, a series of disconnected, fleeting impressions, changing from one moment to the next without logic or any sense of cause and effect. "From our perspective, in fact," Lee Clark Mitchell suggests, "he appears fragmented by the very syntax of his presentation, leaving his emotions, thoughts, and behavior profoundly unaligned."[21]

The confusing spectacle that Henry presents—as he changes from one moment to the next, exchanges one set of interpretations for another—is if anything compounded by the curious absence of any sort of narrative authority or perspective offering clues or directions for understanding and evaluating Henry and his plight. Not only does Crane resort to a limited third-person narrator who seldom takes us out of the range of Henry's perceptions and consciousness, but he also makes unsettling use of free indirect discourse, that is, mingling the voice and perspective of the third-person narrator with the thoughts and perceptions of the central protagonist. Henry's thoughts are frequently presented not in his own words but in those of the narrator, and those ruminations are more often than not contradictory to an unsettling degree. One moment Henry despairingly condemns himself for running and the next he fiercely rationalizes his behavior as the better part of wisdom. The result is that we as readers are never quite sure where the narrator's perspective or voice ends and Henry's begins. And because Henry's thoughts shift as swiftly as his perceptions and his experiences, we are given no stable viewpoint from which to take stock of Henry's actions, thoughts, and character. What emerges, then, is an oddly decentered narrative made up of radically disconnected impressions and thoughts of an equally decentered and disjointed protagonist. As readers we are as hard pressed as Henry to form a coherent sense of character or narrative out of the multiplicity of impressions bombarding us, and consequently, *The Red Badge of Courage* itself emerges as a discontinuous, fragmented narrative, one of radically disconnected incidents, impressions, paragraphs, and sentences.[22]

Hence it comes as something of a jolt when Henry finally decides in the very end that he is at last able to herd all the incidents and all his actions into a coherent narrative of manhood achieved under fire. Rejoining his regiment, Henry goes into battle once again, and this time, impelled by the momentum of the charge, he ends up leading the charge with the company lieutenant and his friend Wilson. When he hears praise for his actions from others, he begins to feel "serene self-confidence" and then later a sort of "wild battle madness" prompting him to imagine a heroic sacrifice on the battlefield (199, 205). Once the battle is over and the regiments regroup to march off, he assumes that he too has reached closure: "Later he began to study his deeds, his failures, and his achievements. Thus, fresh from scenes where many of his usual machines of reflection had been idle, from where he had proceeded sheeplike, he struggled to marshal all his acts" (210). He ponders the memory of "his public deeds" that he sees "paraded in great and shining prominence" (210), and that reflection in turn provides him with a sense of achievement: "He felt a quiet manhood, nonassertive but a sturdy and strong blood. He knew that he would no more quail before his guides wherever they should point. He had left to touch the great death, and found that, after all, it was but the great death. He was a man" (212).

In these last scenes, where Henry congratulates himself on "marshaling" his acts into a coherent narrative of achieved manhood, he suggests nothing so much as a parody of an omniscient narrator placing the last brick of a straightforward, readily comprehensible narrative into place. So unsettling, decentered, and disorienting is the narrative as a whole, flitting from one incident to another with no discernible order, that the "ending" on which Henry finally decides looks decidedly arbitrary, artificial, contrived. It is an ending, ultimately, that underscores Henry's own desperate attempts to find order, authority, and closure, for there is nothing in the preceding narrative to indicate that it is a conclusion that naturally "follows." Indeed Henry's conclusion strikes one as radically incompatible with the discontinuous incidents, perceptions, and desperate efforts at interpretation preceding it. Accordingly, Henry's self-complacent meditation upon his narrative of achieved manhood takes on a strange and distorted air as being decidedly forced and arbitrary—not an ending at all but simply yet another set of interpretations and rationalizations by which Crane's protagonist tries to make sense of the confused muddle of voices, sensations, and incidents on the battlefield. As readers we ponder that ending and hesitate, aware that it is not, after all, a conclusion that "goes without saying."

In this respect, Crane's novel anticipates the modernist technique of defamiliarization first articulated by the Russian literary theorist Victor Shklovsky in a 1917 essay titled "Art as Technique," which draws on pre–World War I French avant-garde art and Jamesian psychology. As Shklovsky explained, "The technique of art is to make objects 'unfamiliar,' to make forms difficult, to increase the difficulty and length of perception because the process of perception is an aesthetic end in itself and must be prolonged. Art is a means of re-experiencing the making of objects, but objects already made have no importance for art."[23] In a word, rendering objects in a strange and disorienting manner brings attention to the process of perception and representation, to the making of art itself. Defamiliarization makes it impossible to assume the easy compatibility between the object being represented and the act of representation itself or even to take this relationship for granted, and as such this technique highlights "artfulness," the material design of paint on a canvas or of words on a page and the sense of order artificially imposed by art itself in a world where no other kind of order seems available.[24]

To a great extent, then, General McClurg was indeed right in his assessment of *The Red Badge of Courage* as "a mere riot of words," for Crane's novel, like the Imagist poetry that would follow his work just a decade after his death, renders perceptions, impressions, and even words rich and strange and thus directs attention to the "design" of narrative and its most atomistic components and to art itself, in Robert Frost's memorable phrase, as "a momentary stay against confusion." In the midst of this "riot of words," Crane's characters—and the novel's readers, for that matter—are never quite sure what they see or hear and where they themselves stand. Looking back at a short stretch of ground covered during a charge, Henry discovers "that the distances, as compared with the brilliant measurings of his mind, were trivial and ridiculous" (195). In a sense, Henry's plight, as well as the plight of readers, can be summed up by the nameless soldier with the "cheery voice" who announces that in the confusion of battle he scarcely knew "which side I was on." Sometimes, he adds, "I was sure 'nough from Ohio, an' other times I could 'a swore I was from th' bitter end of Florida. It was th' most mixed up dern thing I ever see" (152).

Here again *The Red Badge of Courage* offers a striking parallel to Stein's *Three Lives*. For like Crane, Stein disorients the reader and

defamiliarizes her narrative material—the lives of three very marginal women—by resisting narrative coherence and by bringing
attention to the sound, shape, and turns of words and phrases, to
the way words themselves provide in the end the only sense of
order truly available to us. And like Crane again, Stein offers a
world of radically fragmented details—fleeting impressions, conversations, appearances, and incidents—that prompt the efforts of
her characters to impose some sort of interpretive and narrative
coherence in a manner resembling nothing so much as the effort of
modernist writers to impose order on a world of confusion through,
as one student of modernism observes, the "ordering principle" of
art.[25] In that effort, though, they fail time and time again, and Stein's
characters frequently give voice to their own frustration and confusion—and that of the readers as well—by emphasizing their inability to understand the events that happen to them or the people they
encounter.

Stein made a careful effort to achieve that effect of disorientation
and defamiliarization by following the path of Post-Impressionist
painter Paul Cézanne, four of whose paintings she and her brother
Leo bought in 1904, not long after Stein herself moved to Paris. One
of those paintings was a portrait of Madame Cézanne, which Stein
singled out two decades later in *The Autobiography of Alice B. Toklas*
as the inspiration for *Three Lives*.[26] Excited by the avant-garde work
of Cézanne and Picasso, Stein was drawn in particular to the way
that Cézanne's paintings highlighted seeing as an act of interpretation striving to arrange minute sensory impressions into perceptible
order. Accordingly, Cézanne's work brought attention to the play of
details defined by light and color, details that tended to rend asun-
der the conventionally assumed unity between signs—like "patches
of color" on the canvas—and the objects they sought to represent—
like hills, trees, houses, and vistas. It was the way Cézanne's compositions foregrounded the paint on canvas, working against the illusion of offering a "window" view of landscape, for instance, that
fascinated Stein.[27] Decades later, in a 1946 interview, she would
emphasize just how important Cézanne's innovations in composition, undertaken in the last years of the nineteenth century, would
be for her own narrative experiments:

Up to that time composition had consisted of a central idea, to which everything else was an accompaniment and separate but was not an end in itself,

and Cézanne conceived the idea that in composition one thing was as important as another thing. Each part is as important as the whole, and that impressed me enormously, and it impressed me so much that I began to write *Three Lives* under this influence and this idea of composition and I was more interested in composition at that moment, this background of word-system, which had come to me from this reading I had done. I was obsessed by this idea of composition, and the Negro story ["Melanctha"] was the quintessence of it.[28]

Attracting Stein in particular was the underlying anxiety of Cézanne's compositions—what Pablo Picasso, then forming a fast friendship with Stein, shrewdly noted was his predecessor's greatest "lesson" to artists who followed him.[29] For by implying in his compositions that each detail was as important as the whole pattern, Cézanne inserted doubt into the process of perception, assimilation, and comprehension—doubt about the possibility of subordinating details to a recognizable and coherent whole pattern, doubt about the object under scrutiny, doubt about the very act of perception. As art historian Robert Hughes once observed, the statement "This is what I see," implicitly defining paintings that sought to create the illusion of seeing an actual view, became in Cézanne's paintings the question, "Is this what I see?"[30]

It is precisely that anxiety, prompted by a multiplicity of details and voices resisting assimilation into a coherent pattern of narrative, that Stein probes in "Melanctha," the central narrative in her triptych. Anxiety—the fear that no pattern can arrange a multiplicity of details, that no coherent understanding will emerge from a multitude of voices or from the fragmentary experiences of daily life—is the prime incentive behind the long, dense, and torturous discussions between Melanctha and her conventional middle-class lover Dr. Jeff Campbell. The two characters engage in those discussions in an effort to understand each other, only to fail over and over again. Melanctha, the narrator says, knows what it is to have "real wisdom," to be familiar with the complexity of human emotions and sexuality (148). Jeff, in turn, insists upon the importance of living a "regular," disciplined life, one that avoids the roller coaster rides provided by excitement and passion (151). Melanctha's response is to tell him quite simply that he thinks too much to feel, and the result is that Jeff and Melanctha increasingly come to feel that they are speaking two different languages incapable of translation. Each complains repeatedly of not understanding the other—what the other wants and says—and as they pursue their stymied, frustrated dialogue, the language becomes more and more dense and torturous, as though to underscore the difficulties of communicating at all in a world of radically different and competing voices: "It was a struggle, sure to be going on always between them. It was a struggle that was as sure always to be going on between them, as their minds and hearts always were to have different ways of working" (176). But the more Jeff in particular struggles to understand Melanctha and his own feelings for her, the more doubt he feels—not just about their relationship, but about precisely who Melanctha herself is and what he feels for her. Increasingly, he concludes that he does not understand or even know Melanctha at all, "when she was real herself, and honest" (178). She is, he tells himself, "too many for him," and he is unable "to find out the way she really felt now for him" (193).

In a word, Jeff simply cannot make sense of the contradictory elements that make up Melanctha—her intelligence, her intensity of feeling, her suffering, and her sexual adventurousness. Castigating her for failing to "remember," he also, in a sense, charges her with changing her very identity from one moment to the next. She is, he implies, never consistent, never subject to any sort of coherent summary of self, never mindful of the need to link past and present through a unified sense of self-identity. In this respect, his final judgment is quite accurate: she is indeed "too many for him"—a radically disconnected self made up of many incompatible parts who exemplifies in many respects the multiplicity of the public world she restlessly explores—in the streets of Bridgepoint, on the docks, and by the railroads. She herself, the narrator observes, does not know how to tell a story "wholly" because she can never "remember right," never impose unity where none apparently exists, even upon herself, and hence manages "to leave out big pieces which make a story very different" (136).

Not surprisingly, then, both Melanctha and Jeff find themselves defeated by the multiplicity of their own selves—changing from one moment to the next—and that of the world around them, a multiplicity so pronounced that they are defeated even by the effort to arrive at a narrative of their romance in those circuitous and ultimately formless dialogues—why in particular their love has failed and what cause-and-effect sequence can be discerned. Jeff, the narrator tells us, keeps wondering if the failure of their love is his fault, but even scrutinizing himself for culpability in a last-ditch attempt to impose narrative order on their romance turns out to be a failure: "What could he know, who had such slow feeling in him? What could he ever know, who always had to find his way with just thinking" (192).

Even words themselves fail them, meaning one thing on Melanctha's lips and quite another on Jeff's. The more the two characters talk and ponder, probe and question, the less they understand each other until words seem to be tangible obstacles lying between them, sounds and signs seemingly taking on form and substance, piling higher and higher, becoming increasingly obstructive and even suffocating as they talk and talk and talk. In a sense, we as readers find ourselves peering over the barricades of words that come to surround Melanctha and Jeff as they pursue their talks, and so little relation does one paragraph, sentence, or word seem to bear to the next in those dialogues that the very words the two characters first utter and then discard appear to lie between and around them like so much fragmented debris. Repeated over and over again, often with slight variations, their words come to bear a startling resemblance to Cézanne's brush strokes of color, so distinctive and compelling that the viewer must make a genuine and self-conscious effort to see, in the midst of those patches of colors, the overall design and composition, the landscape as a whole.

It is no wonder, then, that the more Melanctha and Jeff talk, the more suspicious they both become of words, of their ability to communicate and understand anything at all. "What words," Jeff asks, "could help him to make their feeling any better?" (210). Indeed, the more words they utter the less likely they are to understand each other and the less susceptible "Melanctha" itself appears to any sort of assimilation into a coherent, comprehensive narrative. And compounding the disintegrating effect of those radically disconnected words is Stein's recourse to free indirect discourse, intertwining the thoughts and words of her characters with those of the third-person narrator, so that the reader never quite knows, as in *The Red Badge of Courage,* where the words and perspective of the narrator end and those of Melanctha and Jeff begin. More than one critic has already noted that the limited vocabulary and simple and sometimes awkward syntax of Melanctha, Anna, and Lena—language emphasizing their lack of education, their marginality, and even their powerlessness—"invades the narrative as a whole" so that the third-person narrator relating their histories sounds remarkably like the characters whose lives are being described.[31] Whether spoken by the characters or wielded by the narrator, the same words and the same sentence structures are used. In "Melanctha," for instance, the sentences frequently tend to be hypotactic, structured by subordinate clauses making connections, and lengthy, as though to underscore the efforts of Jeff and Melanctha to perceive sequence and order in their relationship. In "The Good Anna," in contrast, the sentences tend to be short and paratactic, eschewing subordinate clauses and coordination and thus echoing Anna's own speech and her perspective of the world as a collection of straightforward facts and objects requiring the arrangement of a good housekeeper. And in "The Gentle Lena" the sentences seem to vary between being short, simple, and paratactic and being long, winding, and compound, piling coordinating conjunctions on top of one another, as though to emphasize Lena's gradual but systematic incarceration behind the language of the people around her who plan her life.

The result is a notable diminishment of the third-person narrator's perspective, narrowed to the claustrophobic circumstances of characters' lives. So diminished is that perspective that it seems to emphasize the impossibility of taking an all-encompassing, omniscient view, one that can offer an authoritative and coherent version of these three women's lives. Echoing the words, sentiments, and perspectives of Anna, Melanctha, and Lena, the third-person narrator can neither see farther nor offer more understanding than the characters themselves. *Three Lives,* in short, deliberately eschews an omniscient narrator capable of telling the histories of these three women from a central and stable position and as such decenters and disperses narrative authority, pluralizes viewpoints, and generates a multiplicity of voices.[32] In this respect, *Three Lives,* like *The Red Badge of Courage,* parts company with the naturalist novel, usually marked by an omniscient, far-seeing third-person narrator pondering its subjects with a certain detached and clinical precision. Indeed, if anything, Stein's and Crane's texts repeatedly and self-consciously bring attention to the decentering of narrative authority, and accordingly, they look forward to the suspicion of narrative itself usually associated with modernism.

Indeed, as Harriet Scott Chessman suggests, the absence of authoritative words and of a unified, stable viewpoint underscores the "resistance" of *Three Lives* to ordering itself into a narrative with a hierarchical ranking of events.[33] We find instead an interrogation of the conventional novel itself and its underlying assumptions—that reading and interpretation can uncover a discernible and logical sequence of events, that some events and incidents can be ranked as more important and as more significant than others, that individual elements like separate incidents, characters, and even lone words can themselves eventually find a place in a meaningful coherent whole, that a single narrative can represent the growing complexity and pluralization of American life. Stein fragments her narrative of marginal life in a southern city into three wholly unrelated parts—"The Good Anna," "Melanctha," and "The Gentle Lena"—as though to underscore the difficulty of capturing life in Bridgepoint in a single story. This is a world, *Three Lives* suggests in its form and its content, that is far too fragmentary and pluralized for any one story, any one voice, any one identity to dominate.

Moreover, it is an arena where self-identity itself—coherent, unified, stable—appears to be increasingly problematic. Anna, Melanctha, and Lena often appear to blur and fade into the chorus of voices defining everyday life in Bridgepoint, and in many respects, the deaths abruptly punctuating the endings of all three "lives" come as no surprise at all. Each woman has already demonstrated an unsettling tendency to shift and change from one moment to the next—Melanctha most conspicuously of all. So little coherence is demonstrated by their characters that it is difficult in many respects to trace their individual trajectories. Instead, Melanctha, Anna, and Lena make fleeting appearances—in conversations, in difficulties they encounter, in troubling encounters with other characters—and each appearance seems to change as the circumstances do. Ultimately, those appearances are simply extinguished: Anna dies from the overwork of running a boardinghouse; Melanctha goes from one disappointing relationship to another, suffers the condemnation of friends who self-righteously reject her, and dies abruptly of consumption; Lena becomes more and more "lifeless" in her assigned role as wife and mother and dies giving birth to her fourth baby (270). All three in the end simply fade back into the chorus of voices from which they emerge in brief and periodic spurts. So diminished are all three women by that chorus of voices and by the welter of details and confusion they inhabit that they themselves are reduced to mere fragments and details, much like George Hurstwood in *Sister Carrie* and Frank Norris's protagonist McTeague. We see them, as we see Hurstwood and McTeague, from a far distance—small fragmented details of no particular prominence or importance in the mosaic of public life that defines Stein's Bridgepoint.

What remains, ultimately, is the foregrounding of that mosaic in *Three Lives*—the shifting and perplexing multiplicity of voices, incidents, and even words themselves. If it is difficult to arrange *Three Lives* as a whole into a coherent narrative—or to see narrative patterns even in the individual lives themselves, for that matter—it is because details and fragments loom larger, in a sense, than any overarching, defining narrative structure. Individual words themselves take on a solidity and distinctiveness of their own and become in a sense "artifacts," to borrow Ronald Martin's term, handled and arranged according to the dictates of design and composition rather than presented as a transparent medium giving writers and readers automatic access to the world of experience. The result, as Martin persuasively argues, is something very much like a Cubist painting, featuring sentences and words of equal importance. Stein's wordplay, Martin says, "becomes an assemblage of equivalent details, an atomic collage, a still picture of imagination's passage."[34]

Stein would follow this experiment in narrative Cubism with her radically innovative and unclassifiable text *Tender Buttons,* published in 1914 and immediately hailed and damned for its innovative use of language and its unflinching interrogation of representation as an arbitrary, unstable convention. It is a text, as Jayne Walker suggests, that offers a "brilliantly subversive demonstration of the unbreachable gulf that separates the chaotic plenitude of the sensory world from the arbitrary order of language."[35] Offering what appears to be a mere catalogue of objects and arbitrary descriptions, *Tender Buttons* eschews narrative and the effort of illusionistic representation altogether. In the first section, titled "Objects," for instance, the opening words are as follows:

A carafe, that is a blind glass.
A kind in glass and a cousin, a spectacle and nothing strange a single hurt color and an arrangement in a system to pointing. All this and not ordinary, not unordered in not resembling. The difference is spreading.[36]

Radically experimental and more akin to poetry than prose, *Tender Buttons* thus demonstrates some of the defining traits of the literary modernism to come: its self-conscious break with tradition; its suspicion and even repudiation of narrative unity as irrelevant in an age of disruption, disorder, and fragmentation; and its foregrounding of the arbitrariness and slipperiness of language.[37] In many respects, *Tender Buttons* exemplifies that sense of a radical break with tradition as well as Stein's own later voiced conviction that the modern age was marked by a drastic sense of discontinuity. "So the twentieth century," she declared in her 1939 book *Picasso*, "is . . . a time when everything cracks, when everything is destroyed, everything isolates itself, it is a more splendid thing than a period where everything follows itself."[38]

Tender Buttons, in sum, appeared to have traveled a long distance indeed from nineteenth-century American novels or even the naturalist-tinged narratives produced by Stein herself and Stephen Crane. Both *Tender Buttons* and *Three Lives,* in fact, would leave their stamp on experimental modernist narratives to follow, like Sherwood Anderson's *Winesburg, Ohio* (1919) and Ernest Hemingway's *In Our Time* (1925). Following in Stein's footsteps, Anderson and Hemingway would deliberately violate narrative unity and expectations to emphasize their alliance with modernism's disruption of tradition and its suspicion of narrative in general, and the result would be discontinuous texts resisting and interrogating the conventional novel with its orderly plot, hierarchical rankings of events, and unified, consistent characters. Like *Three Lives* and *Tender Buttons, Winesburg, Ohio* and *In Our Time* lay somewhere between novels and collections, juxtaposing on one hand the broken framework of an overall narrative and on the other hand the individual fragments, whether stories, sketches, or scenes, emerging from the deliberate disruption of narrative form. Above all, these were texts that took their cue from Stein's deliberate fragmentation, following the lead of Cézanne and modernist painting, of unified compositions into equal details resisting subordination to a greater whole. In a word, *Winesburg, Ohio* and *In Our Time,* like *Three Lives* and *Tender Buttons,* function much like early modernist collages of juxtaposed disparate fragments. As Marjorie Perloff explains of collages in general, "Such images do not really cohere, nor are they meant to. Central to the collage is the refusal to suppress the alterity of elements temporarily united in its structure."[39]

Both *Three Lives* and *The Red Badge of Courage,* themselves resistant to the imposition of narrative unity and authority, point the way to this sort of experimentation—to texts made up of fragments and details that remain insistently distinct. Stein's and Crane's narratives anticipate as well the dissolution of authority that would mark the form and content of many modernist novels, like William Faulkner's 1929 novel-collage *The Sound and the Fury*. Through fragmented narratives and the highlighting of doubt and uncertainty, *Three Lives* and *The Red Badge of Courage* revealed, in John Berryman's vivid phrase applied to Crane's novel, the *"refusal to guarantee."*[40] The public arenas they evoke—whether on the battlefield or in a fictional version of Baltimore—resonate with too many conflicting and contradictory voices for any one authoritative voice and view to emerge.

But if *Three Lives* and *The Red Badge of Courage* did indeed look ahead to modernist experiments with the novel, they also hearkened back to an earlier era, one stamped by the entry of new and quarrelsome literary voices into the public sphere and requiring and demanding both recognition and dialogue. These were voices serving notice that the public arena had become considerably more complicated and heterogeneous since the 1840s, when the sphere of political, literary, and public debate appeared to be largely homogeneous and relatively free from bitter contention. They were also voices casting doubt on the project first called for by novelist John W. De Forest of writing the Great American Novel, a single story summing up the spirit and character of the newly reunified nation. In the late nineteenth and early twentieth century, new literary voices and stories made their presence felt among an ever-widening range of the population, from immigrants and African Americans to white women determined to be taken seriously as artists in their own right, and under the weight of their increasingly noisy declamations and quarrels, the very form of the American novel as it had come to be known began to buckle.

Just how momentous those changes were could be discerned in the pivotal Armory Show of avant-garde European and American art held in New York, Chicago, and Boston in 1913 and sponsored by the rebellious American Association of Painters and Sculptors. The show featured paintings and sculpture by Kandinsky, Brancusi, Matisse, Picasso, Redon, Maurice Denis, Seurat, Van Gogh, Gauguin, Duchamp, Delauney, and Kirchner and even featured a special "Cubist Room" with paintings by Duchamp, Picabia, and Braque. Large crowds flocked to the show—totaling 75,000 in New York alone—and controversy dogged it every step of the way. Henri

Matisse was enthusiastically burned in effigy by art students, and the Vice Commission in Chicago, prompted by charges of immorality, solemnly undertook an investigation of the exhibition. What outraged viewers the most was the resolutely antirealistic character of the art. Marcel Duchamp's *Nude Descending a Staircase* was famously renamed *Explosion in a Shingle Factory* by one critic, and when shown the painting, Theodore Roosevelt reportedly asked, "Where is the woman?" and pronounced Duchamp "nuts."[41]

For most Americans it was a first glimpse of modernist art that raised direct questions about representation and the problematic project of representing the world in a "realistic" way, and a good deal of their outrage was no doubt prompted by the show's violation of all their traditional expectations about what paintings and sculpture were supposed to do—in particular, represent the world "out there" in a "realistic fashion." For what paintings like Duchamp's famous *Nude Descending a Staircase* did was to offer fragmented images evoking the process of perception and cognition rather than the illusion of a unified, three-dimensional object. The paintings and sculpture on exhibit at the Armory Show offered multiplicity for unity and fragmentation for narrative wholes, and therein lay its greatest irony for American viewers convinced that these were indeed strange, foreign, and unreadable images. Shocked by pictures that seemingly made no effort to represent "reality" as they thought they knew it, the audiences of the Armory Show were nonetheless looking at an array of paintings and sculptures that were, in one odd and important sense, much more mimetic than they realized. For those European art works that shocked and scandalized American sensibilities served as something of a collective mirror reflecting the very public that came, laughed, criticized, and complained. Staring at Duchamp's famous nude, puzzling over Cubist canvases, clicking their tongues at Matisse's colors, the audiences of the Armory Show were really in some respects looking at themselves—at a public increasingly definable by heterogeneity, pluralization, and fragmentation. The European paintings and sculptures that scandalized their American viewers, that prompted complaints about the chaos, fragmentation, and unreadability of the show's art, offered a revealing glimpse of what the viewers themselves had become—inhabitants of a public sphere marked increasingly by assertions and reassertions of newly defined and defiantly proclaimed identities and stories, of noisy and quarrelsome voices, and of radically shifting and realigned social space.

Upon reflection, then, it is small wonder indeed that the Armory Show provoked such unease. Exported largely from Europe, the paintings and sculptures signaled just how drastically transformed American culture had become by the second decade of the twentieth century. Far less dramatically, but just as firmly, Crane's and Stein's strange and disturbing texts had offered a similar—and equally disturbing—reflection of the contentious, noisy arena that the American public sphere had become. It was an arena that defied easy summary and interpretation and that cast increasing attention—and suspicion—on the very words that were used in public and private exchanges. Partly the creation of elusive texts like *The Red Badge of Courage* and *Three Lives*, of the general proliferation of novels in an ever-multiplying array of forms, that public realm also provided a measure of how far the American novel itself had come since the end of the Civil War. Early wars between sentimentalism and professionalism and quarrels over the meaning and content of realism had given way at century's end to uncertainty and doubt about the very nature of narrative itself. By the early years of the twentieth century, uncertainty and multiplicity—the products of an increasingly fragmented and quarrrelsome public arena—would become indelibly inscribed on the content and form of the American novel.

Notes and References

PREFACE

1. Quoted in Barbara Bardes and Suzanne Gossett, *Declarations of Independence: Women and Political Power in Nineteenth-Century American Fiction* (New Brunswick, N.J.: Rutgers University Press, 1990), 4.

2. Cynthia J. Davis and Kathryn West, *Women Writers in the United States: A Timeline of Literary, Cultural, and Social History* (New York: Oxford University Press, 1996), 79.

3. Bardes and Gossett, *Declarations of Independence,* 4.

4. Cathy N. Davidson argues that the novel served as a "form of education," especially for women, in *Revolution and the Word: The Rise of the Novel in America* (New York: Oxford University Press, 1986), 10.

5. Jürgen Habermas, "The Public Sphere: An Encyclopedia Article (1964)," trans. Sara Lennox and Frank Lennox, *New German Critique* 1, no. 5 (1974): 49. For an overview of this essay and Habermas's theory of the public sphere, see Peter Hohendahl, "Introduction to Habermas," trans. Patricia Russian, *New German Critique* 1, no. 5 (1974): 45–48; and Craig Calhoun, ed., *Habermas and the Public Sphere* (Cambridge, Mass.: MIT Press, 1992).

6. Mary P. Ryan, *Women in Public: Between Banners and Ballots, 1825–1880* (Baltimore: Johns Hopkins University Press, 1990), 8, 19–30, 135, 67.

7. Ibid., 14, 139, 53, 174.

8. Charles Taylor, "The Politics of Recognition," in *Multiculturalism: Examining the Politics of Recognition,* ed. Amy Gutmann (Princeton, N.J.: Princeton University Press, 1994), 26–27, 28, 32–34, 35, 25.

9. Glenna Matthews makes this point about access to the public arena through the genre of the novel in her study, *The Rise of Public Woman: Woman's Power and Woman's Place in the United States, 1630–1970* (New York: Oxford University Press, 1992), 73.

10. Stressing the importance of a marginal group's appropriation of social space as the first step to political empowerment, Ryan cites Henri Lefebvre, who asserts, "Groups, classes and fragments of classes are only constituted and recognized as 'subjects' through generating [producing] a space" (quoted in Ryan, *Women in Public,* 92).

11. See in general Anne C. Rose, *Victorian America and the Civil War* (New York: Cambridge University Press, 1992).

12. See in general *Divided Houses: Gender and the Civil War,* ed. Catherine Clinton and Nina Silber (New York: Oxford University Press, 1992); but in particular, LeeAnn Whites, "The Civil War as a Crisis in Gender," 3–21; Jim Cullen, " 'I's a Man Now': Gender and African American Men," 76–91; George Rable, " 'Missing in Action': Women of the Confederacy," 134–46; Jeanie Attie, "Warwork and the Crisis of Domesticity in the North," 247–59; and Nina Silber, "Intemperate Men, Spiteful Women, and Jefferson Davis," 283–305.

CHAPTER 1

1. Henry James, "Louisa M. Alcott" [review of *Moods*], in *Literary Criticism: Essays on Literature, American Writers, English Writers* (New York: Library of America, 1984), 189.

2. Anne Goodwyn Jones, *Tomorrow Is Another Day: The Woman Writer in the South, 1859–1936* (Baton Rouge: Louisiana State University Press, 1981), 59.

3. David Leverenz, *Manhood and the American Renaissance* (Ithaca, N.Y.: Cornell University Press, 1989), 4, 168.

4. Augusta J. Evans, *St. Elmo* (New York: Hurst & Company, 1866), 349. Subsequent references to this text are cited parenthetically within the chapter.

5. Alfred Habegger, *Gender, Fantasy, and Realism in American Literature* (New York: Columbia University Press, 1982), 3.

6. Susan Coultrap-McQuin, *Doing Literary Business: American Women Writers in the Nineteenth Century* (Chapel Hill: University of North Carolina Press, 1990), 2.

7. Ibid.

8. Nina Baym, *Woman's Fiction: A Guide to Novels by and about Women in America, 1820–1870* (Ithaca, N.Y.: Cornell University Press, 1978), 276.

9. Mary Kelley, *Private Woman, Public Stage: Literary Domesticity in Nineteenth-Century America* (New York: Oxford University Press, 1984), 25–26.

10. William Peary Fidler, *Augusta Evans Wilson, 1835–1909: A Biography* (Tuscaloosa: University of Alabama Press, 1951), 128, 129.

11. Kelley, *Private Woman*, 26.

12. Baym, *Woman's Fiction*, 19–20.

13. Philip Fisher, *Hard Facts: Setting and Form in the American Novel* (New York: Oxford University Press, 1987), 93, 92, 99.

14. Ibid., 99.

15. Isabelle Lehuu, "Sentimental Figures: Reading *Godey's Lady's Book*," in *The Culture of Sentiment: Race, Gender, and Sentimentality in Nineteenth-Century America*, ed. Shirley Samuels (New York: Oxford University Press, 1992), 74.

16. Quoted in Elizabeth Ammons, *Conflicting Stories: American Women Writers at the Turn into the Twentieth Century* (New York: Oxford University Press, 1991), 10.

17. Kelley, *Private Woman*, 145.

18. Coultrap-McQuin, *Doing Literary Business*, 194.

19. Christopher P. Wilson, *The Labor of Words: Literary Professionalism in the Progressive Era* (Athens: University of Georgia Press, 1985), 6–7.

20. Ibid., 9.

21. Jay Martin, *Harvests of Change: American Literature, 1865–1914* (Englewood Cliffs, N.J.: Prentice-Hall, 1967), 5, 17.

22. Wilson, *Labor of Words*, 48.

23. Coultrap-McQuin, *Doing Literary Business*, 32, 41, 48.

24. Quoted in Wilson, *Labor of Words*, 44.

25. Edward Bok, *The Americanization of Edward Bok* (New York: Charles Scribner's Sons, 1920), 292–93.

26. Alexis de Tocqueville, *Democracy in America*, ed. and introd. Phillips Bradley, 2 vols. (New York: Alfred A. Knopf, 1945), 2:61.

27. Michael Anesko, *"Friction with the Market": Henry James and the Profession of Authorship* (New York: Oxford University Press, 1986), 37.

28. See Robert G. Albion, "The 'Communications Revolution,' " *American Historical Review* 37 (1932): 718–20.

29. Burton J. Bledstein, *The Culture of Professionalism: The Middle Class and the Development of Higher Education in America* (New York: W. W. Norton, 1976), 47–48.

30. Lawrence W. Levine, *Highbrow/Lowbrow: The Emergence of Cultural Hierarchy in America* (Cambridge, Mass.: Harvard University Press, 1988), 77.

31. Bledstein, *Culture of Professionalism*, 78, 85, 20.

32. Ibid., 100.

33. Levine, *Highbrow/Lowbrow*, 177, 211, 146.

34. Alan P. Trachtenberg, *The Incorporation of America: Culture and Society in the Gilded Age* (New York: Hill & Wang, 1982), 157.

35. Levine, *Highbrow/Lowbrow*, 139.

36. Michael Davitt Bell, *The Problem of American Realism: Studies in the Cultural History of a Literary Idea* (Chicago: University of Chicago Press, 1993), 26; and Elise Miller, "The Feminization of American Realist Theory," *American Literary Realism* 23 (1990): 30.

37. Alfred Habegger, *Henry James and the "Woman Business"* (New York: Cambridge University Press, 1989), 116.

38. William Dean Howells, "Literary Criticism," in *Selected Literary Criticism, Vol. 1: 1859–1885*, ed. and introd. Ulrich Halfmann, vol. 13 of *A Selected Edition of William Dean Howells* (Bloomington: Indiana University Press, 1993), 1:61.

39. Henry James, "The Lesson of Balzac," in *The Question of Our Speech, The Lesson of Balzac: Two Lectures* (Boston: Houghton, Mifflin, 1905), 56, 57.

40. Henry James to William Dean Howells, Aug. 17, 1908, in *The Letters of Henry James*, ed. Percy Lubbock, 2 vols. (New York: Charles Scribner's Sons, 1920), 2:99.

41. Marcia Jacobson, *Henry James and the Mass Market* (Tuscaloosa: University of Alabama Press, 1983), 10, 13.

42. Henry James, *The Aspern Papers*, in *The Complete Tales of Henry James*, vol. 6: 1884–1888, ed. and introd. Leon Edel, 12 vols. (Philadelphia: J. B. Lippincott, 1963), 6:278. Subsequent references to this text are cited parenthetically within the chapter.

43. Pierre Bourdieu, *Distinction: A Social Critique of the Judgment of Taste*, trans. Richard Nice (Cambridge, Mass.: Harvard University Press, 1984), 228.

44. Henry James, "Preface to *The Ambassadors*" (1909), in *Theory of Fiction: Henry James*, ed. and introd. James E. Miller Jr.(Lincoln: University of Nebraska Press, 1972), 186.

CHAPTER 2

1. Henry James, "Rebecca Harding Davis" [review of *Dallas Galbraith*], in *Literary Criticism: Essays on Literature, American Writers, English Writers* (New York: Library of America, 1984), 225.

2. James, "Rebecca Harding Davis" [review of *Waiting for the Verdict*], in *Literary Criticism*, 21.

3. Michael Davitt Bell, *The Problem of American Realism: Studies in the Cultural History of a Literary Idea* (Chicago: University of Chicago Press, 1993), 37. See in general Alfred Habegger's two volumes on this subject: *Gender, Fantasy, and Realism in American Literature* (New York: Columbia University Press, 1982); and *Henry James and the "Woman Business"* (New York: Cambridge University Press, 1989). Also useful on this subject is David E. Shi, *Facing Facts: Realism in American Thought and Culture, 1850–1920* (New York: Oxford University Press, 1995).

4. Habegger, *Gender, Fantasy, and Realism*, 106.

5. Judith Fetterley, Introduction, *Provisions: A Reader from 19th Century American Women* (Bloomington: Indiana University Press, 1985), 10; Elizabeth Ammons, "Men of Color, Women, and Uppity Art at the Turn of the Century," *American Literary Realism* 23, no. 3 (1991): 14–24; Ammons, *Conflicting Stories: American Women Writers at the Turn into the Twentieth Century* (New York: Oxford University Press, 1991); and Sharon M. Harris, *Rebecca Harding Davis and American Realism* (Philadelphia: University of Pennsylvania Press, 1991).

6. See, for example, Daniel Borus's discussion of these three books constituting the *annus mirabilis* of literary realism (*Writing Realism: Howells, James, and Norris in the Mass Market* [Chapel Hill: University of North Carolina Press, 1989], 15).

7. George Becker focuses on these three tenets in "Introduction: Modern Realism as a Literary Movement," in *Documents of Modern Literary Realism*, ed. George J. Becker (Princeton, N.J.: Princeton University Press, 1963), 23–34.

8. Habegger, *Gender, Fantasy, and Realism*, 38; Shi, *Facing Facts*, 18–19; and Harris, *Rebecca Harding Davis*, 6, 8, 18.

9. William Dean Howells, "Criticism and Fiction," in *Criticism and Fiction and Other Essays by William Dean Howells*, ed. Clara Marburg Kirk and Rudolf Kirk (New York: New York University Press, 1959), 64.

10. Ammons suggests that ". . . the most important characteristic of American realism was its racial, ethnic, sexual, and cultural range" ("Men of Color, Women, and Uppity Art," 24). Similarly, in their introduction to *American Realism and the Canon*, Tom Quirk and Gary Scharnhorst declare: "What we call *literary realism* was in fact composed of a multitude of *isms*: naturalism, impressionism, local colorism, aestheticism, imagism, regionalism, veritism" (Introduction, *American Realism and the Canon*, ed. Tom Quirk and Gary Scharnhorst [Newark: University of Delaware Press, 1994], 20). For a discussion of realism as "a debate with competing definitions of reality" drawing on Howells, Edith Wharton, and Theodore Dreiser, see Amy Kaplan, *The Social Construction of American Realism* (Chicago: University of Chicago Press, 1988), 160.

11. Kaplan, *Social Construction*, 15.

12. Quoted in Janet Holmgren McKay, *Narration and Discourse in American Realistic Fiction* (Philadelphia: University of Pennsylvania Press, 1982), 27.

13. Harris, *Rebecca Harding Davis*, 19.

14. John F. Kasson, *Rudeness and Civility: Manners in Nineteenth-Century Urban America* (New York: Hill & Wang, 1990), 70.

15. Anne C. Rose, *Victorian America and the Civil War* (New York: Cambridge University Press, 1992), 17.

16. Kasson, *Rudeness and Civility*, 115, 117, 5.

17. [John W. De Forest], "The Great American Novel," *Nation*, Jan. 9, 1863: 28, 29.

18. Borus, *Writing Realism*, 139, 101, 25, 4.

19. Quoted in Shi, *Facing Facts*, 100–101.

20. Becker, "Introduction," 6, 33.

21. This phrasing is Kaplan's. She asserts, "To call oneself a realist means to make a claim not only for the cognitive value of fiction but for one's own cultural authority both to possess and dispense access to the real" (*Social Construction*, 13).

22. June Howard, *Form and History in American Literary Naturalism* (Chapel Hill: University of North Carolina Press, 1985), 12.

23. See, for example, McKay, *Narration and Discourse*, 29, 31, 190; and Kaplan, *Social Construction*, 9. See also Harold Kolb Jr., *The Illusion of Life: American Realism as a Literary Form* (Charlottesville: University of Virginia Press, 1969), 64.

24. Robert Shulman, "Realism," in *The Columbia History of the American Novel*, ed. Emory Elliott et al. (New York: Columbia University Press, 1991), 187.

25. Rebecca Harding Davis, *Bits of Gossip* (Boston: Houghton, Mifflin, 1904), 136.

26. See Kenneth S. Lynn, *William Dean Howells: An American Life* (New York: Harcourt Brace Jovanovich, 1971), 109, 113.

27. William Dean Howells, *The Rise of Silas Lapham*, in *Novels 1875–1886* (1885; rpt. New York: Library of America, 1982), 873. Subsequent references to this text are cited parenthetically within the chapter.

28. Davis, *Bits of Gossip*, 122, 124.

29. Ibid., 36, 34.

30. Rebecca Harding Davis, *Waiting for the Verdict* (1868; rpt. Upper Saddle River, N.J.: The Gregg Press, 1968), 244. Subsequent references to this text are cited parenthetically within the chapter.

31. William Dean Howells, Review of *Miss Ravenel's Conversion from Secession to Loyalty*, by John W. De Forest, in *Selected Literary Criticism, Vol. 1: 1859–1885*, ed. and introd. Ulrich Halfmann, vol. 13 of *A Selected Edition of William Dean Howells* (Bloomington: Indiana University Press, 1993), 1:96.

32. John W. De Forest, *Miss Ravenel's Conversion from Secession to Loyalty*, introd. Gordon S. Haight, Rinehart ed. (1867; rpt. New York: Holt, Rinehart and Winston, 1955), 10. Subsequent references to this text are cited parenthetically within the chapter.

33. James, "Rebecca Harding Davis" [review of *Waiting for the Verdict*], 220.

34. James, "The Art of Fiction," in *Literary Criticism*, 52.

35. William Dean Howells, "Dostoyevsky and the More Smiling Aspects of Life," in *Selected Literary Criticism, Vol. 2: 1886–1897*, ed. Donald Pizer, vol. 21 of *A Selected Edition of William Dean Howells* (Bloomington: Indiana University Press, 1993), 2:35.

36. Historians like Linda K. Kerber have warned us for at least the last ten years not to take such literary representations of separate spheres as realistic depictions of actual historical conditions; Kerber herself reminds us that "the idea of separate spheres" is "primarily a trope" (see Linda K. Kerber, "Separate Spheres, Female Worlds, Woman's Place: The Rhetoric of Woman's History," *Journal of American History* 75 (1988): 39 and passim. For recent revisionist approaches to the public and the private, see Dorothy O. Helly and Susan M. Reverby, eds., *Gendered Domains: Rethinking Public and Private in Women's History. Essays from the Seventh Berkshire Conference on the History of Women* (Ithaca, N.Y.: Cornell University Press, 1992).

37. John W. Crowley, "W. D. Howells: The Ever-Womanly," in *American Novelists Revisited: Essays in Feminist Criticism,* ed. Fritz Fleischmann (Boston: G. K. Hall, 1982), 177.

38. Walter Benn Michaels, *The Gold Standard and the Logic of Naturalism: American Literature at the Turn of the Century* (Berkeley: University of California Press, 1987), 41.

39. Ibid., 40.

40. Amy Schrager Lang, "Class and the Strategies of Sympathy," in *The Culture of Sentiment: Race, Gender, and Sentimentality in Nineteenth-Century America,* ed. Shirley Samuels (New York: Oxford University Press, 1992), 130.

41. John Seelye, "The Hole in Howells/The Lapse in Silas Lapham," in *New Essays on* The Rise of Silas Lapham, ed. Donald E. Pease (New York: Cambridge University Press, 1991), 53; and Kaplan, *Social Construction,* 10.

42. See in general Raymond Williams, *The Country and the City* (New York: Oxford University Press, 1973).

CHAPTER 3

1. Susan Gillman, "Regionalism and Nationalism in Jewett's *Country of the Pointed Firs,*" in *New Essays on* The Country of the Pointed Firs, ed. June Howard (New York: Cambridge University Press, 1994), 103. See in general Amy Kaplan, "Nation, Region, and Empire," in *The Columbia History of the American Novel,* ed. Emory Elliott, et al. (New York: Columbia University Press, 1991), 240–66; and Richard H. Brodhead, *Cultures of Letters: Scenes of Reading and Writing in Nineteenth-Century America* (Chicago: University of Chicago Press, 1993).

2. Kaplan, "Nation, Region, and Empire," 252; Brodhead, *Cultures of Letters,* 107–76. See also Dean MacCannell, *The Tourist: A New Theory of the Leisure Class* (New York: Schocken Books, 1976), 3, 13.

3. T. J. Jackson Lears, "From Salvation to Self-Realization: Advertising and the Therapeutic Roots of the Consumer Culture, 1880–1930," in *The Culture of Consumption: Critical Essays in American History, 1880–1980,* ed. Richard Wightman Fox and T. J. Jackson Lears (New York: Pantheon, 1983), 7, 10, 6, 8, 9.

4. Curtis M. Hinsley, "The World as Marketplace: Commodification of the Exotic at the World's Columbian Exposition, 1893," in *Exhibiting Cultures: The Poetics and Politics of Museum Display,* ed. Ivan Karp and Steven D. Lavine (Washington, D.C.: Smithsonian Press, 1991), 344–46.

5. Virginia Domínguez, "The Marketing of Heritage," *American Ethnologist* 13 (1986): 550.

6. Ibid., 547–48.

7. Ibid., 548.

8. Simon J. Bronner, "Object Lessons: The Work of Ethnological Museums and Collections," in *Consuming Visions: Accumulation and Display of Goods in America, 1880–1920,* ed. Simon J. Bronner (New York: Norton, 1989), 224–25. See also James Clifford, "On Collecting Art and Culture," in *The Predicament of Culture: Twentieth-Century Ethnography, Literature, and Art* (Cambridge, Mass.: Harvard University Press, 1988), 215–51.

9. Barbara Kirshenblatt-Gimblett, "Objects of Ethnography," in Karp and Lavine, *Exhibiting Cultures,* 413, 415.

10. See, for example, William Leach, "Strategists of Display and the Production of Desire," in Bronner, *Consuming Visions,* 99–132.

11. Bronner, "Object Lessons," 227–28, 232.

12. See in general Benedict Anderson, *Imagined Communities: Reflections on the Origin and Spread of Nationalism,* rev. ed. (London: Verso, 1991). See also Werner Sollers, "Introduction: The Invention of Ethnicity," in *The Invention of Ethnicity,* ed. Werner Sollers (New York: Oxford University Press, 1989), xii.

13. Kirshenblatt-Gimblett, "Objects of Ethnography," 388–89.

14. Jewett's *The Country of the Pointed Firs,* for example, was first serialized in 1896 in the *Atlantic Monthly* and then issued in book form later that year. See Paula Blanchard, *Sarah Orne Jewett: Her World and Her Work* (New York: Addison-Wesley, 1994), 277.

15. Susan Stewart, *On Longing: Narratives of the Miniature, the Gigantic, the Souvenir, the Collection* (Baltimore: Johns Hopkins University Press, 1984), 165.

16. J. Gerald Kennedy, "From Anderson's *Winesburg* to Carver's *Cathedral:* The Short Story Sequence and the Semblance of Community," in *Modern American Short Story Sequences: Composite Fictions and Fictive Communities,* ed. J. Gerald Kennedy (New York: Cambridge University Press, 1995), 214, 213, 195.

17. Richard Brodhead, for instance, suggests that regionalist short fiction was implicitly situated as "minor" in a period "when long works carried the meaning 'major' " (*Cultures of Letters,* 167).

18. See Kaplan's brief discussion of De Forest's novel, "Nation, Region, and Empire," 240–41.

19. [John W. De Forest], "The Great American Novel," *Nation,* Jan. 9, 1863: 28, 29.

20. Brodhead, *Cultures of Letters,* 118, 178, 177. See also Kaplan, "Nation, Region, and Empire," 251; and Eric J. Sundquist, "Realism and Regionalism," in *The Columbia History of the American Novel,* 502–3.

21. Stuart M. Blumin, *The Emergence of the Middle Class: Social Experience in the American City, 1760–1900* (New York: Cambridge University Press, 1989), 297, 13, 258, 290.

22. Quoted in Rudolf Kirk and Clara M. Kirk, "Abraham Cahan and William Dean Howells: The Story of a Friendship," *American Jewish Historical Quarterly* (1962): 41.

23. Quoted in William L. Andrews, *The Literary Career of Charles W. Chesnutt* (Baton Rouge: Louisiana State University Press, 1980), 25.

24. Ibid., 31–35.

25. Charles W. Chesnutt, *The Conjure Woman*, introd. Robert M. Farnsworth (1899; rpt. Ann Arbor: University of Michigan Press, 1969), 2–3. Subsequent references to this text are cited parenthetically within the chapter.

26. Cahan's portrayal of Jewish immigrant life was preceded in the 1880s by a popular series of novels on German Jewish life by Sidney Luska, the pseudonym for a WASP writer named Henry Harland. Among those novels were *As It Was Written: A Jewish Musician's Story* (1885), *Mrs. Peixada* (1886), *The Yoke of the Thorah* (1887), and *Grandison Mather, or An Account of the Fortunes of Mr. and Mrs. Thomas Gardiner* (1887). Another of Cahan's predecessors in Jewish American fiction was Annie Nathan Meyer (1867–1951), a champion of higher education for women and a novelist, playwright, and essayist, who published the novel *Helen Brent, M.D.* in 1892.

27. Susan K. Harris observes that early immigrant writers in the late nineteenth century "adopted rather than adapted the majority language" ("Problems of Representation in Turn-of-the-Century Immigrant Fiction," in *American Realism and the Canon*, ed. Tom Quirk and Gary Scharnhorst [Newark: University of Delaware Press, 1994], 135).

28. Jules Chametzky, *From the Ghetto: The Fiction of Abraham Cahan* (Amherst: University of Massachusetts Press, 1977), 53, 15.

29. Abraham Cahan, *Yekl and the Imported Bridegroom and Other Stories of the New York Ghetto*, introd. Bernard G. Richards (1896; rpt. New York: Dover, 1970), 13. Subsequent references to this text are cited parenthetically within the chapter.

30. Kirshenblatt-Gimblett, "Objects of Ethnography," 412.

31. Sandra A. Zagarell, "*Country*'s Portrayal of Community and the Exclusion of Difference," in Howard, *New Essays on* The Country of the Pointed Firs, 39.

32. Sarah Orne Jewett, *The Country of the Pointed Firs*, in *Novels and Stories* (1896; rpt. New York: Library of America, 1994), 377. Subsequent references to this text are cited parenthetically within the chapter.

33. Quoted in Louis Henza, "*A White Heron*" *and the Question of Minor Literature* (Madison: University of Wisconsin Press, 1984), 47.

34. Blanchard, *Sarah Orne Jewett*, 110, 110–14.

35. Elizabeth Ammons, "Material Culture, Empire, and Jewett's *Country of the Pointed Firs*," in Howard, *New Essays on* The Country of the Pointed Firs, 92.

36. Ibid., 91.

37. Chametzky, *From the Ghetto*, 3.

38. Ibid., 34–35.

39. Kirk and Kirk, "Abraham Cahan and William Dean Howells," 34.

40. Ibid., 28; Chametzky, *From the Ghetto*, 49.

41. Sollers, "Introduction," xii, xiv–xv.

42. Renato Rosaldo, "Imperialist Nostalgia," *Representations*, special issue on "Memory and Counter-Memory," ed. Natalie Zemon Davis and Randolph Starn, no. 26 (1989): 107–8.

43. *The Journals of Charles W. Chesnutt*, ed. Richard Brodhead (Durham, N.C.: Duke University Press, 1993), 139, 140.

44. Ben Slote, "Listening to 'The Goophered Grapevine' and Hearing Raisins Sing," *American Literary History* 6 (1994): 684.

45. Quoted in John F. Callahan, *In the African-American Grain: The Pursuit of Voice in Twentieth-Century Black Fiction* (Urbana: University of Illinois Press, 1988), 56.

46. Andrews, *Literary Career*, 69–73.

47. Eric J. Sundquist, *To Wake the Nations: Race in the Making of American Literature* (Cambridge, Mass.: Harvard University Press, 1993), 363.

48. Ibid., 369.

49. Quoted in Andrews, *Literary Career*, 69–70.

50. See in general Blumin's argument in *The Emergence of the Middle Class*.

51. Andrews, *Literary Career*, 36–37, 1, 3–10.

CHAPTER 4

1. Robyn Wiegman, *American Anatomies: Theorizing Race and Gender* (Durham, N.C.: Duke University Press, 1995), 15.

2. James Weldon Johnson, *The Autobiography of an Ex-Coloured Man*, introd. Henry Louis Gates Jr. (1912; rpt. New York: Random House/Vintage, 1989), 204. Subsequent references to this text are cited parenthetically within the chapter.

3. Thomas F. Gossett, *Race: The History of an Idea in America* (New York: Schocken Books, 1965), 69, 83.

4. Susan Gillman, "The Mulatto, Tragic or Triumphant? The Nineteenth-Century American Race Melodrama," in *The Culture of Sentiment: Race, Gender, and Sentimentality in 19th Century America*, ed. Shirley Samuels (New York: Oxford University Press, 1992), 228.

5. Frances Smith Foster, Introduction to *A Brighter Day Coming: A Frances Ellen Watkins Harper Reader*, ed. Frances Smith Foster (New York: Feminist Press, 1990), 13.

6. See, for example, Rayford W. Logan, *The Negro in American Life and Thought: The Nadir, 1871–1901* (New York: Dial Press, 1954).

7. See in general Joel Williamson, *The Crucible of Race: Black/White Relations in the American South Since Emancipation* (New York: Oxford University Press, 1984), 327–40.

8. Ibid., 185.

9. See in general Joseph Boskin, *Sambo: The Rise and Demise of an American Jester* (New York: Oxford University Press, 1986).

10. Frances Ellen Watkins Harper, "The Colored People in America," in Foster, *A Brighter Day Coming*, 99.

11. Reginald Horsman, *Race and Manifest Destiny: The Origins of American Racial Anglo-Saxonism* (New York: Cambridge University Press, 1981), 134.

12. Gossett, *Race*, 65, 67, 69.

13. Michael Omi and Howard Winant, *Racial Formation in the United States from the 1960s to the 1990s*, 2d ed. (New York: Routledge, 1994), 14–15.

14. Quoted in Michael Banton, *Racial Theories* (Cambridge, UK: Cambridge University Press, 1987), 78.

15. George Fredrickson, *White Supremacy: A Comparative Study in American and South African History* (New York: Oxford University Press, 1981), 130.

16. F. James Davis, *Who Is Black? One Nation's Definition* (University Park: Pennsylvania State University Press, 1991), 12, 55, 58.

17. Thomas Dixon, *The Leopard's Spots* (1902; rpt. Ridgewood, N.J.: Irvington, 1967), 244.

18. Davis, *Who Is Black?*, 22; Eric J. Sundquist, *To Wake the Naions: Race in the Making of American Literature* (Cambridge, Mass.: Harvard–Belknap Press, 1993), 393.

19. Davis, *Who Is Black?*, 56.

20. Gossett, *Race*, 69, 77–82, 83.

21. Omi and Winant, *Racial Formation*, 15.

22. Frances E. W. Harper, *Iola Leroy, or Shadows Uplifted*, introd. Frances Smith Foster, Schomburg Library of Nineteenth-Century Black Woman Writers (1892; rpt. New York: Oxford University Press, 1988), 107. Subsequent references to this text are cited parenthetically within the chapter.

23. Mark Twain, *The Tragedy of Pudd'nhead Wilson and the Comedy of Those Extraordinary Twins* (1894; rpt. New York: Oxford University Press, 1996), 123. Subsequent references to this text are cited parenthetically within the chapter.

24. Eric J. Sundquist, "Mark Twain and Homer Plessy," in *Mark Twain's Pudd'nhead Wilson: Race, Conflict, and Culture*, ed. Susan Gillman and Forrest G. Robinson (Durham, N.C.: Duke University Press, 1990), 65.

25. Eric Lott, "Mr. Clemens and Jim Crow: Twain, Race, and Blackface," in *The Cambridge Companion to Mark Twain*, ed. Forrest G. Robinson (New York: Cambridge University Press, 1995), 146.

26. See, for example, Richard Dyer on the invisibility of whiteness in film in "White," *Screen* 29 (1988): 48–68. The most notable commentator on the literary uses of blackness to invent and define whiteness is Toni Morrison, who asserts: "Africanism is the vehicle by which the American self knows itself as not enslaved, but free; not repulsive but desirable; not helpless, but licensed and powerful; not history-less, but historical; not damned, but innocent; not a blind accident of evolution, but a progressive fulfillment of destiny" (*Playing in the Dark: Whiteness and the Literary Imagination*, William E. Massey Sr. Lectures in the History of American Civilization 1990 (Cambridge, Mass.: Harvard University Press, 1992), 52.

27. See in general Bertram Wyatt-Brown, *Southern Honor: Ethics and Behavior in the Old South* (New York: Oxford University Press, 1982).

28. Sandra Gunning, *Race, Rape, and Lynching: The Red Record of American Literature, 1890–1912* (New York: Oxford University Press, 1996), 14.

29. Michael Rogin, "Frances Galton and Mark Twain: The Natal Autograph in *Pudd'nhead Wilson*," in Gillman and Robinson, *Mark Twain's Pudd'nhead Wilson*, 76.

30. Elizabeth Young, "Warring Fictions: *Iola Leroy* and the Color of Gender," in *Subjects and Citizens: Nation, Race, and Gender from Oroonoko to Anita Hill*, ed. Michael Moon and Cathy Davidson (Durham, N.C.: Duke University Press, 1995), 304.

31. Hazel V. Carby, *Reconstructing Womanhood: The Emergence of the Afro-American Woman Novelist* (New York: Oxford University Press, 1988), 93.

32. Samira Kawash, *"The Autobiography of an Ex-Coloured Man:* (Passing for) Black Passing for White," in *Passing and the Fictions of Identity,* ed. Elaine K. Ginsburg (Durham, N.C.: Duke University Press, 1996), 63.

33. Quoted in Eugene Levy, *James Weldon Johnson: Black Leader, Black Voice* (Chicago: University of Chicago Press, 1973), 127.

34. Ibid. See also ibid., 133.

35. Kawash, *"The Autobiography,"* 60.

36. Harper, " 'Almost Constantly Either Traveling or Speaking' " [Columbiana, Georgia (?)], Feb. 20, 1870, in Foster, *Brighter Day Coming,* 126–27.

37. John Ernest, *Resistance and Reformation in Nineteenth-Century African-American Literature: Brown, Wilson, Jacobs, Delaney, Douglass, and Harper* (Jackson: University Press of Mississippi, 1995), 203.

38. Nancy Bentley, "White Slaves: The Mulatto Hero in Antebellum Fiction," in Moon and Davidson, *Subjects and Citizens,* 198.

39. Kenneth W. Warren, "Troubled Black Humanity in *The Souls of Black Folk* and *The Autobiography of an Ex-Coloured Man,"* in *The Cambridge Companion to American Realism and Naturalism: Howells to London,* ed. Donald Pizer (New York: Cambridge University Press, 1995), 273.

40. Gunning, *Race, Rape, and Lynching,* 55.

41. Susan Gillman, " 'Sure Identifiers': Race, Science, and the Law in *Pudd'nhead Wilson,"* in Gillman and Robinson, *Mark Twain's* Pudd'nhead Wilson, 96.

42. Ibid., 95. See also Lott, "Mr. Clemens and Jim Crow," 148.

43. Gillman, " 'Sure Identifiers,' " 96.

CHAPTER 5

1. Paula Giddings, *When and Where I Enter: The Impact of Black Women in Race and Sex in America* (New York: Bantam Books, 1984), 80; Lynne Vallone, *Disciplines of Virtue: Girls' Culture in the Eighteenth and Nineteenth Centuries* (New Haven, Conn.: Yale University Press, 1995), 28.

2. Mary P. Ryan, *Women in Public: Between Banners and Ballots, 1825–1880* (Baltimore: Johns Hopkins University Press, 1990), 26; Lisa Tickner, "Men's Work? Masculinity and Modernism," in *Visual Culture: Images and Interpretations,* ed. Norman Bryson, Michael Ann Holly, and Keith Moxey (Hanover, N.H.: Wesleyan University Press–University Press of New England, 1994), 48.

3. Bram Dijkstra, *Evil Sisters: The Threat of Female Sexuality and the Cult of Manhood* (New York: Alfred A. Knopf, 1996), 34.

4. Charlotte Perkins Gilman, *The Man-Made World or, Our Androcentric Culture* (New York: Charlton Co., 1911; rpt. Johnson Rept. Corp., 1971), 24.

5. See in general Elizabeth Ammons, *Conflicting Stories: American Women Writers at the Turn into the Twentieth Century* (New York: Oxford University Press, 1992), 3–19.

6. Barbara Hochman, *"The Awakening* and *The House of Mirth:* Plotting Experience and Experiencing Plot," in *The Cambridge Companion to American Realism and Naturalism: Howells to London,* ed. Donald Pizer (New York:

Cambridge University Press, 1995), 211. See also Ammons, *Conflicting Stories*, 4–5.

7. Shari Benstock, *No Gifts from Chance: A Biography of Edith Wharton* (New York: Scribner's, 1994), 139; Elizabeth Ammons, *Edith Wharton's Argument with America* (Athens: University of Georgia Press, 1980), 38.

8. Linda Wagner-Martin, *The House of Mirth: A Novel of Admonition* (Boston: Twayne, 1990), 5; and Benstock, *No Gifts from Chance*, 150.

9. R. W. B. Lewis, *Edith Wharton: A Biography* (New York: Harper & Row, 1975), 155; and Millicent Bell, "Introduction: A Critical History," in *The Cambridge Companion to Edith Wharton*, ed. Millicent Bell (New York: Cambridge University Press, 1995), 10. See also Sandra M. Gilbert and Susan Gubar, *No Man's Land: The Place of the Woman Writer in the Twentieth Century: Sexchanges*, vol. 2 (New Haven, Conn.: Yale University Press, 1989), 139; and Ammons, *Edith Wharton's Argument*, 3.

10. Hazel V. Carby, Introduction to *The Magazine Novels of Pauline Hopkins*, Schomburg Library of Nineteenth-Century Black Women Writers (New York: Oxford University Press, 1988), xxx.

11. Claudia Tate, *Domestic Allegories of Female Desire: The Black Heroine's Text at the Turn of the Century* (New York: Oxford University Press, 1992), 148.

12. Hazel V. Carby, *Reconstructing Womanhood: The Emergence of the Afro-American Woman Novelist* (New York: Oxford University Press, 1987), 121–22.

13. Carby, Introduction, xxix.

14. Ryan, *Women in Public*, 74–75.

15. Kate McCullough, "Slavery, Sexuality, and Genre: Pauline Hopkins and the Representation of Female Desire," in *The Unruly Voice: Rediscovering Pauline Elizabeth Hopkins*, ed. John Cullen Gruesser (Urbana: University of Illinois Press, 1996), 22. See also Ryan, *Women in Public*, 73; and Sandra Gunning, *Race, Rape, and Lynching: The Red Record of American Literature, 1890–1912* (New York: Oxford University Press, 1996), 10.

16. Vallone, *Disciplines of Virtue*, 24.

17. Pauline E. Hopkins, *Contending Forces: A Romance Illustrative of Negro Life North and South*, introd. Richard Yarborough, Schomburg Library of Nineteenth-Century Black Women Writers (1900; rpt. New York: Oxford University Press, 1988), 14. Subsequent references to this edition are cited parenthetically within the chapter.

18. Gilman, *The Man-Made World*, 104–5.

19. Ryan, *Women in Public*, 135, 19.

20. Glenna Matthews, *The Rise of Public Woman: Woman's Power and Woman's Place in the United States, 1630–1970* (New York: Oxford University Press, 1992), 4.

21. Ibid., 4, 120, 128, 130.

22. See in general Drew Gilpin Faust, "Altars of Sacrifice: Confederate Women and the Narratives of War," in *Divided Houses: Gender and the Civil War*, ed. Catherine Clinton and Nina Silber (New York: Oxford University Press, 1992), 171–99.

23. Rachel Bowlby, *Just Looking: Consumer Culture in Dreiser, Gissing, and Zola* (New York: Methuen, 1985), 11, 19.

24. Matthews, *Rise of Public Woman*, 151.

25. See in general Carroll Smith-Rosenberg, "The New Woman as Androgyne: Social Disorder and Gender Crisis, 1870–1936," in *Disorderly Conduct: Visions of Gender in Victorian America* (New York: Oxford University Press, 1985), 245–96; see also Ammons, *Conflicting Stories*, 5–7.

26. Wagner-Martin, *The House of Mirth: A Novel of Admonition*, 3.

27. David Shi, *Facing Facts: Realism in American Thought and Culture, 1850–1920* (New York: Oxford University Press, 1995), 91.

28. Matthews, *Rise of Public Woman*, 148.

29. Quoted in Gilbert and Gubar, *No Man's Land: Sexchanges*, vol. 2, 49.

30. Tate, *Domestic Allegories*, 138.

31. Giddings, *When and Where I Enter*, 76, 75, 83.

32. Ibid., 86.

33. Richard Yarborough, Introduction, in Hopkins, *Contending Forces*, xxxii; Giddings, *When and Where I Enter*, 86–87, Williams quoted, 86–87.

34. Ryan, *Women in Public*, 75; and Matthews, *Rise of Public Woman*, 4.

35. Quoted in Nancy Walker, *The Disobedient Writer: Women and Narrative Tradition* (Austin: University of Texas Press, 1995), 25.

36. Ryan, *Women in Public*, 74–75.

37. Smith-Rosenberg, "New Woman as Androgyne," 257–62, 265–73.

38. Molly Hite, *The Other Side of the Story: Structures and Strategies of Contemporary Feminist Narratives* (Ithaca, N.Y.: Cornell University Press, 1989), 5; and Vallone, *Disciplines of Virtue*, 34, 156. See in general Nancy K. Miller, *The Heroine's Text: Reading in the French and English Novel, 1722–1782* (New York: Columbia University Press, 1980).

39. Edith Wharton, *The House of Mirth*, in *Novels* (1905; rpt. New York: Library of America, 1985), 18. Subsequent references to this text are cited parenthetically within the chapter.

40. Ammons, *Conflicting Stories*, 80, 78.

41. Quoted in Lewis, *Edith Wharton*, 155.

42. See, for example, Gunning, *Race, Rape, and Lynching*, 10. See also Carby, *Reconstructing Womanhood*, 20–39.

43. Carby, *Reconstructing Womanhood*, 131–32; see also McCullough, "Slavery, Sexuality, and Genre," 25.

44. Candace Waid, *Edith Wharton's Letters from the Underworld: Fictions of Women and Writing* (Chapel Hill: University of North Carolina Press, 1991), 28.

45. Hopkins, Preface, in *Contending Forces*, 13.

46. Edith Wharton, *A Backward Glance* (1929; rpt. New York: Charles Scribner's Sons, 1962), 294. For a good account of Wharton's resistance to any alliance with fellow women writers, see Waid, *Edith Wharton's Letters*, 7, 11.

47. Wharton, *A Backward Glance*, 2; and Benstock, *No Gifts from Chance*, 46.

48. Wharton, *A Backward Glance*, 112, 115; and Benstock, *No Gifts from Chance*, 59.

49. See Wharton, *A Backward Glance*, 197–212.

50. Quoted in Ammons, *Conflicting Stories*, 78.

51. Carby, *Reconstructing Womanhood*, 133, 144; and C. K. Doreski, "Inherited Rhetoric and Authentic History: Pauline Hopkins at the *Colored American Magazine*," in Gruesser, *The Unruly Voice*, 73.

52. Note, for instance, the subtitle of Wagner-Martin's book on *The House of Mirth: A Novel of Admonition.*

CHAPTER 6

1. Gail Bederman, *Manliness* and *Civilization: A Cultural History of Gender and Race in the United States, 1880–1917* (Chicago: University of Chicago Press, 1995), 14. See also Irene Gammel, *Sexualizing Power in Naturalism: Theodore Dreiser and Frederick Philip Grove* (Calgary: University of Calgary Press, 1994), 2–3; and Lisa Tickner, "Men's Work? Masculinity and Modernism," in *Visual Culture: Images and Interpretations,* ed. Norman Bryson, Michael Ann Holly, and Keith Moxey (Hanover, N.H.: Wesleyan University Press–University Press of New England, 1994), 49.

2. Richard Lingeman, *Theodore Dreiser: At the Gates of the City, 1871–1907* (New York: G. P. Putnam's Sons, 1986), 288. See also Gammel, *Sexualizing Power,* 33.

3. Gammel makes this observation as well (*Sexualizing Power,* 49), drawing from critical perspectives developed by David Baguley in *Naturalist Fiction: The Entropic Vision* (Cambridge, UK: Cambridge University Press, 1990), 84.

4. Tickner, for one, writes: "The battle of the sexes (for pro- and antifeminists, especially men) and the exploration of a modern, self-determined identity (particularly by women) is *the* modern subject matter, even when talk of speed, electricity, cars, planes, and war dominates the manifest content of a work" ("Men's Work?," 44). Donald Pizer makes much the same observation in asserting that sex first makes its appearance in naturalist texts as "the great theme of modern art" (*The Theory and Practice of American Literary Naturalism* [Carbondale: Southern Illinois University Press, 1993], 20). See also the three-volume examination of gender battles in modernism, *No Man's Land: The Place of the Woman Writer in the Twentieth Century,* by Sandra M. Gilbert and Susan Gubar: *The War of the Words,* vol. 1 (New Haven, Conn.: Yale University Press, 1988); *Sexchanges,* vol. 2 (New Haven, Conn.: Yale University Press, 1989); and *Letters from the Front,* vol. 3 (New Haven, Conn.: Yale University Press, 1994).

5. June Howard, *Form and History in American Literary Naturalism* (Chapel Hill: University of North Carolina Press, 1985), 39. Michael Davitt Bell notes succinctly, ". . . it is hard to imagine any coherent 'school' that could include the authors of *The Red Badge of Courage, McTeague,* and *Sister Carrie* (*The Problem of American Realism: Studies in the Cultural History of a Literary Idea* [Chicago: University of Chicago Press, 1993], 111).

6. Pizer, *Theory and Practice,* 14.

7. George J. Becker, "Introduction: Modern Realism as a Literary Movement," in *Documents of Modern Literary Realism,* ed. George J. Becker (Princeton, N.J.: Princeton University Press, 1963), 35.

8. Rachel Bowlby, *Just Looking: Culture in Dreiser, Gissing, and Zola* (New York: Methuen, 1985), 9–10. See also Pizer, *Theory and Practice,* 16.

9. Paul Civello, *American Literary Naturalism and Its Twentieth-Century Transformations* (Athens: University of Georgia Press, 1994), 7.

10. Cynthia Eagle Russett, *Darwin in America: The Intellectual Response, 1865–1912* (San Francisco: Freeman, 1976), 35.

11. Civello, *American Literary Naturalism*, 8–9.

12. Quoted in ibid., 25. See also Pizer, *Theory and Practice*, 18–19.

13. Civello, *American Literary Naturalism*, 23, 25; Lee Clark Mitchell, *Determined Fictions: American Literary Naturalism* (New York: Columbia University Press, 1989), 11, 19, 33; Barbara Hochman, *The Art of Frank Norris, Storyteller* (Columbia: University of Missouri Press, 1988), 5.

14. Richard Slotkin, *The Fatal Environment: The Myth of the Frontier in the Age of Industrialization, 1800–1890* (New York: Harper/Perennial, 1985), 286–87, 288–89.

15. Alan Trachtenberg, *The Incorporation of America: Culture and Society in the Gilded Age* (New York: Hill & Wang, 1982), 38–39.

16. Howard, *Form and History*, ix.

17. Harold Kaplan, *Power and Order: Henry Adams and the Naturalist Tradition in America* (Chicago: University of Chicago Press, 1981), 17.

18. See, for example, Daniel H. Borus, *Writing Realism: Howells, James, and Norris in the Mass Market* (Chapel Hill: University of North Carolina Press, 1989), 114; Donna M. Campbell, *Resisting Regionalism: Gender and Naturalism in American Fiction, 1885–1915* (Athens: Ohio University Press, 1997), passim; Alfred Habegger, *Gender, Fantasy, and Realism in American Literature* (New York: Columbia University Press, 1982), 65; Barbara Hochman, "*The Awakening* and *The House of Mirth*: Plotting Experience and Experiencing Plot," in *The Cambridge Companion to American Realism and Naturalism: Howells to London*, ed. Donald Pizer (New York: Cambridge University Press, 1995), 212–13; Mark Seltzer, *Bodies and Machines* (New York: Routledge, 1992), 156; David E. Shi, *Facing Facts: Realism in American Thought and Culture, 1850–1920* (New York: Oxford University Press, 1995), 218; and Christopher P. Wilson, *The Labor of Words: Literary Professionalism in the Progressive Era* (Athens: University of Georgia Press, 1985), xiv, 1, 58. See also Bell, *Problem of American Realism*, passim; Gammel, *Sexualizing Power*, 2–3, 49; and Howard, *Form and History*, 179.

19. Bert Bender, *The Descent of Love: Darwin and the Theory of Sexual Selection in American Fiction, 1871–1926* (Philadelphia: University of Pennsylvania Press, 1996), 7, 11.

20. Quoted in ibid., 18.

21. Ibid., xi.

22. Bram Dijkstra, *Evil Sisters: The Threat of Female Sexuality and the Cult of Manhood* (New York: Alfred A. Knopf, 1996), 34–35.

23. Tickner, "Men's Work?," 48.

24. Ibid., 48. See also Dijkstra, *Evil Sisters*, 34–35.

25. Dijkstra, *Evil Sisters*, 34.

26. Slotkin, *Fatal Environment*, 286, 289; Trachtenberg, *Incorporation of America*, 56, 65–66.

27. Bederman, *Manliness and Civilization*, 12.

28. See in general Bertram Wyatt-Brown, *Southern Honor: Ethics and Behavior in the Old South* (New York: Oxford University Press, 1982); and Elliott Gorn, " 'Gouge and Bite, Pull Hair and Scratch': The Social Signifi-

cance of Fighting in the Southern Backcountry," *American Historical Review* 90 (1985): 18–43.

29. Clyde Griffen, "Reconstructing Masculinity from the Evangelical Revival to the Waning of Progressivism: A Speculative Synthesis," in *Meanings for Manhood: Constructions of Masculinity in Victorian America*, ed. Mark C. Carnes and Clyde Griffen (Chicago: University of Chicago Press, 1990), 183, 185, 191, 198. See also Bederman, *Manliness and Civilization*, 12.

30. Griffen, "Reconstructing Masculinity," 183, 198, 199.

31. E. Anthony Rotundo, *American Manhood: Transformations of Masculinity from the Revolution to the Modern Era* (New York: Basic Books, 1993), 249.

32. Herbert Sussman, "The Study of Victorian Masculinity," *Victorian Literature and Culture* 20 (1993): 372.

33. See Elaine Showalter, *Sexual Anarchy: Gender and Culture at the Fin de Siècle* (New York: Viking, 1990), 7–8, 3.

34. Bederman, *Manliness and Civilization*, 15; Showalter, *Sexual Anarchy*, 14.

35. George Chauncey, *Gay New York: Gender, Urban Culture, and the Making of the Gay Male World, 1890–1940* (New York: Basic Books, 1994), 48, 47.

36. Eve Kosofsky Sedgwick, *Between Men: English Literature and Male Homosocial Desire* (New York: Columbia University Press, 1985), 88–89, and *Epistemology of the Closet* (Berkeley: University of California Press, 1990), 185.

37. Sedgwick, *Epistemology of the Closet*, 146–47.

38. Wilson, *Labor of Words*, 144; Amy Kaplan, "Nation, Region, and Empire," in *The Columbia History of the American Novel*, ed. Emory Elliott, et al. (New York: Columbia University Press, 1991), 249; and Shi, *Facing Facts*, 218.

39. Bell, *Problem of American Realism*, 119.

40. Quoted in ibid., 117.

41. See in general Gayle Rubin, "The Traffic in Women: Notes toward a Political Economy of Sex," in *Toward an Anthropology of Women*, ed. Rayna Reiter (New York: Monthly Review Press, 1975), 157–210. Sedgwick follows this argument in her examination of "Gender Asymmetry and Erotic Triangles" in *Between Men*, 21–27 and passim.

42. Theodore Dreiser, *Sister Carrie* (1900; rpt. Philadelphia: University of Pennsylvania Press, 1981), 95. Subsequent references to this text are cited parenthetically within the chapter.

43. Frank Norris, *McTeague: A Story of San Francisco*, in *Novels and Essays* (1899; rpt. New York: Library of America, 1986), 303. Subsequent references to this text are cited parenthetically in the chapter.

44. Howard, *Form and History*, 182. See also Philip Fisher, *Hard Facts: Setting and Form in the American Novel* (New York: Oxford University Press, 1987), 128–75.

45. See, for example, Fisher, *Hard Facts*, 170.

46. See, for example, ibid., 161–62.

47. Quoted in Lingeman, *Theodore Dreiser*, 150.

48. Edward and Madeline Vaughn Abbot, "*McTeague*," in *Critical Essays on Frank Norris*, ed. Don Graham (Boston: G. K. Hall, 1980), 11.

49. Donald Pizer argues in an early article that Norris saw woman's "correct function" as that of "a man's woman." The three novels of his mid-

dle period—*Moran of the Lady Letty* (1898), *Blix* (1899), and *A Man's Woman* (1900)—all focus, Pizer asserts, on "the correct sexual roles for man and woman" ("The Masculine-Feminine Ethic in Frank Norris's Popular Novels," in Graham, *Critical Essays on Frank Norris*, 45.

50. George M. Spangler, "The Structure of *McTeague*," in Graham, *Critical Essays on Frank Norris*, 93, 95. See also John J. Conder, *Naturalism in American Fiction: The Classic Phase* (Lexington: University Press of Kentucky, 1984), 70.

51. Chauncey, *Gay New York*, 36–41, 34.

52. See Gammel, *Sexualizing Power*, 66. See also Scott Zaluda, "The Secrets of Fraternity: Men and Friendship in *Sister Carrie*," in *Theodore Dreiser: Beyond Naturalism*, ed. Miriam Gogol (New York: Viking Press, 1995), 84.

53. Lingeman, *Theodore Dreiser*, 26, 276, 269. See also Miriam Gogol, " 'That oldest boy don't wanta be here': Fathers and Sons and the Dynamics of Shame in Theodore Dreiser's Novels," in Gogol, *Theodore Dreiser: Beyond Naturalism*, 96.

54. June Howard reads naturalist novels in general as marked by an impetus to define the middle-class reader in terms of lower-class figures presented as Other and carefully confined to the pages of the novel (*Form and History*, 127, 140, 150, 151, and passim).

55. Joseph R. McElrath Jr., "Frank Norris: A Biographical Essay," in Graham, *Critical Essays on Frank Norris*, xli.

56. Mitchell, *Determined Fictions*, xiv, 11.

57. Both Bowlby and Howard suggest that naturalist narratives seem peculiarly disjointed and discontinuous, evoking, in Bowlby's words, "a social reality that appears simply as . . . a succession of separate images or scenes" (Bowlby, *Just Looking*, 16; Howard, *Form and History*, 167).

CHAPTER 7

1. The phrase is borrowed from anthropologist Victor Turner, who uses it to discuss liminality. See "Liminality and Communitas," in *The Ritual Process: Structure and Anti-Structure* (Ithaca, N.Y.: Cornell University Press, 1969), 95.

2. See, for example, George Levine, *The Realistic Imagination: English Fiction from Frankenstein to Lady Chatterley* (Chicago: University of Chicago Press, 1981), 20.

3. See Edmund Wilson's discussion of Stein and her influence in his *Axel's Castle* (New York: Charles Scribner's Sons, 1931), 237–44.

4. Christopher Benfey, *The Double Life of Stephen Crane* (New York: Alfred A. Knopf, 1992), 107.

5. [Alexander C. McClurg], "The Red Badge of Hysteria," *Dial* 20 (16 Apr. 1896): 227–28; rpt. in *Critical Essays on Stephen Crane's* The Red Badge of Courage, ed. Donald Pizer (Boston: G. K. Hall, 1990), 42, 41.

6. Harold Frederic, "Stephen Crane's Triumph," *New York Times*, Jan. 26, 1896: 22; rpt. in Pizer, *Critical Essays*, 36.

7. [Anonymous], "Fiction, but Not Novels," *Kansas City Star*, Dec. 18, 1909: 5; rpt. in *Critical Essays on Gertrude Stein*, ed. Michael J. Hoffman (Boston: G. K. Hall, 1986), 26.

8. Quoted in Linda Wagner-Martin, *"Favored Strangers": Gertrude Stein and Her Family* (New Brunswick, N.J.: Rutgers University Press, 1995), 87.

9. Benfey, *Double Life*, 106.

10. Quoted in Lee Clark Mitchell, Introduction, in *New Essays on* The Red Badge of Courage, ed. Lee Clark Mitchell (New York: Cambridge University Press, 1986), 6.

11. Hutchins Hapgood, [Letter to Gertrude Stein, 22 Apr. 1906], in Hoffman, *Critical Essays*, 25.

12. Wyndham Lewis, "Tests for Counterfeit in the Arts and The Prose-Song of Gertrude Stein," in *Time and Western Man* (1927; rpt. Boston: Beacon Press, 1957), 49–51; rpt. in Hoffman, *Critical Essays*, 55.

13. Quoted in Mitchell, Introduction, in *New Essays*, 5.

14. Stephen Crane, *The Red Badge of Courage: An Episode of the American Civil War*, in *Prose and Poetry* (1895; rpt. New York: Library of America, 1984), 83. Subsequent references to this text are cited parenthetically within the chapter.

15. Mitchell, Introduction, in *New Essays*, 16; Benfey, *Double Life*, 104.

16. Donald Pizer notes that for Crane, war served as a metaphor for life itself in all its confusion and contradictions (*The Theory and Practice of American Literary Naturalism* [Carbondale: Southern Illinois University Press, 1993], 96).

17. Wagner-Martin, *"Favored Strangers,"* 77.

18. Lena is described as the "victim" of a "conventional plot and framework" and her aunt as the determined narrator of the plot by Janice L. Doane in *Silence and Narrative: The Early Novels of Gertrude Stein* (Westport, Conn.: Greenwood Press, 1986), 80, 78.

19. Gertrude Stein, *Three Lives*, in *Writings 1903–1932* (1909; rpt. New York: Library of America, 1998), 79. Subsequent references to this text are cited parenthetically within the chapter.

20. James Nagel brings attention to "the epistemological nature of Crane's narrative methods" in *Stephen Crane and Literary Impressionism* (University Park: Pennsylvania State University Press, 1980), 86.

21. Lee Clark Mitchell, *Determined Fictions: American Literary Naturalism* (New York: Columbia University Press, 1989), xiv.

22. See, for example, readings of the novel by Donald Pease, "Fear, Rage, and the Mistrials of Representation in *The Red Badge of Courage*, in *American Realism: New Essays*, ed. Eric J. Sundquist (Baltimore: Johns Hopkins University Press, 1982), 157; and Michael Davitt Bell, *The Problem of American Realism: Studies in the Cultural History of a Literary Idea* (Chicago: University of Chicago Press, 1993), 138, 139, 146. See also Nagel's discussion of the discontinuous impressions marking the narrative of *The Red Badge of Courage* (*Stephen Crane and Literary Impressionism*, 50–60).

23. Quoted in Jayne L. Walker, *The Making of a Modernist: Gertrude Stein from* Three Lives *to* Tender Buttons (Amherst: University of Massachusetts Press, 1984), 16.

24. See Walker's explanation, ibid., 15–16.

25. Astradur Eysteinsson, *The Concept of Modernism* (Ithaca, N.Y.: Cornell University Press, 1990), 9.

26. Walker, *Making of a Modernist*, 2, 19.

27. Ibid., 12. The best explanation of Cézanne's impact on Stein's writing is in ibid., 1–18.

28. Quoted in ibid., 13.

29. Quoted in ibid., 4.

30. Robert Hughes, *The Shock of the New* (New York: Alfred A. Knopf–Random House, 1980), 18.

31. Walker, *Making of a Modernist*, 23.

32. Harriet Scott Chessman, *The Public Is Invited to Dance: Representation, the Body, and Dialogue in Gertrude Stein* (Stanford, Calif.: Stanford University Press, 1989), 21.

33. Ibid., 51.

34. Ronald E. Martin, *American Literature and the Destruction of Knowledge* (Durham, N.C.: Duke University Press, 1991), 182, 205.

35. Walker, *Making of a Modernist*, xviii.

36. Gertrude Stein, *Tender Buttons*, in *Writings 1903–1932*, 313.

37. See, for example, an overview of modernism in Eysteinsson, *Concept of Modernism*, 1–102.

38. Quoted in Martin, *American Literature*, 180.

39. Marjorie Perloff, *The Futurist Moment: Avant-Garde, Avant Guerre, and the Language of Rupture* (Chicago: University of Chicago Press, 1986), xix.

40. John Berryman, *Stephen Crane: A Critical Biography*, rev. ed. (1950; New York: Farrar, Straus, Giroux, 1977), 287–88.

41. William R. Everdell, *The First Moderns: Profiles in the Origins of Twentieth-Century Thought* (Chicago: University of Chicago Press, 1997), 327–28. See also Meyer Schapiro, "Introduction of Modern Art in America: The Armory Show," in *Modern Art: 19th and 20th Centuries, Selected Papers* (New York: George Braziller, 1979), 135–78.

Selected Bibliography

PRIMARY WORKS

Adams, Henry. *Democracy*. 1880.
———. *Esther*. 1884.
Albert, Octavia Victoria Rogers. *The House of Bondage, or, Charlotte Brooks and Other Slaves*. 1890.
Alcott, Louisa May. *Little Women; or, Meg, Jo, Beth, and Amy*. 2 vols. 1868–69.
———. *An Old-Fashioned Girl*. 1870.
———. *Little Women and Good Wives*. 1871.
———. *Little Men: Life at Plumfield with Jo's Boys*. 1871.
———. *Work: A Story of Experience*. 1873.
———. *Eight Cousins; or, The Aunt-Hill*. 1875.
———. *Rose in Bloom: A Sequel to "Eight Cousins."* 1876.
———. *Jo's Boys and How They Turned Out*. 1886.
Alger, Horatio. *Ragged Dick; or, Street Life in New York with the Boot-Blacks*. 1868.
———. *Luck and Pluck; or, John Oakley's Inheritance*. 1869.
Allen, James Lane. *The Reign of Law: A Tale of the Kentucky Hemp Fields*. 1900.
Atherton, Gertrude. *The Californians*. 1898.
Austin, Mary. *A Woman of Genius*. 1912.
Bellamy, Edward. *Looking Backward 2000–1887*. 1888.
———. *Equality*. 1897.
Boyesen, H. H. *The Golden Calf*. 1892.
———. *The Social Strugglers*. 1893.
Cable, George Washington. *The Grandissimes: A Story of Creole Life*. 1880.
———. *Madame Delphine*. 1881.
———. *Dr. Sevier*. 1884.
———. *John March, Southerner*. 1894.
———. *The Cavalier*. 1901.
Cahan, Abraham. *Yekl: A Tale of the New York Ghetto*. 1896.
———. *The White Terror and the Red: A Novel of Revolutionary Russia*. 1905.
———. *The Rise of David Levinsky*. 1917.
Callahan, Sophia Alice. *Wynema: A Child of the Forest*. 1891.
Cather, Willa. *Alexander's Bridge*. 1912.
———. *O Pioneers!* 1913.
———. *The Song of the Lark*. 1915.
Chesnutt, Charles W. *The Conjure Woman*. 1899.
———. *The House behind the Cedars*. 1900.
———. *The Marrow of Tradition*. 1901.
———. *The Colonel's Dream*. 1905.
Chopin, Kate. *At Fault*. 1890.
———. *The Awakening*. 1899.

Churchill, Winston. *A Modern Chronicle*. 1910.

Crane, Stephen. *Maggie, A Girl of the Streets (A Story of New York)*. 1893; rev. ed., 1896.

———. *The Red Badge of Courage: An Episode of the American Civil War*. 1895.

———. *George's Mother*. 1896.

Davis, Rebecca Harding. *Life in the Iron-Mills*, in *Atlantic Monthly*. 1861.

———. *Margaret Howth: A Story of Today*. 1862.

———. *Dallas Galbraith*. 1868.

———. *Waiting for the Verdict*. 1868.

———. *Put Out of the Way*. 1870.

———. *John Adross*. 1874.

———. *A Law unto Herself*. 1878.

———. *Natasqua*. 1886.

———. *Dr. Warrick's Daughters*. 1896.

———. *Frances Waldeaux*. 1897.

Davis, Richard Harding. *Soldiers of Fortune*. 1897.

———. *The King's Jackal*. 1899.

———. *Episodes in Van Bibber's Life*. 1899.

———. *In the Fog*. 1901.

De Forest, John W. *Miss Ravenel's Conversion from Secession to Loyalty*. 1867.

———. *Overland*. 1871.

———. *Kate Beaumont*. 1872.

———. *Honest John Vane*. 1875.

———. *Playing the Mischief*. 1875.

———. *Irene the Missionary*. 1879.

———. *A Lover's Revolt*. 1898.

Dixon, Thomas. *The Leopard's Spots: A Romance of the White Man's Burden*. 1902.

———. *The Clansman*. 1905.

———. *The Traitor*. 1907.

Dreiser, Theodore. *Sister Carrie*. 1900.

———. *Jennie Gerhardt*. 1911.

———. *The Financier*. 1912.

———. *The Titan*. 1914.

———. *The "Genius."* 1915.

Du Bois, W. E. B. *The Quest of the Silver Fleece*. 1911.

Dunbar, Paul Laurence. *The Uncalled*. 1896.

———. *The Love of Landry*. 1900.

———. *The Fanatics*. 1901.

———. *The Sport of the Gods*. 1902; as *The Jest of Fate*. 1902.

Eaton, Edith Maud (as Sui Sin Far). *Mrs. Spring Fragrance*. 1912.

Eaton, Winnifred (as Onoto Watanna). *Miss Nume of Japan*. 1900.

———. *A Japanese Nightingale*. 1901.

Eggleston, Edward. *The Hoosier School-Master*. 1871; rev. ed., 1892.

———. *The End of the World: A Love Story*. 1872.

———. *The Mystery of Metropolisville*. 1873.

———. *The Circuit Rider: A Tale of the Heroic Age*. 1874.

———. *Roxy*. 1878.

———. *The Hoosier School-Boy*. 1882.

———. *The Graysons: A Story of Illinois.* 1888.
———. *The Faith Doctor: A Story of New York.* 1891.
Evans, Augusta Jane (Wilson). *Beulah.* 1859.
———. *Macaria.* 1863.
———. *St. Elmo.* 1866.
———. *Vashti: or "Until Death Do Us Part."* 1869.
———. *Infelice.* 1875.
Foote, Mary Hallock. *The Led-Horse Claim: A Romance of a Mining Camp.* 1883.
———. *The Chosen Valley.* 1892.
Fox, John Jr. *The Trail of the Lonesome Pine.* 1908.
Frederic, Harold. *Seth's Brother's Wife: A Study of Life in the Greater New York.* 1887.
———. *The Lawton Girl.* 1890.
———. *In the Valley.* 1890.
———. *The Return of the O'Mahony.* 1892.
———. *The Damnation of Theron Ware.* 1896; as *Illumination.* 1896.
———. *March Hares.* 1896.
———. *Gloria Mundi.* 1898.
———. *The Market-Place.* 1899.
Freeman, Mary E. Wilkins. *A Humble Romance.* 1887.
———. *A New England Nun.* 1891.
———. *Jane Field.* 1892.
———. *Pembroke.* 1894.
———. *The Heart's Highway.* 1900.
———. *The Portion of Labor.* 1901.
———. *The Debtor.* 1905.
———. *The Green Door.* 1910.
French, Alice (as Octave Thanet). *We All.* 1891.
Fuller, Henry Blake. *The Chatelaine of La Trinité.* 1892.
———. *The Cliff-Dwellers.* 1893.
———. *With the Procession.* 1895.
Gale, Zona. *Romance Island.* 1906.
———. *Mothers to Men.* 1911.
———. *Heart's Kindred.* 1915.
———. *A Daughter of the Morning.* 1917.
———. *Birth.* 1918.
Garland, Hamlin. *Jason Edwards: An Average Man.* 1892.
———. *A Member of the Third House.* 1892.
———. *A Spoil of Office.* 1892.
———. *Rose of Dutcher's Coolly.* 1895; rev. ed., 1899.
Gilman, Charlotte Perkins. "The Yellow Wall-Paper," in *New England Magazine.* 1892.
———. *What Diantha Did.* 1910.
———. *Herland.* 1915.
Glasgow, Ellen (anon.).*The Descendant.* 1897.
———. *Phases of an Inferior Planet.* 1898.
———. *The Voice of the People.* 1900.

————. *The Battle-Ground*. 1902.

————. *The Deliverance*. 1904.

————. *The Wheel of Life*. 1906.

————. *The Ancient Law*. 1908.

————. *The Romance of a Plain Man*. 1909.

————. *The Miller of Old Church*. 1911.

————. *Virginia*. 1913.

————. *Life and Gabriella*. 1916.

Grant, Robert. *Unleavened Bread*. 1900.

Grey, Zane. *The Heritage of the Desert*. 1910.

————. *Riders of the Purple Sage*. 1912.

————. *Desert Gold*. 1913.

Griggs, Sutton E. *Imperium in Imperio: A Study of the Negro Race Problem*. 1899.

————. *Overshadowed*. 1901.

————. *The Hindered Hand: or, The Reign of the Repressionist*. 1905.

————. *Pointing the Way*. 1908.

Harland, Henry (as. Sidney Luska). *As It Was Written: A Jewish Musician's Story*. 1885.

————. *Mrs. Peixada*. 1886.

————. *A Land of Love*. 1887.

————. *The Yoke of the Thorah*. 1887.

————. *Grandison Mather, or An Account of the Fortunes of Mr. and Mrs. Thomas Gardiner*. 1889.

Harper, Frances Ellen Watkins. *Minnie's Sacrifice*. 1869.

————. *Sowing and Reaping*. 1876–77.

————. *Trials and Triumphs*. 1888.

————. *Iola Leroy; or Shadows Uplifted*. 1892.

Harris, Joel Chandler. *Uncle Remus: His Songs and His Sayings: The Folklore of the Old Plantation*. 1880.

————. *Sister Jane*. 1896.

————. *Gabriel Tolliver: A Story of Reconstruction*. 1902.

Hay, John. *The Bread-Winners: A Social Study*. 1884.

Hearn, Lafcadio. *Chita: A Memory of Last Island*. 1889.

————. *Youma: The Story of a West-Indian Slave*. 1890.

Hopkins, Pauline. *Contending Forces: A Romance Illustrative of Negro Life North and South*. 1900.

————. *Hagar's Daughter: A Story of Southern Caste Prejudice*. 1902.

————. *Winona: A Tale of Negro Life in the South and Southwest*. 1902.

————. *Of One Blood, or the Hidden Self*. 1903.

Howe, Edgar W. *The Story of a Country Town*. 1883.

Howells, William Dean. *Their Wedding Journey*. 1872.

————. *A Chance Acquaintance*. 1873.

————. *A Foregone Conclusion*. 1874.

————. *The Lady of the Aroostook*. 1879.

————. *The Undiscovered Country*. 1880.

————. *Doctor Breen's Practice*. 1881.

————. *A Modern Instance*. 1882.

———. *A Woman's Reason*. 1883.

———. *The Rise of Silas Lapham*. 1885.

———. *Indian Summer*. 1886.

———. *The Minister's Charge; or, The Apprenticeship of Lemuel Barker*. 1886.

———. *April Hopes*. 1887.

———. *Annie Kilburn*. 1888.

———. *A Hazard of New Fortunes*. 1889.

———. *The Shadow of a Dream*. 1890.

———. *An Imperative Duty*. 1891.

———. *Mercy*. 1892; as *The Quality of Mercy*. 1892.

———. *The World of Chance*. 1893.

———. *The Coast of Bohemia*. 1893.

———. *A Traveler from Altruria*. 1894.

———. *The Day of Their Wedding*. 1896.

———. *A Parting and a Meeting*. 1896.

Hum-ishu-ma (Mourning Dove). *Cogewea; The Half Blood* (written 1912–14). 1927.

Jackson, Helen Hunt. *Mercy Philbrick's Choice*. 1876.

———. *Ramona: A Story*. 1884.

James, Henry. *Roderick Hudson*. 1875.

———. *The American*. 1877.

———. *Watch and Ward*. 1878.

———. *The Europeans: A Sketch*. 1878.

———. *Daisy Miller: A Study*. 1878.

———. *The Portrait of a Lady*. 1881.

———. *Washington Square*. 1881.

———. *The Bostonians*. 1886.

———. *The Princess Casamassima*. 1886.

———. *The Reverberator*. 1888.

———. *The Aspern Papers*. 1888.

———. *The Tragic Muse*. 1890.

———. *The Other House*. 1896.

———. *The Spoils of Poynton*. 1897.

———. *What Maisie Knew*. 1897.

———. *The Two Magics: The Turn of the Screw, Covering End*. 1898.

———. *The Awkward Age*. 1899.

———. *The Sacred Fount*. 1901.

———. *The Wings of the Dove*. 1902.

———. *The Ambassadors*. 1903.

———. *The Golden Bowl*. 1904.

———. *The Outcry*. 1911.

Jewett, Sarah Orne. *Deephaven*. 1877.

———. *A Country Doctor*. 1884.

———. *A Marsh Island*. 1885.

———. *The Country of the Pointed Firs*. 1896.

———. *The Tory Lover*. 1901.

Johnson, James Weldon (anon.). *The Autobiography of an Ex-Coloured Man*. 1912.

Johnston, Mary. *To Have and to Hold*. 1902.
———. *The Long Roll*. 1911.
———. *Hagar*. 1913.
———. *The Witch*. 1914.
Lewis, Sinclair. *Our Mr. Wrenn*. 1914.
———. *The Trail of the Hawk*. 1915.
Libby, Laura Jean. *A Fatal Wooing*. 1883.
London, Jack. *The Call of the Wild*. 1903.
———. *The Sea-Wolf*. 1904.
———. *White Fang*. 1906.
———. *The Iron Heel*. 1908.
———. *Martin Eden*. 1909.
———. *Burning Daylight*. 1910.
———. *The Valley of the Moon*. 1913.
Major, Charles. *When Knighthood Was in Flower*. 1898.
Matthews, Victoria Earle. *Aunt Lindy: A Story Founded on Real Life*. 1893.
Meyer, Annie Nathan. *Helen Brent, M.D: A Social Study*. 1892.
Murfree, Mary Noailles (as Charles Egbert Craddock). *In the Tennessee Mountains*. 1884.
———. *The Prophet of the Great Smoky Mountains*. 1885.
———. *In the "Strange People's" Country*. 1891.
Norris, Frank. *McTeague*. 1899.
———. *The Octopus*. 1901.
———. *The Pit*. 1903.
———. *Vandover and the Brute*. (written 1894–95) 1914.
Page, Thomas Nelson. *In Ole Virginia; or, Marse Chan and Other Stories*. 1887.
———. *Red Rock: A Chronicle of Reconstruction*. 1898.
———. *Gordon Keith*. 1903.
———. *John Marvel, Assistant*. 1909.
Phelps, Elizabeth Stuart. *Up Hill; or, Life in the Factory*. 1865.
———. *The Gates Ajar*. 1868.
———. *Hedged In*. 1870.
———. *The Silent Partner*. 1871.
———. *The Story of Avis*. 1877.
———. *Doctor Zay*. 1882.
———. *A Singular Life*. 1895.
Phillips, David Graham. *The Great God Success*. 1901.
———. *A Woman Ventures*. 1902.
———. *The Master-Rogue: The Confessions of a Croesus*. 1903.
———. *The Deluge*. 1905.
———. *The Fortune Hunter*. 1906.
———. *Light-Fingered Gentry*. 1907.
———. *Old Wives for New*. 1908.
———. *The Hungry Heart*. 1909.
———. *The Grain of Dust*. 1911.
———. *The Price She Paid*. 1912.
———. *Susan Lenox: Her Fall and Rise*. 1917.
Poole, Ernest. *The Voice of the Street*. 1906.

Sheldon, Charles M. *In His Steps*. 1896.

Sinclair, Upton. *The Jungle*. 1906.

Southworth, E.D.E.N. *The Fatal Marriage*. 1869.

———. *Self-Raised; or, From the Depths*. 1876.

———. *Why Did He Wed Her?* 1884.

Stein, Gertrude. *Three Lives*. 1909.

———. *The Making of Americans*. (written 1903–6) 1925.

Stowe, Harriet Beecher. *Uncle Tom's Cabin*, 1851, 1852.

———. *Oldtown Folks*. 1869.

———. *My Wife and I*. 1871.

———. *Pink and White Tyranny*. 1871.

———. *We and Our Neighbors*. 1875.

———. *Poganuc People*. 1878.

Stuart, Ruth McEnery. *Napoleon Jackson: The Gentleman of the Plush Rocker*. 1902.

Tourgée, Albion. *'Toinette*. 1874, 1881.

———. *A Fool's Errand: By One of the Fools*. 1879.

———. *Hot Plowshares*. 1883.

Twain, Mark. *The Adventures of Tom Sawyer*. 1876.

———. *The Prince and the Pauper*. 1882.

———. *Adventures of Huckleberry Finn*. 1884, 1885.

———. *A Connecticut Yankee in King Arthur's Court*. 1889.

———. *The Tragedy of Pudd'nhead Wilson, and The Comedy of Those Extraordinary Twins*. 1894.

Ventura, Luigi Donato. *Peppino*. 1886.

Wharton, Edith. *The Touchstone*. 1900.

———. *The Valley of Decision*. 1902.

———. *Sanctuary*. 1903.

———. *The House of Mirth*. 1905.

———. *The Fruit of the Tree*. 1907.

———. *Madame de Treymes*. 1907.

———. *Ethan Frome*. 1911.

———. *The Reef*. 1912.

———. *The Custom of the Country*. 1913.

Wister, Owen. *The Virginian*. 1902.

Woolson, Constance Fenimore. *For the Major*. 1883.

———. *Jupiter Lights*. 1889.

SECONDARY WORKS

Ammons, Elizabeth. *Conflicting Stories: American Women Writers at the Turn into the Twentieth Century*. New York: Oxford University Press, 1991.

———. *Edith Wharton's Argument with America*. Athens: University of Georgia Press, 1980.

———. "Men of Color, Women, and Uppity Art at the Turn of the Century." *American Literary Realism* 23, no. 3 (1991): 14–24.

Anderson, Benedict R. *Imagined Communities: Reflections on the Origin and Spread of Nationalism*, rev. ed. London: Verso, 1991.

Andrews, William L. *The Literary Career of Charles W. Chesnutt*. Baton Rouge: Louisiana State University Press, 1980.

Anesko, Michael. *"Friction with the Market": Henry James and the Profession of Authorship*. New York: Oxford University Press, 1986.

Baguely, David. *Naturalist Fiction: The Entropic Vision*. Cambridge, UK: Cambridge University Press, 1990.

Banton, Michael. *Racial Theories*. Cambridge, UK: Cambridge University Press, 1987.

Bardes, Barbara, and Suzanne Gossett. *Declarations of Independence: Women and Political Power in Nineteenth-Century American Fiction*. New Brunswick, N.J.: Rutgers University Press, 1990.

Baym, Nina. *Woman's Fiction: A Guide to Novels by and about Women in America, 1820–1870*. Ithaca, N.Y.: Cornell University Press, 1978.

Becker, George, ed. *Documents of Modern Literary Realism*. Princeton, N.J.: Princeton University Press, 1963.

Bederman, Gail. *Manliness and Civilization: A Cultural History of Gender and Race in the United States, 1880–1917*. Chicago: University of Chicago Press, 1995.

Bell, Michael Davitt. *The Problem of American Realism: Studies in the Cultural History of a Literary Idea*. Chicago: University of Chicago Press, 1993.

Bell, Millicent, ed. *The Cambridge Companion to Edith Wharton*. New York: Cambridge University Press, 1995.

Bender, Bert. *The Descent of Love: Darwin and the Theory of Sexual Selection in American Fiction, 1871–1926*. Philadelphia: University of Pennsylvania Press, 1996.

Benfey, Christopher. *The Double Life of Stephen Crane*. New York: Alfred A. Knopf, 1992.

Benstock, Shari. *No Gifts from Chance: A Biography of Edith Wharton*. New York: Scribner's, 1994.

Berthoff, Warner. *The Ferment of Realism: American Literature, 1884–1919*. New York: Cambridge University Press, 1965.

Blanchard, Paula. *Sarah Orne Jewett: Her World and Her Work*. New York: Addison-Wesley Publishing Co., 1994.

Bledstein, Burton J. *The Culture of Professionalism: The Middle Class and the Development of Higher Education in America*. New York: W. W. Norton, 1976.

Blumin, Stuart M. *The Emergence of the Middle Class: Social Experience in the American City, 1760–1900*. New York: Cambridge University Press, 1989.

Borus, Daniel H. *Writing Realism: Howells, James, and Norris in the Mass Market*. Chapel Hill: University of North Carolina Press, 1989.

Bourdieu, Pierre. *Distinction: A Social Critique of the Judgement of Taste*. Trans. Richard Nice. Cambridge, Mass.: Harvard University Press, 1984.

Bowlby, Rachel. *Just Looking: Consumer Culture in Dreiser, Gissing, and Zola*. New York: Methuen, 1985.

Brodhead, Richard H. *Cultures of Letters: Scenes of Reading and Writing in Nineteenth-Century America*. Chicago: University of Chicago Press, 1993.

Bryson, Norman, Michael Ann Holly, and Keith Moxey, eds. *Visual Culture: Images and Interpretations*. Hanover, N.H.: Wesleyan University Press–University Press of New England, 1994.

Buell, Lawrence. *New England Literary Culture: From Revolution through Renaissance.* New York: Cambridge University Press, 1986.

Campbell, Donna M. *Resisting Regionalism: Gender and Naturalism in American Fiction, 1885–1915.* Athens: Ohio University Press, 1997.

Carby, Hazel. Introduction. *The Magazine Novels of Pauline Hopkins.* New York: Oxford University Press, 1988. xxix–l.

———. *Reconstructing Womanhood: The Emergence of the Afro-American Woman Novelist.* New York: Oxford University Press, 1987.

Chametzky, Jules. *From the Ghetto: The Fiction of Abraham Cahan.* Amherst: University of Massachusetts Press, 1977.

Chauncey, George. *Gay New York: Gender, Urban Culture, and the Making of the Gay Male World, 1890–1940.* New York: Basic Books, 1994.

Chessman, Harriet Scott. *The Public Is Invited to Dance: Representation, the Body, and Dialogue in Gertrude Stein.* Stanford, Calif.: Stanford University Press, 1989.

Civello, Paul. *American Literary Naturalism and Its Twentieth-Century Transformations.* Athens: University of Georgia Press, 1994.

Clinton, Catherine, and Nina Silber, eds. *Divided Houses: Gender and the Civil War.* New York: Oxford University Press, 1992.

Conder, John J. *Naturalism in American Fiction: The Classic Phase.* Lexington: University Press of Kentucky, 1984.

Conn, Peter. *The Divided Mind: Ideology and Imagination in America, 1890–1917.* New York: Cambridge University Press, 1983.

Coultrap-McQuin, Susan. *Doing Literary Business: American Women Writers in the Nineteenth Century.* Chapel Hill: University of North Carolina Press, 1990.

Davis, F. James. *Who Is Black? One Nation's Definition.* University Park: Pennsylvania State University Press, 1991.

[De Forest, John W.]. "The Great American Novel." *Nation,* Jan. 9, 1863: 27–29.

Dijkstra, Bram. *Evil Sisters: The Threat of Female Sexuality and the Cult of Manhood.* New York: Alfred A. Knopf, 1996.

Dimock, Wai-Chee. "Debasing Exchange: Edith Wharton's *The House of Mirth.*" *PMLA* 100 (1985): 783–92.

Dittman, Linda. " 'When Privilege Is No Protection': The Woman Artist in *Quicksand* and *The House of Mirth.*" In *Writing the Woman Artist: Essays on Poetics, Politics, and Portraiture.* Ed. Suzanne Jones. Philadelphia: University of Pennsylvania Press, 1991. 133–54.

Doane, Janice L. *Silence and Narrative: The Early Novels of Gertrude Stein.* Westport, Conn.: Greenwood Press, 1986.

Donovan, Josephine. *New England Local Literature: A Women's Tradition.* New York: Frederick Ungar, 1983.

Elliott, Emory, et al., eds. *The Columbia History of the American Novel.* New York: Columbia University Press, 1991.

Ernest, John. *Resistance and Reformation in Nineteenth-Century African-American Literature: Brown, Wilson, Jacobs, Delany, Douglas, and Harper.* Jackson: University Press of Mississippi, 1995.

Eysteinsson, Astradur. *The Concept of Modernism.* Ithaca, N.Y.: Cornell University Press, 1990.

Fisher, Philip. *Hard Facts: Setting and Form in the American Novel.* New York: Oxford University Press, 1987.

Fishkin, Shelley Fisher. *Was Huck Black? Mark Twain and African-American Voices.* New York: Oxford University Press, 1993.

Foster, Frances Smith. Introduction. *A Brighter Day Coming: A Frances Ellen Watkins Harper Reader.* Ed. Frances Smith Foster. New York: The Feminist Press, 1990. 3–40.

Fox, Richard Wightman, and T. J. Jackson Lears, eds. *The Culture of Consumption: Critical Essays in American History, 1880–1980.* New York: Pantheon, 1983.

Freedman, Jonathan. *Professions of Taste: Henry James, British Aestheticism, and Commodity Culture.* Stanford, Calif.: Stanford University Press, 1990.

Gammel, Irene. *Sexualizing Power in Naturalism: Theodore Dreiser and Frederick Philip Grove.* Calgary: University of Calgary Press, 1994.

Giddings, Paula. *When and Where I Enter: The Impact of Black Women in Race and Sex in America.* New York: Bantam Books, 1984.

Gilbert, Sandra M., and Susan Gubar. *No Man's Land: The Place of the Woman Writer in the Twentieth Century.* 3 vols. New Haven, Conn.: Yale University Press, 1988, 1989, 1994.

Gillman, Susan, and Forrest G. Robinson, eds. *Mark Twain's* Pudd'nhead Wilson: *Race, Conflict, and Culture.* Durham, N.C.: Duke University Press, 1990.

Gilman, Charlotte Perkins. *The Man-Made World or, Our Androcentric Culture.* New York: Charlton Co., 1911.

Ginsberg, Elaine K., ed. *Passing and the Fictions of Identity.* Durham, N.C.: Duke University Press, 1996.

[Godkin, E. L.]. "Female Influence." *Nation,* July 25, 1867: 73–74.

———. "The Other Side of the Question." *Nation,* Oct. 17, 1867: 316–17.

Gogol, Miriam, ed. *Theodore Dreiser: Beyond Naturalism.* New York: New York University Press, 1995.

Goldberg, David Theo, ed. *Anatomy of Racism.* Minneapolis: University of Minnesota Press, 1990.

Goodman, Susan. *Edith Wharton's Women: Friends and Rivals.* Hanover, N.H.: University Press of New England, 1990.

Gossett, Thomas F. *Race: The History of an Idea in America.* New York: Schocken Books, 1965.

Graham, Don, ed. *Critical Essays on Frank Norris.* Boston: G. K. Hall, 1980.

Griffen, Clyde. "Reconstructing Masculinity from the Evangelical Revival to the Waning of Progressivism: A Speculative Synthesis." In *Meanings for Manhood: Constructions of Masculinity in Victorian America.* Ed. Mark C. Carnes and Clyde Griffen. Chicago: University of Chicago Press, 1990. 183–204.

Gruesser, John Cullen, ed. *The Unruly Voice: Rediscovering Pauline Elizabeth Hopkins.* Urbana: University of Illinois Press, 1996.

Gunning, Sandra. *Race, Rape, and Lynching: The Red Record of American Literature, 1890–1912.* New York: Oxford University Press, 1996.

Gutmann, Amy, ed. *Multiculturalism: Examining the Politics of Recognition.* Princeton, N.J.: Princeton University Press, 1994.

Habegger, Alfred. *Gender, Fantasy, and Realism in American Literature*. New York: Columbia University Press, 1982.

———. *Henry James and the "Woman Business."* New York: Cambridge University Press, 1989.

Habermas, Jürgen. "The Public Sphere." *New German Critique* 1, no. 3 (1974): 49–55.

Harris, Sharon M. *Rebecca Harding Davis and American Realism*. Philadelphia: University of Pennsylvania Press, 1991.

Helly, Dorothy, and Susan M. Reverby, eds. *Gendered Domains: Rethinking Public and Private in Women's History. Essays from the Seventh Berkshire Conference on the History of Women*. Ithaca, N.Y.: Cornell University Press, 1992.

Henza, Louis. *"A White Heron" and the Question of Minor Literature*. Madison: University of Wisconsin Press, 1984.

Hochman, Barbara. *The Art of Frank Norris, Storyteller*. Columbia: University of Missouri Press, 1988.

Hoffman, Michael J., ed. *Critical Essays on Gertrude Stein*. Boston: G. K. Hall, 1986.

Horsman, Reginald. *Race and Manifest Destiny: The Origins of American Racial Anglo-Saxonism*. Cambridge, Mass.: Harvard University Press, 1981.

Howard, June. *Form and History in American Literary Naturalism*. Chapel Hill: University of North Carolina Press, 1985.

———, ed. *New Essays on* The Country of the Pointed Firs. New York: Cambridge University Press, 1994.

Howells, William D. *Literature and Life: Studies*. New York: Harper & Brothers, 1911.

———. *Selected Literary Criticism. Vol. I: 1859–1885*. Introd. Ulrich Halfmann. Vol. 13 of *A Selected Edition of William Dean Howells*. Bloomington: Indiana University Press, 1993.

Jacobson, Marcia. *Henry James and the Mass Market*. Tuscaloosa: University of Alabama Press, 1983.

James, Henry. *Literary Criticism: Essays on Literature, American Writers, English Writers*. New York: Library of America, 1984.

Kaplan, Amy. *The Social Construction of American Realism*. Chicago: University of Chicago Press, 1988.

Kaplan, Harold. *Power and Order: Henry Adams and the Naturalist Tradition in American Fiction*. Chicago: University of Chicago Press, 1981.

Karp, Ivan, and Steven D. Lavine, eds. *Exhibiting Cultures: The Poetics and Politics of Museum Display*. Washington, D.C.: Smithsonian Press, 1991.

Kasson, John F. *Rudeness and Civility: Manners in Nineteenth-Century Urban America*. New York: Hill & Wang, 1990.

Kelley, Mary. *Private Woman, Public Stage: Literary Domesticity in Nineteenth-Century America*. New York: Oxford University Press, 1984.

Kennedy, Gerald J., ed. *Modern American Short Story Sequences: Composite Fictions and Fictive Communities*. New York: Cambridge University Press, 1995.

Kerber, Linda K. "Separate Spheres, Female Worlds, Woman's Place: The Rhetoric of Woman's History." *Journal of American History* 75 (1988): 9–39.

Ladd, Barbara. *Nationalism and the Color Line in George W. Cable, Mark Twain, and William Faulkner.* Baton Rouge: Louisiana State University Press, 1996.

Levine, George. *The Realistic Imagination: English Fiction from Frankenstein to Lady Chatterley.* Chicago: University of Chicago Press, 1981.

Levine, Lawrence W. *Highbrow/Lowbrow: The Emergence of Cultural Hierarchy in America.* Cambridge, Mass.: Harvard University Press, 1988.

Levy, Eugene. *James Weldon Johnson: Black Leader, Black Voice.* Chicago: University of Chicago Press, 1973.

Lichtenstein, Nelson. "Authorial Professionalism and the Literary Marketplace, 1885–1900." *American Studies* 19, no. 1 (1978): 35–53.

Lingeman, Richard. *Theodore Dreiser: At the Gates of the City, 1871–1907.* New York: G. P. Putnam's Sons, 1986.

Lott, Eric. "White Like Me: Racial Cross-Dressing and the Construction of American Whiteness." In *Cultures of United States Imperialism,* ed. Amy Kaplan and Donald E. Pease. Durham, N.C.: Duke University Press, 1993, 474–95.

———. *Love and Theft: Blackface Minstrelsy and the American Working Class.* New York: Oxford University Press, 1993.

McKay, Janet Holmgren. *Narration and Discourse in American Realistic Fiction.* Philadelphia: University of Pennsylvania Press, 1982.

Martin, Jay. *Harvests of Change: American Literature, 1865–1914.* Englewood Cliffs, N.J.: Prentice-Hall, 1967.

Martin, Ronald. *American Literature and the Destruction of Knowledge.* Durham, N.C.: Duke University Press, 1991.

———. *American Literature and the Universe of Force.* Durham, N.C.: Duke University Press, 1981.

Matthews, Glenna. *The Rise of Public Woman: Woman's Power and Woman's Place in the United States, 1630–1970.* New York: Oxford University Press, 1992.

Michaels, Walter Benn. *The Gold Standard and the Logic of Naturalism: American Literature at the Turn of the Century.* Berkeley: University of California Press, 1987.

Miller, Elise. "The Feminization of American Realist Theory." *American Literary Realism* 23, no. 1 (1990): 20–41.

Mitchell, Lee Clark. *Determined Fictions: American Literary Realism.* New York: Columbia University Press, 1989.

———, ed. *New Essays on The Red Badge of Courage.* New York: Cambridge University Press, 1986.

Moon, Michael, and Cathy Davidson, eds. *Subjects and Citizens: Nation, Race, and Gender from Oroonoko to Anita Hill.* Durham, N.C.: Duke University Press, 1995.

Morrison, Toni. *Playing in the Dark: Whiteness and the Literary Imagination.* William E. Massey Sr. Lectures in the History of American Civilization 1990. Cambridge, Mass.: Harvard University Press, 1992.

Omi, Michael, and Howard Winant. *Racial Formation in the United States from the 1960s to the 1990s,* 2d ed. New York: Routledge, 1994.

Pease, Donald E., ed. *New Essays on The Rise of Silas Lapham.* New York: Cambridge University Press, 1991.

Pizer, Donald. *The Cambridge Companion to Realism and Naturalism: Howells to London.* New York: Cambridge University Press, 1995.

———, ed. *Critical Esays on Stephen Crane's* The Red Badge of Courage. Boston: G. K. Hall, 1990.

———, ed. *New Essays on* Sister Carrie. New York: Cambridge University Press, 1991.

———, *Realism and Naturalism in Nineteenth-Century American Literature,* rev. ed. Carbondale: Southern Illinois University Press, 1984.

———. *The Theory and Practice of American Literary Naturalism.* Carbondale: Southern Illinois University Press, 1993.

Pollack, Griselda. *Vision and Difference: Femininity, Feminism, and Histories of Art.* London: Routledge, 1988.

Quirk, Tom, and Gary Scharnhorst, eds. *American Realism and the Canon.* Newark: University of Delaware Press, 1994.

Robinson, Forrest G., ed. *The Cambridge Companion to Mark Twain.* New York: Cambridge University Press, 1995.

Rose, Anne C. *Victorian America and the Civil War.* New York: Cambridge University Press, 1992.

Rotundo, E. Anthony. *American Manhood: Transformations of Masculinity from the Revolution to the Modern Era.* New York: Basic Books, 1993.

Rubin, Gayle. "The Traffic in Women: Notes toward a Political Economy of Sex." In *Toward an Anthropology of Women,* ed. Rayna Reiter. New York: Monthly Review Press, 1975. 157–210.

Ryan, Mary P. *Women in Public: Between Banners and Ballots, 1825–1880.* Baltimore: Johns Hopkins University Press, 1990.

Samuels, Shirley, ed. *The Culture of Sentiment: Race, Gender, and Sentimentality in Nineteenth-Century America.* New York: Oxford University Press, 1992.

Sears, John F. *Sacred Places: American Tourist Attractions in the Nineteenth Century.* New York: Oxford University Press, 1989.

Sedgwick, Eve Kosofsky. *Between Men: English Literature and Male Homosocial Desire.* New York: Columbia University Press, 1985.

———. *Epistemology of the Closet.* Berkeley: University of California Press, 1990.

Seltzer, Mark. *Bodies and Machines.* New York: Routledge, 1992.

Shi, David. *Facing Facts: Realism in American Thought and Culture, 1850–1920.* New York: Oxford University Press, 1995.

Showalter, Elaine. *Sexual Anarchy: Gender and Culture at the Fin de Siècle.* New York: Viking, 1990.

Smith-Rosenberg, Carroll. *Disorderly Conduct: Visions of Gender in Victorian America.* New York: Oxford University Press, 1985.

Slotkin, Richard. *The Fatal Environment: The Myth of the Frontier in the Age of Industrialization, 1800–1890.* New York: Harper/Perennial, 1985.

Sollers, Werner, ed. *The Invention of Ethnicity.* New York: Oxford University Press, 1989.

Stowe, William W. *Balzac, James, and the Realistic Novel.* Princeton, N.J.: Princeton University Press, 1983.

Sundquist, Eric J., ed. *American Realism: New Essays.* Baltimore: Johns Hopkins University Press, 1982.

————. *To Wake the Nations: Race in the Making of American Literature.* Cambridge, Mass.: Harvard University Press, 1993.

Sussman, Herbert. "The Study of Victorian Masculinity." *Victorian Literature and Culture* 20 (1993): 366–77.

Tate, Claudia. *Domestic Allegories of Political Desire: The Black Heroine's Text at the Turn of the Century.* New York: Oxford University Press, 1992.

————. "Pauline Hopkins: Our Literary Foremother." In *Conjuring: Black Women, Fiction, and Literary Tradition,* ed. Marjorie Pryse and Hortense J. Spillers. Bloomington: Indiana University Press, 1985. 53–66.

Vallone, Lynne. *Disciplines of Virtue: Girls' Culture in the Eighteenth and Nineteenth Centuries.* New Haven, Conn.: Yale University Press, 1995.

Wagner-Martin, Linda. *"Favored Strangers": Gertrude Stein and Her Family.* New Brunswick, N.J.: Rutgers University Press, 1995.

————. *The House of Mirth: A Novel of Admonition.* Boston: Twayne, 1990.

Waid, Candace. *Edith Wharton's Letters from the Underworld: Fictions of Women and Writing.* Chapel Hill: University of North Carolina Press, 1991.

Walker, Jayne L. *The Making of a Modernist: Gertrude Stein from* Three Lives *to* Tender Buttons. Amherst: University of Massachusetts Press, 1984.

Walker, Nancy. *The Disobedient Writer: Women and Narrative Tradition.* Austin: University of Texas Press, 1995.

Warren, Kenneth W. *Black and White Strangers: Race and American Literary Realism.* Chicago: University of Chicago Press, 1993.

West, James L. W. III. *American Authors and the Literary Marketplace Since 1900.* Philadelphia: University of Pennsylvania Press, 1988.

Wharton, Edith. *A Backward Glance.* 1934; rpt. New York: Charles Scribner's Sons, 1962.

Wiegman, Robyn. *American Anatomies: Theorizing Race and Gender.* Durham, N.C.: Duke University Press, 1995.

Wilson, Christopher P. *The Labor of Words: Literary Professionalism in the Progressive Era.* Athens: University of Georgia Press, 1985.

Ziff, Larzer. *The American 1890s: Life and Times of a Lost Generation.* New York: Viking Press, 1966.

Index

in, 125, 147; male self-definition
in, 134–35; plot of decline in,
138–41, 148; pluralized public
sphere in, 143–45; stereotype of
"fairy" in, 145–46; suspicion of
femininity in, 140; and traffic in
women, 134, 139; uncertainty of
manhood in, 143–46. *See also*
masculinity, white; Norris,
Frank; plot of decline; traffic in
women
men, black: dual perspective of,
90–91; self-definition of, 89–90;
stereotypes of, 71, 74, 82, 84
men, white: and competition with
women, 124, 131; and public
sphere, 125, 131; and social
change, 125
Michaels, Walter Benn, 39
middle class, white: boundaries of,
71; definition of, 50–51, 69;
emergence of, 43, 44–45, 50;
and ethnological collections, 47;
as "imagined community," 49;
and local color fiction, 48, 50; as
readers, 54. *See also* local color
fiction
Miller, Nancy, 105
Mitchell, Lee Clark, 153
modernism, xv; and absence of
narrative authority, 166; and
collage, 169; experimentation in,
148; interrogation of novel in,
148, 166; and language, 169; and
multiplicity, 172; narrative techniques of, 150; and naturalism,
125, 148; resistance to narrative
in, 166, 172; and suspicion of
narrative, 166, 168–69; traits of,
121, 125, 168–69. See also *Red
Badge of Courage, The*; *Three Lives*
modernist novels, rejection of sentimentalism in, 6. *See also* modernism; narrative
mulatto figure, the, 93

narrative: and authority, 125, 150,
151, 159; fragmentation of, xv,

49, 125, 148, 159; free indirect
discourse in, 159; modernist,
121; resistance to, xv, 150, 151
narrative, Richardsonian, 100; and
fallen women, 100; and virtuous
women, 100. *See also* marriage
plot; Richardson, Samuel
naturalism: definitions of, 126, 148;
and determinism, 126, 149; and
diminished individuals, 149;
and evolutionary theory, 126;
influence of science in, 126;
masculine character of, 149; and
modernism, 125, 148; traits of,
126, 149. *See also* determinism;
McTeague; naturalist novels; *Sister Carrie*
naturalist novels, 169; determinism
in, 148; and diminished individuals, 148; and fragmentation of
self, 125; gender battles in, 125,
128; heredity in, 148; masculine
character of, 128; and modernism, 125, 148; omniscient
narrator in, 166; plot of decline
in, 135; sexual selection in, 128;
suspicion of narrative in, 125.
See also Darwin, Charles; evolutionary theory; *McTeague*; naturalism; plot of decline; *Red
Badge of Courage, The*; sexual
selection, theory of; *Sister Carrie*;
Three Lives
Norris, Frank, 21, 133; *McTeague*,
123, 125, 134, 143, 148; and plot
of decline, 138; and Zola, Émile,
127. *See also* masculinity, white;
McTeague; naturalism; Zola,
Émile
nostalgia, commodification of, 48
Nott, Josiah Clark, 74

Omi, Michael, 74

Page, Thomas Nelson, 50
Page, Walter Hines, 11, 51
passing: anxiety about, 75; novel
of, 87; statistics for, 75

The Author

Susan V. Donaldson teaches nineteenth- and twentieth-century American literature at the College of William and Mary, where she has been on the faculty since 1985. She is coeditor, with Anne Goodwyn Jones, of *Haunted Bodies: Gender and Southern Texts,* and editor of a 1995 special double issue of *The Faulkner Journal* on Faulkner and sexuality. She has also published and lectured widely on William Faulkner, Eudora Welty, Walker Percy, and general topics on southern literature and culture and is currently completing a book on the politics of storytelling in modern southern literature and painting.

The Editor

Herbert Sussman is professor of English at Northeastern University. His publications in Victorian literature include *Victorian Masculinities: Manhood and Masculine Poetics in Early Victorian Literature and Art; Fact into Figure: Typology in Carlyle, Ruskin, and the Pre-Raphaelite Brotherhood;* and *Victorians and the Machine: The Literary Response to Technology.*